Ministers Decide

Ministers Decide

A Personal Memoir
of the
Thatcher Years

———

NORMAN FOWLER

CHAPMANS
1991

Chapmans Publishers Ltd
141–143 Drury Lane
London WC2B 5TB

BRITISH LIBRARY CATALOGUING IN PUBLICATION DATA

Fowler, Norman
Ministers decide.
1. Great Britain. Politics – Biographies
I. Title
320.092

ISBN 1–85592–511–7

First published by Chapmans 1991

Photoset in Linotron Ehrhardt by
Rowland Phototypesetting Ltd
Bury St Edmunds, Suffolk
Printed and bound in Great Britain by
Butler & Tanner Ltd, Frome and London

For Fiona

Contents

Illustrations

Preface

When I started this book Margaret Thatcher was still Prime Minister and seemed certain to lead the Conservative Party into a fourth general election. In the autumn of 1990 the position changed dramatically. The resignation of the Deputy Prime Minister, Sir Geoffrey Howe, set the stage for a leadership election. The eventual result was the election of a new leader, John Major, the youngest Prime Minister this century, and the end of the Thatcher years.

This book is intended as my personal recollections of those years. I had served with Margaret Thatcher from the very beginning of her leadership in February 1975. When I resigned from the Government at the beginning of 1990, only Geoffrey Howe remained from that original Shadow Cabinet team. I do not attempt to chronicle every development over the fifteen-year period but rather to describe the events in which I was most closely involved. I also seek to describe the life of a minister from the euphoria of appointment to the difficulties of resignation. In short this is the book of a journalist who became a politician, not the work of a political historian.

The book takes its title from one of Margaret Thatcher's best-known replies. It was just before Nigel Lawson's resignation as Chancellor of the Exchequer in 1989 when she was challenged in the House of Commons on the influence of one of her advisers, Sir Alan Walters. Her reply was: 'Advisers advise; Ministers decide.'

It is not a bad commentary on the Thatcher years. It was ministers, not advisers, who drove through the distinctive policies like privatization and industrial relations reform. Ultimately it was also ministers who decided that Margaret Thatcher's period as Prime Minister was at an end.

Norman Fowler,
March 1991

CHAPTER 1

The Election of Margaret Thatcher

Punch

I did not vote for Margaret Thatcher in the leadership election of 1975. In my five years in the House of Commons I had come across her rarely, and my closest encounters had been after the defeat of the Heath Government in 1974. She was often to be seen at lunchtime patiently waiting with her tray in the downstairs refreshment room of the House of Commons – affectionately known by Members of Parliament as the 'greasy spoon'. For back-benchers this was a favourite spot for a quick cheap meal. Former Cabinet ministers, however, were thin on the ground. Had I thought about it I would have seen the obvious contrast between this democratic picture of Margaret Thatcher and the picture most often presented in the press of a stiff, rather starchy, middle-class lady from an outer London suburb. But I did not think about it any more than I thought about her as a future leader of the Conservative Party. In my view such a prospect seemed remote.

Margaret Thatcher had been Education Secretary throughout the Heath Government, but her period of office had not been counted an overwhelming success by many of us backbenchers. In particular, her action in discontinuing free school milk for some schoolchildren to make a measly £8 million saving had been counted a classic political disaster: the maximum row for the minimum gain. She became 'Thatcher the Milk Snatcher' and although newspaper sub-editors love such alliteration – any mistake I made attracted the headline 'Fowler's Howler' – it was a tag that stuck. When it came to the leadership election itself I was not regarded by Margaret's campaign managers as one of her natural allies. Although Ted Heath's supporters thought (rightly) that I was sufficient of a floating voter to merit two free lunches with the great man, I was never offered the glass of claret which came from the Thatcher camp. The nearest I came to their campaign was innumerable cups of coffee in the members' tea room at the House of Commons with Margaret's chief of staff, Airey Neave. In short, I did not expect that I would spend the next fifteen years working closely with the woman

who has had more effect on post-war Britain than any other
political leader.

The story of Margaret Thatcher's election to the leadership of the
Conservative Party really starts in the autumn of 1973. The Heath
Government faced a crisis. Having introduced an incomes policy,
they needed the acquiescence of the miners to make it work. The
Government had bent over backwards to make agreement possible,
writing in a specific exception to allow groups working 'unsocial
hours' to have more than the general 8 to 9 per cent increase. The
exception was tailor-made for the miners but they would not play.
They remembered only too well their strength in 1972, when they
had taken on the Government and won a massive pay increase.
Some of the leaders of the National Union of Mineworkers, like
the Communist Mick McGahey, thought they could do the same
again and destroy the incomes policy too. So as 1973 ended,
there was a dangerous deadlock between the Government and the
union. Thus far there had been only an overtime ban, but the
prospect was advancing of an all-out strike. How should the
Government respond to this threat? The Conservative Party was
deeply divided.

Many in the party thought that we should sweat it out. We had
a comfortable majority of around thirty and we had another sixteen
months to go before a general election needed to be called. The
argument went that governments were elected to govern and that
meant governing in the bad times as well as the good. Another view
was put by Enoch Powell, who at that stage was still a Conservative
backbencher, albeit a notably disgruntled one. His view was that
the introduction of an incomes policy was against everything that
the party had stood for in the 1970 general election and there was
no moral basis on which we could go to the country. To some of
us, however, the issue was not incomes policy: the issue was union
power. The last four years had seen strike after strike, and industry
after industry had been laid low. There had been strikes in electricity supply, the Post Office, the motor-car industry, local
government, the railways – and now, to add to the disruption, the
miners were in dispute for the second time in two years. Massed
pickets, votes in car parks and periodic violence characterized the
times. The country was verging on the kind of industrial chaos

that finally overtook us in the 'winter of discontent' four years
later. The Government had sought to bring some sanity to the
area by its reform of the industrial relations law, but its whole
democratic authority was now being challenged. That was the *real*
issue we faced.

Parliament resumed in early January 1974. At two meetings of
the 1922 Committee, which represents all Conservative backbenchers, we considered the crisis. I was one of those who argued
for an early election and, although opinion was still divided, it
seemed to me that this view had majority support. There then
followed the weeks that settled the fate of the Heath Government.
I would be the first to concede that Ted was presented with an
appallingly difficult decision. Understandably, he was reluctant to
plunge the country into an election months before it was strictly
necessary. Understandably, he wanted to take every opportunity
possible to reach an agreement with the miners' leaders, however
unlikely such an agreement seemed. Equally he recognized only
too well that the party was not united. The Whips' Office, whose
very *raison d'être* was to advise him of opinion in the party, was
reputed to be split down the middle. Nevertheless what was clear
– and clear then, not just with hindsight – was that if there were
to be a general election, speed was of the essence. It is difficult
enough to keep a three-week election campaign to a single issue,
but it is totally impossible if you have a three-week preliminary
debate. The press, the public and the politicians themselves will
tire of the one issue and inevitably drag in others. To win the
public debate, the Government needed to act quickly and decisively. Instead, we went into a period of 'will he?' or 'won't he?'

Possible early dates for an election slipped past. As the days
went by and still no election was called, you could see Labour
MPs cheering up before your eyes. Finally, on 7 February 1974,
when even so-called 'hawks' like myself were becoming reconciled
to a long slog with the NUM and an election in 1975, Ted Heath
announced that the issue would be decided at the polls.

Election day was set for 28 February. In every respect it was a
thoroughly miserable month. The lights went out; the snow came
down; the three-day working week continued; and the Director-
General of the CBI suggested that the industrial relations
legislation which we had long laboured to put on the statute book

should be repealed. To cap it all, in the middle of the election campaign the Pay Board put out a report which appeared, at first glance, to suggest that the Coal Board had its figures wrong and that the miners *were*, in fact, underpaid. 'The Great Pit Blunder' thundered the *Daily Mail* across its front page. The public suspended judgement. There was no love for the unions, but nor was there much affection for a Government which had taken Britain shivering through a bitter winter.

The result on polling day was that Conservative and Labour were almost equal in terms of votes cast, but in terms of seats Labour had a slender lead of 301 to 297 with the minority parties holding the balance of power. What had really done us the damage was the vote for Jeremy Thorpe's Liberal Party. Their support had trebled to over six million. For the Liberals it proved to be a marvellous pitch on which to bat. To the fury of Conservative and Labour candidates alike, the Liberals posed as the reasonable men of the centre against both the extremes of right and left. As such, they caught the mood of much of the public. On the question of whether the country was to be run by the Government or the unions, several million people in effect abstained and said that they would prefer to be asked another question.

From a personal point of view the election had not been unsuccessful. I had been first elected to Parliament in 1970, having won for the Conservatives the Labour marginal seat of South Nottingham, but the constituency had almost immediately perished in redistribution. In 1972 I had been adopted as candidate for Sutton Coldfield, some 40 miles to the West on the edge of Birmingham. In February 1974, Sutton Coldfield was one of the Liberals' target seats after they had achieved a surprising success in the county council elections. They were optimistic that they would win, but in the event we outpostered and outcanvassed them and I was elected with a majority of almost 12,000 – with Labour losing its deposit.

Coming from a marginal seat, I was not used to seeing my votes get a table ahead of my nearest opponent as the ballot papers were laid out in neat bundles of twenty. But any satisfaction I had on that score was soon dispersed once I returned to Westminster. The tensions in the party were considerable. Enoch Powell's last-minute decision not to fight his Wolverhampton seat, and then to advise the public to vote Labour, had not helped either the election or the morale of the party. Above all, there was foreboding that the initiative was now with Harold Wilson's Labour Government. He could choose his time for the inevitable second election and, in the meantime, bring forward a number of measures designed to win votes. He chose to increase pensions by 29 per cent – an increase which was never matched in the years of Labour Government to follow.

The October general election of 1974 was not as bad for us as it could have been. The public who had withheld support for eight months previously declined to be stampeded into giving Wilson an overwhelming majority. Labour increased its vote by a mere 2 per cent. Although this gave them a forty-seat lead over us, it was just short of an overall majority in the House of Commons. As later events were to show, this was a perilous hold. Nevertheless, if there were doubts about who had won the election there was no doubt who had lost it. There had been no perceptible movement to change the leader of the Conservative Party between February and October, with the prospect of an election ever imminent. But this was no longer the position. The prospect now was for a long haul of several years to the next election. All attention turned to the future of Edward Heath.

By any measure Ted was extremely vulnerable. He had lost two general elections in a row and three elections out of four as leader of the party. He also had his fair share of enemies. Inevitably, any leader offends by not promoting a backbencher who considers himself ready for office – and he risks making a life-long enemy of any minister he has promoted and then sacks. But Ted Heath had not indulged in the frequent reshuffles which became such a part of Margaret Thatcher's style. He had to make changes when, for example, Reggie Maudling resigned following the Poulson affair. Nevertheless, the significance of the Heath approach was not how many ministers were sacked but how few. He was loyal to his team and he expected loyalty from them. That would appear to make Ted the kind of leader that most people would want to follow, and does nothing to explain the sometimes bitter personal hostility he was facing in 1974. One senior backbencher at the time confided to me that he did not want a leadership election yet. He would like the uncertainty to drag on for a little longer. 'Heath has not suffered enough,' he observed chillingly.

In part the hostility resulted from what was seen as the Heath style. My first memories of Ted Heath were in university politics fifteen years earlier. Then he was a popular visitor to the weekend conferences that we undergraduates used to organize. He was popular for this reason. Some senior figures whisked in, gave their speech and were away. In those days Ted always appeared to have time to talk and indeed appeared happiest when surrounded by a group of young people. That was emphatically not the kind of reputation that he had by 1974 after almost four years in Downing Street. Stories abounded of him being bodily propelled into the smoking room of the House of Commons to meet Conservative backbenchers and on arrival subsiding in total silence behind a copy of the *Evening Standard.* His supporters excused him as 'unclubbable'; his enemies wrote him off as unapproachable, aloof and autocratic. I believe that had he done more to cultivate the backbenches Ted would almost certainly have remained leader. As it was, when he was in need of friends they failed to rally.

There was, of course, another, more fundamental case against Ted Heath. At its extreme it was that he had taken the party down paths which we should never even have considered let alone followed. The introduction of a statutory incomes policy was one idea many Tories found quite impossible to accept; an industrial policy which propped up hopeless companies was another. My views were not quite so black and white. For one thing, it seemed to me that much of the criticism of Ted Heath's policies camou-flaged the deep hostility of some Tory MPs to our entry into the Common Market. There was no way that they would ever forgive the former Prime Minister for leading us into Europe in 1973. What did seem to me self-evident was that the party had lost its way. What did we stand for? I was not much impressed by all the talk in the last stages of the October election of national coalition. Even coalitions need some kind of programme. The attraction of a call for all good men of whatever party to come to the aid of the nation is more apparent than real. Coalition is not a building designed to last.

However, there was a central theme of policy which Ted Heath himself had once embraced, and which was capable of uniting the party and, more important, of attracting the public. What I wanted was a party which mixed economic and industrial radicalism with social commitment. My view was best put by R. A. Butler, a politician who twice almost became Prime Minister, who said that Conservatives stand for 'private enterprise but without selfishness'. It remains my most fundamental political belief that private enterprise is the best way of creating wealth, but that the beneficiaries of such wealth should include the sick, the old and the poor. For anyone with those views there was only one person who could be seen as an alternative to Ted Heath in 1974 – and that was Keith Joseph.

Keith Joseph had been one of the undoubted successes of the Heath Government. Throughout his period as Social Services Secretary he had been responsible for both the health service and social security. As I was to find out ten years later, it was an immensely demanding job. One of the images I still carry is of Keith leaving the Commons in his ministerial car in the early hours of the morning after a long night of voting, with the reading light on, and still working on his papers. A number of ministers have made something of their appetite for work and the early hour at which they start, but there were not many ministers who devoured as much paper as Keith. Added to this, he has the first-class mind of a fellow of All Souls and, above all, a commitment and interest in social reform entirely at odds with the picture so often painted of a free-market ideologue content to see the weakest go to the wall. Although I did not know it then, Keith Joseph is one of the gentlest men in politics and also one of the least devious. That may have prevented him from reaching the absolute pinnacle of political life, but it makes him one of the best men that I knew in fifteen years on the front bench.

In 1974, however, my vantage point was very much from the back benches. The nearest I had come to the front bench was a two-year spell as Parliamentary Private Secretary at the Northern Ireland Office, but that unpaid and slightly dogsbody job had finished when the Government fell. From the back benches Keith seemed to have most of the attributes necessary to be leader of the party. He was intellectually tough but an attractive speaker who was sometimes awarded a warm standing ovation from the Conservative Party Conference. He was not frightened of challenging accepted ideas with his own: he once called for more millionaires and more bankrupts

as a way of illustrating what the market economy had to offer. Above
all, he was a man of total honesty.

After the October election – in which my majority in Sutton
Coldfield had remained virtually unchanged – I returned to Westminster to be sworn in for the new Parliament. Rumour was rife
about the leadership but, as the party rules then stood, an election
could be forced only on the retirement of the old leader. Ted
showed neither an inclination to retire nor any desire to engineer
an immediate vote of confidence – which he could well have won.
Nevertheless, the assumption on the back benches was that a way
should be found to give the party an opportunity to choose. If there
were to be a contest, it was my view that Keith Joseph should be
persuaded to stand. So together with another colleague, Norman
Lamont, I went to see Keith in his tiny office reserved for the
Shadow Cabinet at the House of Commons. We put it to him that
he should stand for the leadership and that if he did we would support him. He listened to what we said; thanked us for our support;
but did not absolutely commit himself to the battle. For one thing
there was as yet no leadership election. Nevertheless, there was no
doubt in my mind that once there was a contest Keith would run.

Shortly after our meeting, I left for Istanbul in search of some
autumn sun – the two elections of 1974 having given us snow in
February and driving rain in October. It was in Istanbul that I read
the *Sunday Times'* account of a speech Keith had given to the
Edgbaston Conservative Association on Saturday 19 October.
Before the election he had challenged some of the fashionable
assumptions on economic policy and he had now moved on to the
social policy. His message was stark:

> The balance of our population, our human stock, is threatened.
> A recent article in *Poverty*, published by the Child Poverty Action
> Group, showed that a high and rising proportion of children are
> being born to mothers least fitted to bring children into the
> world and bring them up. They are born to mothers who were
> first pregnant in adolescence in socio-economic classes four and
> five. Many of these girls are unmarried, many are deserted or
> divorced or soon will be. Some are of low intelligence, most of
> them of low educational attainment. ... They are producing
> problem children, the future unmarried mothers, delinquents,

denizens of our borstals, subnormal educational establishments, prisons and hostels for drifters.

There was an immediate storm. The speech was compared with Enoch Powell's 'rivers of blood' immigration warning. It appeared to be a totally uncharacteristic piece of sensationalism on Keith's part – dressed up in the language of the sociologist. Keith was genuinely taken aback by the reaction, and admitted in typically frank style that the speech had been naive and misjudged. Although he protested that his concern for problem families was of long standing, and that he had coined the phrase 'the cycle of deprivation', this did nothing to deflect the criticism. Ted Heath's supporters could hardly believe their luck or suppress their glee that Ted's main rival had so obviously stumbled. Indeed, there seemed some doubt whether Ted would now have a challenger at all given that Willie Whitelaw was Chairman of the Party and therefore effectively debarred from challenging the leader.

There was no question that Keith had stumbled badly. If he had had the time, he could have put the matter right. People forget even the most controversial statements. After all, the problem he was pointing to was real and important. But Keith did not have the time to allow people to forget or to have second thoughts. A leadership election was clearly going to take place in the next few months.

Keith did not withdraw from the prospective contest straight away. But on 18 November 1974, he wrote to me and to one or two other supporters. It proved to be a historic letter. Without it, Margaret Thatcher would never have been elected leader of the Conservative Party. Keith wrote:

You have very kindly expressed your wish that I should compete for the leadership. I have told you that I have been considering whether to run. I have now concluded that I am not willing, and must therefore at once let you know. I am writing similarly to a few others.

Such a decision must, of course, be difficult and personal. It may cause some disappointment – and some pleasure! But one factor that did *not* enter into my thoughts was any unwillingness to stand against Ted.

Since I've not said publicly that I would run but have simply kept my options open I am under no obligation to make a public statement saying that I am not standing. But if asked I shall reply in the sense of this letter.

The Edgbaston speech had effectively destroyed Keith's position as a potential leadership candidate. It may have been unfair but it illustrates a truth about any leadership election. Unless there is an anointed crown prince as Eden was to Churchill, everything depends on the last months leading up to the election itself. Years of patient work can be blown away by the bad luck of being in an unpopular dispute at the time the election takes place, or, as in Keith's case, by one poorly judged speech. Keith could have gone on. He would probably have attracted a good vote, but he no longer had a chance of winning. Had he persevered, however, it would have had one fundamental effect. It would have made it impossible for any candidate from the 'right' of the party to have challenged Ted Heath.

As his letter shows, Keith was far too honest to pretend that he wanted anything other than a change of direction for the Conservative Party and a change of leader. He could have argued that a challenge would have been bad for the unity of the party or uttered any one of a dozen similar excuses. His letter specifically contemplated a challenge to Ted Heath and prepared the ground for it.

Meeting Keith in the Members' Lobby of the House of Commons a few hours after I had received his letter, I expressed my regret at his decision. He had clearly reached it after the kind of merciless, self-critical assessment that only Keith would carry out. I believe that Edgbaston had persuaded him that he did not have all the qualities necessary to be leader. We talked for a few minutes. At the end of the conversation, he paused and said that I might like to consider transferring my support to a candidate who he believed would run – that candidate was Margaret Thatcher.

My immediate reaction was less than ecstatic and it is on record. At the time, I was contributing to the Peterborough column in the *Daily Telegraph* – a position which had been occupied by Bill Deedes who had moved to the editor's chair. My comment was this:

Though both Sir Keith and Mr Whitelaw have now contracted out ... there is still likely to be a challenger from within the Shadow Cabinet. The most likely is Mrs Margaret Thatcher, unquestionably a beneficiary of Sir Keith's decision. Whether her support inside the Parliamentary party is as broad based as Sir Keith's is perhaps more doubtful.

As a prediction of what was to happen eventually, it was wide of the mark. As a description of the position in mid-November, it was not so far out. The immediate reaction of many inside the party to the Thatcher candidacy was incredulity. She had run only one government department; she had no experience in foreign affairs; and as far as I could judge she had no great personal following. That she managed to win the election less than two months later was certainly a tribute to her, but it was also a tribute to some brilliant staff work by the head of her campaign, Airey Neave.

Airey Neave was a deceptive man. With his silver hair and correct black suits he looked every inch the lawyer he had once been. He was neither flamboyant nor extrovert. He was the anti-thesis of the politician with a view on every subject and I suspect disliked that breed intensely. He preferred to prepare and know his ground thoroughly before committing himself. He was a private man and as such an easy man to overlook. However, those who did, did so at their peril. There was no question that he had real steel and both physical and moral courage. It was a tragic irony that having survived the war – including imprisonment in and escape from Colditz – Airey should have been murdered just before the 1979 general election by a terrorist bomb which exploded as he drove out of the underground car park at the House of Commons.

Airey had entered politics following the war and from 1957 to 1959 had been a junior minister in Harold Macmillan's Government. In 1959 he fell ill and had to resign. He made a strong recovery and, returning to Westminster, he went to see the party's Chief Whip to receive the bleak message that his ministerial career was finished. The Chief Whip was Ted Heath. Anyone who doubts the effect of personal feeling in politics has only to examine this episode. Although disputes are often set out in ideological terms, at the heart of many you can find the personal element. Airey deeply resented the way he felt he had been discarded and the way it had been done. Whether rightly or wrongly he blamed Heath, and with the prospect of a leadership contest Airey was in search of a candidate. He had first offered his services to Edward du Cann but du Cann had decided not to stand. He next offered his services to Margaret Thatcher whom he had known since their days at the Bar. If Keith Joseph gave the Thatcher campaign some of its intellectual force, Airey Neave gave it political clout.

Airey ran the Thatcher campaign more like a secret service operation than a standard political campaign. While the leaders of the Heath campaign issued statements confidently predicting victory, Airey Neave and his team, notably Bill Shelton and George Gardiner, were quietly and patiently canvassing the views of every member of the Parliamentary party. Airey trusted no one in the Heath camp – as I witnessed for myself in the tea room in the House of Commons. Over yet another cup of coffee I was chatting with Airey about the progress of his campaign. We were the only Tory members in the room. Suddenly Peter Walker, a former member of Ted Heath's Cabinet and a leading member of his re-election team, joined us. As soon as Peter sat down, Airey embarked on an entirely unstoppable lecture on his experiences at the Nuremberg war trials where he had served the indictments on some of the most notorious Nazis like Goering and Streicher. The lecture proceeded for almost ten minutes before Peter departed, having thanked Airey for the 'fascinating' break. Once he had gone Airey returned to our discussion.

Over the weeks of the campaign Airey made many converts but in spite of his gentle persuasion I voted for Ted Heath. Why? Partly there was a question of loyalty. In late November I had been recruited into the Shadow team. There had been a number of calls for Heath to bring new people onto the front bench but he was reluctant – and probably in no position to make the gaps which were necessary if new faces were to be fitted in. In the end he appointed Sally Oppenheim as consumer affairs spokesman and myself as a junior spokesman on Home Office affairs. I have the distinction of being the last front bench appointment that Ted Heath ever made.

Ironically, I was put under the command of the Shadow Home Secretary, Keith Joseph – although Keith had nothing to do with my appointment and was only told after I had accepted. For me it was an ideal job as in those days my expertise was the Home Office. I had been Home Affairs Correspondent of *The Times* for over four years in the 1960s. But there were other factors that influenced my vote apart from loyalty to a boss or even job satisfaction. In the constituencies, opinion was strongly in favour of Ted Heath and my own association in Sutton Coldfield was no exception. Above all, however, I shared the view of many of my contemporaries that Margaret Thatcher presented the wrong image as far as the party was concerned, and that we would suffer gravely if we appeared to leave the centre ground of politics.

The result of the contest was announced in an upstairs committee room of the House of Commons at 4 p.m. on Tuesday 4 February by the chairman of the 1922 Committee, Edward du Cann. To my frank astonishment the result was:

Margaret Thatcher	130
Edward Heath	119
Hugh Fraser	16

The effect on some colleagues was instantaneous. I remember one literally jumping with joy. Sad to report, in time he became just as disillusioned with Margaret Thatcher as he had been with Ted Heath. In any party you have a number who for one reason or another – sometimes but not always frustrated ambition – appear to be in a state of permanent disillusionment.

Apart from surprise, my immediate reaction was sadness for Ted. He had been awkward and at times autocratic but he had also achieved a great deal – notably he had led us into the Common Market where his will and judgement had been crucial against the opposition of a determined anti-market group of Tory MPs, not to mention the bulk of the Labour Party. I still find it difficult to take seriously Labour's pretensions to be the natural party of Europe. Ted Heath's attempt to reform industrial relations law had also been right and he had one other enormous merit: his commitment in areas like social services was deep and genuine and his hatred of unemployment was clear for all to see. This may have led him into some wrong policies but many of his aims and attitudes were ones that I shared.

As it was, however, he had been delivered a stunning rebuff. There would have to be a second round in the election because although Margaret Thatcher was top of the poll, she had not received the required 15 per cent majority. But for Ted Heath it was the end. There was no prospect of him recovering his position and a few hours later he resigned. In truth there was now no chance of anyone else catching Margaret Thatcher. She had a lead which could only get bigger as others joined the bandwagon. Her most serious rival was Willie Whitelaw. The way was now clear for him to stand but the opportunity of victory had disappeared.

If no one was going to catch Margaret, there was one thing that could be achieved. Potential candidates for the leadership could in Enoch Powell's words leave their 'visiting cards' by achieving a respectable vote in the second round. Such candidates would also be well placed for good positions in the new Shadow Cabinet. Within hours of the election result, it became clear that a small group was backing Jim Prior, not with the aim of winning but of making him a strong man in the new regime. A number of us decided to do the same for Geoffrey Howe.

Geoffrey Howe was the natural political successor to Keith Joseph. He believed in financial prudence, a reduction in personal and capital taxation, control of public spending and practical help to new small businesses rather than vast subsidies to collapsing old industries. Just as significantly, he had a commitment to social reform. He had been a leading member of the committee which had proposed laws to prohibit racial discrimination and had headed an important mental hospital inquiry. As a member of the Heath Government he had been responsible for the legislation to reform industrial relations and for the European Communities Act. The point so often forgotten about Geoffrey was just how creative a politician he was. He delighted in new ideas: he brought forward and developed many of the policies that characterized the Thatcher years. The partnership between him and Margaret Thatcher may have ended in tears and recriminations but particularly up to 1983 it was remarkably effective.

Geoffrey Howe had struggled to get into Parliament in 1964, only to lose his marginal seat of Bebbington in 1966. He had then been selected for Reigate in a televised selection conference against the stiff competition of the former television star, Christopher Chataway. Not for the first or last time he was helped by his wife Elspeth. There was no doubt that the Howes had made many sacrifices for politics, and Geoffrey's political luck looked ready to change when he was promoted from Solicitor-General to the Cabinet and made Minister for Trade and Consumer Affairs in the autumn of 1973. Six months later the Government fell and Geoffrey was back in Opposition. He picked himself up and settled down to the vast social services brief which he had inherited from Keith Joseph.

On the Tuesday night of Margaret Thatcher's first-round victory, a group of us met in Geoffrey's house in Lambeth. It included Leon Brittan, Ken Clarke and myself from the Bow Group. There was the late and much lamented David Walder, both a politician and a distinguished writer who died in 1978 at the age of forty-nine, and the irrepressible Ian Gow who fifteen years later was to be killed by an IRA car bomb. In overall charge was Tony Buck, an old friend from Geoffrey's Trinity Hall days in Cambridge and the Member of Parliament for Colchester. The meeting went on into the early hours of the morning for the good reason that Geoffrey required some persuasion that he should run. He had been a junior member of Heath's Cabinet and even now his position was at best middle rank. On the other hand he certainly had as much claim as Jim Prior to the leadership. In politics people tend to put on you the value you put on yourself: you need to take yourself seriously. There was not a dog's chance of Geoffrey winning, but we had to persuade him that he would not be left with a derisory vote which far from strengthening his position would weaken it. Conceivably, the presence in his drawing room of a small football team of supporters helped to persuade him and we left him seeking to find Elspeth (who was abroad in Canada) to tell her the news.

When the lists closed there were four candidates against Margaret Thatcher: Willie Whitelaw, Geoffrey Howe, Jim Prior and the former Transport Minister, John Peyton. According to a leading Thatcher campaign manager, George Gardiner, there was only one campaign that really gave them any cause for concern and that was ours. This was on the basis that we might attract natural Thatcher votes. Viewed from our side, that looked like one of the least of her problems. There was no way that the Thatcher bandwagon was going to be stopped by us or by anyone else. In Sutton Coldfield over the weekend I was able to take the views of my local association – a process which was made rather academic by the *Sunday Times* naming me as a leading Howe supporter. As association members rang in, it rapidly became clear that the tide had turned decisively in Margaret Thatcher's favour. Nevertheless, our own campaign was having some modest success. When we returned to Westminster on the Monday, Tony Buck was able to report that we had twenty-five firm pledges. Sadly, when it came to the poll that translated into nineteen actual votes – providing a cautionary tale for any would-be candidates in leadership elections. Estimates of support can be appreciably amiss. Some play the whole field and appear on everybody's canvass returns; some are too polite to say 'no'; and some simply change their minds during the progress of the campaign.

Whatever our problems in assessing support, there was no doubting the overall result:

Margaret Thatcher	146
William Whitelaw	79
Geoffrey Howe	19
James Prior	19
John Peyton	11

Our team met back in Tony Buck's room. The mood was gloomy. The vote was seen as a break with the past. As in other parts of the party there were fears that the new leader would not attract working-class voters in the Midlands and the North – a view which proved spectacularly inaccurate. I was deputed to go to the BBC to appear on the early-evening *Nationwide* programme, where representatives from all the five campaigns were to be interviewed. Not surprisingly the Whitelaw camp, represented by Christopher Tugendhat, was the most disappointed but everyone had basically the same message: 'The election is over. Whatever our views may have been in the past, the aim now must be to unite.'

The weekend after the election I went up to the Swinton Conservative College in Yorkshire to give a lecture. Following my session I drove back with a fellow lecturer, Bill Deedes. He had been a Cabinet minister in the Macmillan Government and when he left the front bench he did what all former ministers should do but do not always quite manage: he kept a kindly eye on new backbenchers, encouraged them and never, but never, confided how much better things were when he was in power. Tentatively I raised my own position. I said that I hoped I would be able to stay with the Home Office but, frankly, Margaret Thatcher owed me no favours. Tactfully, Bill replied that she would need 'young men like you'. My expectations, however, were not great. I had not voted for Margaret Thatcher on either the first or the second ballot – when a number of former Heath voters had changed position – and I saw no reason why I should remotely figure in her plans.

I was a little surprised on the Monday, therefore, to get a note from the Whips' Office asking me to see Margaret Thatcher in the Shadow Leader's Office in the House of Commons.

Margaret was sitting alone and was quick to come to the point: 'I would like you to take over social services,' she said.

Ah well, I thought, that's not too bad. If I can't stay at the Home Office then social services is the next best thing. I wondered idly who would be head of the team, and then it struck me that she had said 'take over'.

'You mean, head the team?' I asked.

'That's right,' she said. 'I am moving Geoffrey to be Shadow Chancellor and I would like you to take over from him. I would like you to continue some of the campaigns you have been so good at.'

In a state of some shock, I murmured, 'If you think I can do it. I have never done social services before.' I doubt if there has ever been such a subdued response to the prospect of spectacular promotion.

'We have all got new things to learn,' Margaret replied. 'I have spent all my time in home departments. I now need to learn about foreign affairs.'

Through a slight fog I gathered that my deputies were to be my old Cambridge friend Ken Clarke, and Gerry Vaughan who, as a practising consultant, was an undoubted expert on the health service. The interview was over. I left sworn to secrecy, as the announcement was not to be made for another twenty-four hours, and still in a state of considerable shock. Indeed, every time the telephone rang in my Westminster flat I half expected a call to say that Margaret had had second thoughts.

Nevertheless, as planned, the announcement was made on Tuesday 18 February. The headlines were for the recall of Reggie Maudling as Shadow Foreign Secretary and for the sacking of six of the previous Heath Cabinet, including Robert Carr and Peter Walker. Significantly, all Margaret Thatcher's opponents in the leadership elections were to be given Shadow Cabinet posts and these included two which were entirely crucial for the Thatcher revolution. Willie Whitelaw was appointed deputy leader of the party and, in a total vindication of our nineteen-vote campaign, Geoffrey Howe was made Shadow Chancellor. So why did Margaret Thatcher appoint me? Clearly she wanted to bring the divisions of the last few months to an end and was wisely determined not to be surrounded just by her own supporters. I was not quite sure what to make of her remarks about my 'campaigns', however. My most successful backbench campaign had been to get the age of jury service reduced to eighteen, but as this had involved voting against the then Conservative Government I doubted that was what Margaret had in mind.

What was true was that I was a Midlands member. The demography of our defeats in the elections of 1974 was truly awful. The party of one nation had suffered to such an extent that less than a third of Conservative seats were held in the Midlands or the North. If we were to get back into government that position had to be put right and put right quickly. Not for the first time did I thank my guardian angel for taking me to the Midlands as a journalist in the early 1960s, as a candidate in the late 1960s and as a Midlands MP since 1970.

Although he has never confirmed it, to this day I suspect the crucial factor in my promotion was the advice of Keith Joseph. I had been fortunate in working with Keith, shadowing in the Home Office. This was a policy area I knew backwards but the same could not be said for social services. I had taken over as spokesman on a massive policy area where my interest was great but my knowledge was sketchy. It was a point made even by my friends. At its politest, the view was that it was a good idea to put me in the Shadow Cabinet but social services was a daunting first jump.

Nevertheless, social services it was and, at just thirty-seven, I was the youngest member of Margaret Thatcher's first Shadow Cabinet.

CHAPTER 2

The Cambridge Mafia

Evening Standard

I harbour the delusion that I am too young to write an autobiography. This book is intended as my personal recollection of the fifteen years starting with Margaret Thatcher's election as Leader of the Conservative Party and continuing to my resignation from her Cabinet at the beginning of 1990 at the age of fifty-one. Nevertheless, I need to explain my viewpoint and from where I came. My political attitudes had been formed long before I joined the Shadow Cabinet and indeed long before I was elected to the House of Commons in 1970. Unquestionably the biggest influence on my life was Cambridge, where I went in 1958, ostensibly to read law. My real ambition, however, was to take part in the world of Cambridge politics. At that time there were a number of undergraduates with the same idea.

In October 1960, I became Chairman of the Cambridge University Conservative Association. My vice-chairman was Peter Temple-Morris, now the Conservative MP for Leominster; and my head of recruiting was an undergraduate from Selwyn who even in those days looked younger than his years, John Gummer. We had provided an exceptional fare of speakers for the coming term. A whole bevy of Government ministers had agreed to come to Cambridge during the next two months. They included Cabinet ministers like Lord Kilmuir, Charles Hill, John Boyd-Carpenter, John Hare and even the Chief Whip, Martin Redmayne. But our greatest coup had been to persuade Harold Macmillan, the Prime Minister, to speak. We had a record recruiting campaign and were riding high.

October also marked the start of the debating year at the Cambridge Union. Traditionally we started with the debate that 'This House has no confidence in the Government' – a motion which was tabled irrespective of which party was in power. The previous year when John Boyd-Carpenter and I had led for the Government we had won comfortably. We were confident that we would also take the 1960 debate in our stride, but we had reckoned without the effect that individual speeches can have upon Union debates. There are no whips to drive voters into the right lobby. Undergraduates make up their own minds on the basis of the debate itself – a dangerous procedure which is never likely to be introduced at Westminster.

After the opening speeches, honours were about even. The motion was proposed by Tony Firth, one of the most brilliant of our Cambridge generation. He had a later successful career in television but died at the tragically early age of forty-two. He was countered with an able defence by the then President of the Union, Leon Brittan. It was now the turn of the visiting speakers. For Labour, George Brown made a speech designed to appeal to an undergraduate audience of the time. It was to the effect that any old government could provide economic prosperity but only Labour could provide social progress. It was a persuasive speech and is still the basis of the Labour case – in spite of all past experience with Labour governments who have provided neither great economic success nor much social advance. Speaking for the Government side was Hugh Fraser, at that time a junior defence minister.

It was, sadly, one of the most disastrous speeches that I ever heard at the Cambridge Union. Fraser entirely misjudged the mood of his audience and threatened that Labour would reintroduce sweet rationing, which was not regarded as one of the great moral issues of the time. Then, with a huge sweep, he knocked his glass of water flying over the Union secretary and finally dropped his whole speech on to the floor. It was the kind of speech that is any politician's nightmare. It says much for Hugh Fraser's character that following the opening speeches he managed to go round complimenting the undergraduates on *their* speeches.

When the debate opened up I tried to lead a counter-attack. I was rewarded by George Brown listening attentively to my argument and then delivering himself of a marvellously double-edged compliment. He turned to Tony Firth and in a fully audible aside growled: 'Very good – but he should be on our side.' Others too stood by the Government flag – including Nick Budgen, who later was elected as MP for Wolverhampton South-West when Enoch Powell refused to stand in the general election of February 1974. But it was all to no avail. When the votes were counted at midnight our defeat was clear.

Bernard Ingham would not have been pleased with the press following the debate. In those days we had only one newspaper to worry about. That was the undergraduate newspaper *Varsity* whose anonymous political columnist wrote under the pseudonym of Napoleon Boot and in the style of Cross-Bencher in the *Sunday Express*. His verdict was terse:

> Wailing and gnashing of teeth: the state totters, and everyone is wondering who is to face Mac when he comes (if he comes). Norman Fowler is keeping a stiff upper lip but he knows, and Boot knows, that something very precious, something very dear to our hearts, has been lost. We have shattered that touching old Cambridge tradition, unbroken in living memory, that the Union never defeats a government when it's in. O tempora! O mores! O Norman!

A day or two after the debate I was working in my rooms at Trinity Hall – which I shared with another future Tory MP and Minister, Peter Viggers. There was a knock at the door. Two young undergraduates a year behind me entered and explained the purpose of their visit. They were worried at the damage the Union debate had done to the Conservative cause and they wanted urgent action to correct the position. The first of the undergraduates was a law student from Caius College called Kenneth Clarke and the second another law student from Peterhouse named Michael Howard. Twenty years later I recruited Ken Clarke as my Parliamentary Secretary at the Department of Transport. Thirty years later when I left the Government I handed over the Department of Employment to Michael Howard.

Everything now depended upon Macmillan's visit. We had written to the Prime Minister more in hope than expectation and had been amazed to get an affirmative reply. All the predictions were that he would pull out at the last moment but as the weeks ticked by it became clear that, barring a catastrophe, the great man would actually appear. This sent the Labour Club into a panic. They had booked the Cambridge Union for a meeting the same night and had refused to move over for Macmillan. That left us in the Examination Halls and the Labour Club with the problem of how to find an audience for their visiting speaker, Barbara Castle. Their solution was for Mrs Castle to challenge Macmillan to a debate so that Cambridge could hear the 'respective positions' of the two parties. We rejected the idea as merely a device to muscle in on our meeting. I then contacted Number 10 for the first time in my life and a couple of days later a reply from the Prime Minister went to Mrs Castle. Labour were badly split on defence policy and on nationalization. Macmillan observed wryly that to refer to the 'respective positions' of the two parties 'highly oversimplified' the position inside the Labour Party.

At 5.42 on the evening of Friday 28 October, I met the Prime Minister at Cambridge railway station. He was obviously pleased with his reply to Mrs Castle and almost his first words were to see if I liked the gibe at Labour. Nervously I escorted him to the Garden House Hotel where a room and a huge array of drinks had been laid on. We had first approached the University Arms but they had replied curtly that they were full. I often wondered if the hotel's management ever knew how dismissively they had turned away the Prime Minister. Macmillan's Parliamentary Private Secretary was an enormous bluff Ulster Unionist MP called Knox Cunningham and he was dispatched to the Examination Halls to check on the arrangements – in particular the position of the lectern. Macmillan was too vain to wear glasses for his speeches and so it was important that the lectern was just the right height.

Arranging dinner for the Prime Minister had been as fraught as getting him a wash and brush up. On hearing that he was coming the Master of my college, the distinguished constitutional lawyer Ivor Jennings, had written to me saying that doubtless I would regard it as 'appropriate' that the Prime Minister should be entertained at top table. I, an undergraduate, had the ticklish job of writing back to him to say as tactfully as I could that the suggestion was wildly inappropriate and that I believed the Prime Minister had come to Cambridge to speak to undergraduates. Perhaps the Master would like to come to the meeting and the reception we were organizing in Trinity Hall afterwards, I suggested in a spirit of compromise. Back came the magisterial reply that the Master would come to the reception as it was in *his* college, but that his days of listening to political speeches were over. He used to write them.

Instead of top table, we took Macmillan to Leon Brittan's rooms in Trinity. Leon had the best set of rooms of my contemporaries and even managed to get a new carpet out of the college for the occasion. As the dinner started, there came a more and more insistent chant of 'We want Mac' from outside in the Great Court. 'Are the natives friendly?' asked Macmillan, and having been assured that they were he leapt to the window, having previously seemed elderly and rather immobile. He thanked the crowd for their welcome which he put down to the fact that he was Chancellor of Oxford. Back at the table the Prime Minister reminisced. Politics, he observed, was much less vituperative than when he first started out. 'In those days everyone came from the same background – and you can be much ruder to members of your own family.'

In the meeting itself Macmillan set out the kind of philosophy which had attracted most of us to the Conservative Party in the first place. The 1959 election campaign had been attacked as purely materialistic: 'You've never had it so good.' Confronting the argument, Macmillan said that a material prosperity provided the opportunity for spiritual and intellectual advance and gave the prosperous nation the opportunity to help the poorer. Nor did he think that Britain's days of world influence were over. We might not have the territory we once had but we had the priceless advantage of the natural inventiveness, hard work and genius of the British people. He then led into a discussion of the nuclear deterrent in the kind of way that only Macmillan could:

I can never get out of my mind seeing an audience like this of young men that my whole life and that of those of my generation has been dominated not by economic problems, however grave, not even by social problems, but by foreign policy. Foreign policy and defence are basic to all other problems.

For over ninety minutes the Prime Minister spoke and answered questions. He joked and bantered and by the end had the audience eating out of his hand. It was a virtuoso performance and I am glad to say was the recovery event which Messrs Clarke and Howard had ordered me to stage.

By any standards, the Cambridge of the late 1950s and early 1960s produced an exceptional number of politicians, including no fewer than eight Cabinet ministers for different Thatcher administrations: Leon Brittan, Ken Clarke, John Gummer,

Michael Howard, David Howell, John Nott, Norman Lamont and myself. In addition there have been two European Commissioners – Christopher Tugendhat and Leon Brittan – and a whole raft of ministers and MPs like Peter Lloyd, Peter Viggers, Peter Temple-Morris, Hugh Dykes, Nick Budgen and Michael Latham.

When I first went up to Trinity Hall in 1958, John Nott was making funny speeches at the Union which often played on his military service as a regular officer. Christopher Tugendhat seemed to speak in every one of the frequent religious debates we had then. When he went down his place was taken by John Gummer, who even in those days was a quite outstanding orator, although underestimated by his contemporaries. Leon Brittan was effortlessly turning his hand to anything he was asked to do. To no one's surprise he came down with a first, having also found the time to be President of the Union and Chairman of the Conservative Association.

The Cambridge of that period also produced much more in other fields, and doubtless much better. David Frost and Peter Cook were at the Cambridge Footlights; Derek Jacobi and Ian McKellen were at the amateur dramatic club. As for broadcasting, Kings Parade teemed with future television producers and reporters. In my small college alone we had Peter Pagnamenta, John Gau and Peter Hill who at different times have made major contributions to the output of BBC current affairs. In addition a whole host of others have scaled the heights of their chosen careers – lawyers, academics, scientists, businessmen. I make no claim, then, of exceptional merit for the so-called 'Cambridge Mafia' of politicians. I would claim, however, that they symbolized some of the important changes taking place in Britain at the time.

The first point to make about the Cambridge Mafia is that many of us were a long way from the background of the archetypal Conservative politician. Some had been to well-known public schools, but they were thin on the ground. David Howell had been to Eton and Christopher Tugendhat to Ampleforth. Altogether more typical were the number of us who were products of day grammar schools. Ken Clarke went to Nottingham High School; Michael Howard to Llanelli Grammar School; Peter Viggers to Portsmouth Grammar School; Hugh Dykes to Weston-super-

Mare Grammar School; while I went to the King Edward VI Grammar School in Chelmsford.

Several of us were also first-generation university students. It was not that our parents had lacked the ability to go to university, but that they had not had the opportunity. My own father had gone to evening classes in Manchester for three years at the beginning of the 1920s to get his engineer's qualification at what was then called the Municipal College of Technology. Years later, when I was Employment Secretary, I was invited by Roland Smith, the Chairman of British Aerospace, to launch a fund-raising drive for the University of Manchester Institute of Science and Technology and found that this was what my father's old evening college had become. Evening classes must have been a peculiarly difficult way of gaining a qualification after an already hard day's work and my generation was much more fortunate. University education had opened up (thanks to R. A. Butler's education reforms) and with the help of state and county grants many more students were able to go to university. Even so, I can certainly remember several very good students at my school who did not go on to university when it was quite clear that, in terms of ability, they could have walked into a place at Cambridge or anywhere else.

For those of us who did go to university, there were all the opportunities you had ever dreamed of – in fact there were rather too many. I spent three years at Cambridge happily engaged in politics, debating and journalism, not to mention the time spent cycling up the long hill to the strictly segregated women's college of Girton. In all this my law, which I was mistakenly reading and which I quietly loathed, came a poor second.

I even filled my vacations with the extra curricular. During one summer I worked for that excellent evening newspaper, the *Oxford Mail*, and to my delight I found that I had discovered an alternative career to the law. For the next two vacations I worked for none less than *The Times*. I was extraordinarily lucky to get the chance and, again, there was something peculiarly 1960s about it all. I only did so because the then editor of *The Times*, William Haley, came to talk to a meeting in Cambridge. 'How do we get a job on *The Times*?' asked one undergraduate more in jest than with any expectation of a serious reply. Haley was rather an austere and humourless man and he replied without the trace of a smile: 'You write to Mr Maurice Green, the deputy editor, and ask for a vacation attachment. If we like you we will consider you for a traineeship.' It was an enormous cheek but I followed the instructions and eventually graduated to Printing House Square.

Yet life at Cambridge was not entirely, or even mainly, a *Lucky Jim* progression. Undergraduate careers were taken seriously. Having reached university, we were anxious to make the most of it and were ambitious about what we wanted. Many of the staff on *Varsity* had their eyes firmly set on Fleet Street; the performers from Footlights saw the potential of television. Even so, it is doubtful whether the benches of the Cambridge Union in the early 1960s were swarming with bright young men who had already set their eyes on Number 10. For most of us, simply becoming a Member of Parliament seemed a difficult enough ambition.

I had wanted to be a politician from the age of twelve or thirteen. I was fascinated by the radio debates each week on *Any Questions?* and my heroes were politicians like Ted Leather, Bob Boothby and Stephen McAdden – who was years later the chairman of a number of House of Commons Standing Committees on which I served. Of my contemporaries at school who took an interest in politics, the balance was on the side of Labour. My support for the Tories was a reaction to the rather miserable post-war years of austerity but, most of all, it was opposition to the authoritarian model of socialism which was then dominant. Even in those days I was no supporter of turning industry into a series of impersonal bureaucratic corporations. To me, politics offered the opportunity of changing things for the better. Above all, I felt that politics was a worthwhile pursuit – although it was far too early to talk about it as a career.

At Cambridge I began to realize that my long-held ambition to be an MP was perhaps not so impossible after all. There were certainly undoubted stars who came to Cambridge who dazzled with their quality. I remember an epic debate on Europe between Dick Crossman and Bob Boothby. When Crossman sat down you wondered how anyone could conceivably follow him; when Boothby sat down you wondered how anyone could fail to support him. I recall also the passion of a red-haired Paul Johnson, then editor of the *New Statesman*, laying into the Government. These were people you wished to emulate but doubted whether you ever would.

As Hugh Fraser unfortunately showed, however, not all senior politicians impressed in quite the same way. Some suffered terrible stage fright and needed a couple of very stiff drinks before they were ready to face these fierce Cambridge audiences. Others were simply unimpressive. Having listened to a rather tedious speech from the then Chancellor of the Exchequer, Selwyn Lloyd, I recall one of my friends remarking, 'I could do as well as that'. Doubtless there are undergraduates at Cambridge today thinking precisely the same thoughts as they listen to *us*. There is nothing like getting close to politicians to make politics appear more accessible.

Yet in many ways the most striking feature of the Cambridge Mafia of politicians was that virtually all of us who reached West-minster were Conservatives. David Owen, who was quietly going about his medical studies at the same time, is the obvious excep-tion; given the performance of middle parties over the last thirty years, perhaps it is no surprise that he is the sole representative. Outstanding Cambridge Liberals like Brian Walsh, now one of the leading members of the Northern Bar, have concentrated on their profession. As for Labour, they did virtually nothing to recruit undergraduate talent. David Lea became Deputy General Sec-retary of the TUC, but at times Labour and the unions seemed deliberately to turn their backs on the universities. One of my friends in the Labour Club – an outstanding lawyer – sought a career with the TUC. He was told there was only one way in and that was to start work on the shop floor, hope to get union office and then work your way up. He persevered with the Labour Party but then, like David Owen and so many others, he became disillu-sioned with this reactionary old-style party. Labour simply did not come to terms with the education revolution. In contrast the Conservatives welcomed the chance to get their hands on what they saw as able new recruits.

So what kind of Conservatives were we? In those days the terms 'wet' and 'dry' had not been invented. Had they been, most of us would surely have been categorized as 'wets'. In the main we were in favour of joining Europe and supported the wind of change in Africa. We took a determinedly liberal view on most social issues, and although unemployment was not an issue we assumed it was unthinkable for it ever to return to pre-war levels. If we were to rebel against the official line, it was much more likely to be to the left than the right. I moved the motion that 'Public schools do more harm than good'; and I remember Michael Howard proposing that 'South Africa's present policies are incompatible with membership of the Commonwealth'.

One must, however, attach a health warning to Union debates. You were not necessarily expected to agree with the motion you were proposing. The skill was to take up any brief and make a competent speech. The point is made by a note I still have from John Nott, when he was President of the Union, in 1959. Inviting me to speak in a debate, he wrote:

I would be grateful if you would speak in the debate on the motion that 'This House believes that fox-hunting is revolting and disgusting'. It would very much help if you would agree to speak on either side.

The point remains. We were not automatically Conservative and thirty years earlier you would have found some of us in other parties.

Neither we nor Cambridge generally were liberal on all issues, however. At the beginning of 1961 I took over as Political Editor of *Varsity*, and ran a campaign to get women admitted to the Union. Women had entered the university sixty years earlier but the 600 women undergraduates were barred from Union membership. Supported by Michael Howard and about half a dozen other members of the Union Committee, we wrote to all Union members condemning the arguments against admission as 'either illogical or based on prejudice'. Nevertheless it was those arguments – 'people would not listen to them as speakers: they would look at them as women' – which carried the day. We needed a 75 per cent vote and we failed.

Such, then, was the general setting of the Cambridge Mafia, but it is perilous to generalize about the views and motivation of close on two dozen undergraduates who happened to be at one university at the same time. Most were not financially ambitious – and yet John Nott ended up as one of the highest paid executives in the country. Most belonged to the liberal wing of the Conservative Party – but that does not accurately position Nick Budgen. Most were not devoutly religious – but that does not remotely include John Gummer. We were certainly not a mafia in the sense that we spent all our time together. College was the centre of Cambridge life for me as for everyone else. Some of my most lasting friendships were made at Trinity Hall. Nor, when we left, did we act as an entirely self-supporting group. Given that we spent a good deal of the time competing with one another for the same constituencies, that was impossible. Yet we have remained friends in spite of the inevitable vicissitudes of politics.

In the final analysis, I can only set out what impact my early years had on my political beliefs and hope that there might be one or two echoes from others of my generation. My parents had moved south during the depression at the beginning of the 1930s. With his engineering qualifications my father found a job with Hoffman's, a company which made ball bearings in Chelmsford in Essex. My mother had qualified as a teacher thanks to the remarkable effort of her own mother, Ellen. Ellen Baker had been widowed in her mid thirties – her husband dying of tuberculosis – and had then brought up four children alone in an age when social security benefits for one-parent families of this kind did not exist. She took over running the substantial shop in Sale in Manchester where her husband had been the manager and by sheer hard work and skill made herself irreplaceable. She was a fighter and her reward was to see all four children well educated and set up with professional careers.

My own mother began her teaching career in Manchester and Sale with classes of over fifty. Both she and my father saved to buy the neat semi-detached house in Chelmsford where they spent their whole married life. To begin with, my mother was unable to work in Essex. Unemployment was high and the rule was that married women did not need jobs in the same way as married men. When the war broke out all that changed and women teachers were in great demand.

I was born in 1938, just before the war began, and my earliest memories are of the sound of high-flying aircraft. We had an American air force base nearby and Chelmsford was on the direct route to London as well as being a target in its own right.

Hoffman's and Marconi's were bombed reasonably frequently and replacing ceilings and windows was an ordinary feature of the early war years. As the war progressed the raids fell away, although there was still the hazard of the V1 and V2 rockets. In the last months our gang of children were able to make friends with the Italian prisoners of war who were brought in to keep the rivers clear.

My education started at the Kings Road infants school, about a quarter of a mile from my house, and progressed on to the primary school. Here one of my best subjects was football. My goalkeeping career peaked at about the age of ten, however, when I was in the team which won the Chelmsford schools cup. It was a good footballing school and a couple of years behind me at Kings Road was Geoff Hurst who scored the winning goals in England's World Cup victory of 1966. Alas, I did not remotely possess his skill and application. I did, however, manage to pass the 11 plus examination and win entry to what everyone called 'the Grammar School'.

It was desperately early to start dividing up young children and there were some at Kings Road who, given more encouragement, could have made the academic cut. This was not a reason for abolishing the grammar schools as happened in so many parts of the country (although happily not Chelmsford). The King Edward VI School celebrated its four hundredth anniversary when I was there and it is impossible to replace that academic tradition. When I arrived I felt inordinately and unjustifiably satisfied with the reasonably high place I had secured in the 11 plus and for the next few years I freewheeled. My report book in the early years is full of comments like 'He possesses great natural energy which he must direct into his school work' and 'He should do better than this'. The real trouble was that I was bored both with the lessons and with life as a very junior boy in a big school. I have over-compensated ever since by consistently taking on too much and avoiding all prospect of boredom.

Academically I was sometimes in the top set and sometimes not. By chance I happened to be in the top set in my fourth year when the headmaster, Nigel Fanshawe, formerly a house master at Eton, changed the rules. We were all entered for a basic set of O levels a year early and told that if we passed we would go straight into the sixth form. By the slimmest of possible margins I scraped through English and Mathematics and on this slender academic foundation was told to choose three A levels as well as to catch up on French and the appalling Latin.

For the first time in my life I started to work. Originally the plan had been that I should be an accountant. Like many of his generation, my father was concerned that I should have a professional qualification and was not at all impressed with my talk about politics. He had had to struggle hard to find a good job. He recognized that if accountants and lawyers did not quite rule the world, they had a degree of security which was quite absent from politics. He was interested in talking politics but regarded as fanciful any idea that I might practise it. Indeed, it had not even been a foregone conclusion that I would go into the sixth form at all. One idea was that I should start articles straight after the fifth year. Fortunately for me and the accountancy profession, that plan was defeated by my abrupt promotion to the sixth form. But it explains why, when I won a place at Cambridge, I agreed to read law rather than the history I would have infinitely preferred. My father's argument was that law was a serious qualification. What would I do with history? My reply now, thirty years on, is what have I ever done with law? My emphatic advice for anyone going to university is to read what you are best at and above all what you most enjoy.

Between school and university there was a stage in my life which was to have a lasting impact. This was national service. In September 1956, I was instructed to report to Warley Barracks near Brentwood to start two years' service with the Essex Regiment. I was issued with a thick khaki battledress, boots, belt, beret and all the other accoutrements of army uniform. Our days were spent marching to and fro across the parade ground learning the unpolitical art of the about-turn. Evenings were devoted to polishing the brass on our webbing and shining our black boots, first applying a hot spoon to the toe-cap in an effort to achieve a surface which was smooth and could be worked up to a mirror finish. We were woken at 6 a.m., ate in the cookhouse and had our hair clipped to a short regulation length. It was all a considerable shock and one or two, on the face of it very tough and burly characters, were over the wall and heading back home within days of arrival. My stay at Warley was cut short for a different reason.

The regiment decided that they would have a go at picking out 'potential leaders' and giving them a special form of basic training. The result was that I packed all my belongings into a kitbag and set off to Bury St Edmunds to join a mixed group of selected youth from both Essex and Suffolk. We soon found that special training simply meant more uncomfortable and intensive training. The Suez Crisis was developing and there was a certain spring in the step of the regular officers and NCOs as they put us through our paces. There was the prospect of real action rather than the tedious target practice on the Thetford ranges.

Army discipline was like nothing I have experienced before or since. The whole idea was to instil unquestioning obedience to anyone of the rank of lance-corporal and above, while we all lived in awe and dread of the most important man at the barracks, the regimental sergeant-major. One day he drilled us without being told that immediately preceding the parade we had all been inoculated against every known disease. The result was that it was difficult to raise our arms, let alone swing them. No less than three men had been marched off to the guardhouse for idleness on parade before we collectively plucked up courage to raise the subject with the RSM. He stopped the parade but it did not avail our three colleagues who were still put on a charge – on the grounds that they should have spoken earlier.

It was at Bury St Edmunds that I received the only injury of my army career. This was a broken nose inflicted by a soldier allegedly playing on my side at hockey who wielded his stick in the style of Jack Nicklaus driving off the first tee. But there were also moments of pure magic. I remember to this day an afternoon when we found our way by map through the peaceful Suffolk countryside in an autumn sunlight which picked out the greens and golds of the hedgerows and trees.

The aim of our training was to prepare us for the demands of the War Office Selection Board in Wiltshire. It was their task to decide whether we were not only potential leaders but also potential officers. For although we were in the army for only two years, there was a second lieutenant's cane in every national serviceman's knapsack. The two memorable parts of the selection process were the initiative test and the speech. Anyone who knows me will readily confirm that a grasp of practical things like the inside of car engines is not one of my greatest attributes. Here I was, then, with a section of men to get over a small ravine complete with an oil drum. I had been told that the solution did not matter. What mattered was how you approached it and that above all you should show leadership qualities. That was all very well, but for the life of me I could not even begin to see how this blasted oil drum, let alone the other soldiers, were going to get across. Fortunately, I had two soldiers in my section from another regiment which believed in preparing their entrants for these tests. They knew the oil drum procedure backwards. All I had to do was to give sound accompaniment and pretend that I knew what the hell my men were doing.

The subject for the speech was left to the candidate. I decided to summarize two articles I had read in the *Observer* about the recovery of the Volkswagen car company in Germany. The speech went well, but then I was asked why I had chosen this subject. I could hardly say that I had just read it in the papers last weekend so I mumbled something about it being a good example. Only later when I went to Germany did I discover how accurate my flip reply had been. Britain in the mid-1950s was already beginning to fall behind.

The result of the selection board was that I passed and was sent off to Eaton Hall, just outside Chester, as an officer-cadet. Up to this point I had rather enjoyed the army. Eaton Hall I loathed. For the first time in my life I came up against class. Grammar schools can be criticized for creaming off the more able children but within my school I can remember no divisions because of money or background. At Eaton Hall I learned that the Britain of the 1950s was still a class-ridden society. Schools were graded – with grammar schools coming bottom of the league – and so too were regiments.

When I started my national service, my basic choice was between the army and the air force. I picked the army and it was therefore natural to join my local regiment. At Eaton Hall I soon discovered that there were all kinds of gradation in regiments. County regiments like the Essex were certainly socially better than a corps like the Service Corps but they were some way behind, for example, light infantry regiments whose main claim to fame was that they marched at about double the normal pace. At the top of this social tree you found men in tanks on the basis that they used to be hussars on horses. This was a world I had not even glimpsed before.

Personally, I hate an atmosphere in which you are constantly seeking to establish that you are keener than the man next to you. Yet that was the essence of officer-cadet school. I will, however, make one concession. Much of our training was in the hands of two wonderfully named warrant officers – Regimental Sergeant-Major Lynch and Company Sergeant-Major Blood. I don't think either of them ever uttered the famous words: 'I call you "sir" and you call me "sir". The difference is that *you* mean it.' But it would have been surprising if that had not been their attitude to these eighteen-year-old national servicemen whom they had been sent. They responded by providing a no doubt deliberately uncomfortable passage but one that held us in good stead.

Military service could be for real. A few months earlier, an officer-cadet had passed out from Eaton Hall and had been part of the Suez invading forces at Port Said. Once there, he had against all instructions struck off on his own in a jeep and had been kidnapped. A search was mounted but the unfortunate young officer had been suffocated as he was being hidden. For all the value of our military training, however, I hated every minute of the barrack-room talk comparing schools. I remember one product of a public school I had never heard of talking about the product of another public school I had never heard of and saying in a wildly patronizing way: 'He's very proud of his school – best not to tell him that it's not a very good one.' Three years later at Cambridge I remember meeting one of my old Eaton Hall platoon. It was November the fifth and the occasion in those days of foolish battles between town and gown. 'Ah Norman,' he said, 'are you coming out tonight to beat up the Teds?' I had no doubt who was the real Teddy Boy.

Nevertheless, whatever my feelings were about Eaton Hall it was necessary to pass out successfully. The nightmare was that you would be 'returned to unit' without a commission. One cadet, so it was said, had taken this prospect so seriously that he had hanged himself. I never reached those depths of despair but I received an unmistakable message at the half-way point. At this stage you marched into your company commander's office, saluted, read your assessment, saluted again and marched off. My half-term report read: 'This officer-cadet is content to drift through with a general attitude of amused tolerance.'

Secretly I was quite pleased with that assessment, but I also had enough sense to recognize the danger signals. For the next two months I sought to exhibit greater enthusiasm. I led a platoon attack at a battle camp set in some beautiful snow-covered hills in North Wales. This was adjudged a modest success by the visiting Brigadier, although strangely he likened it to 'Piccadilly Circus at the rush hour'. I also delivered the mandatory lecture which was described by my platoon commander as the best yet – very much the first time I had come top in any of my army subjects. At any rate, I did enough to pass out on 15 March 1957 as a fully-fledged Second Lieutenant and I have never been so pleased to leave anywhere as I was to leave Eaton Hall.

In contrast, the rest of my national service, which I spent with the Essex Regiment in Dortmund, passed off pleasantly enough. People tell me at political meetings from time to time that national service should be reintroduced. But that depends from what viewpoint you approach the question. I found my two years a useful transition between school and university. Indeed my standard of living has never recovered. At the grand age of nineteen I shared a batman, who did things like polish my boots and press my uniform, with Neil Macfarlane, a future Minister of Sport and a fellow national service subaltern. In the evening I was able to dine in the splendour of the officers' mess with the regimental band playing in the background. Drink was cheap and cigarettes even cheaper.

For many, however, national service was a long exercise in boredom. There was not enough for the Rhine Army to do. There was no war to fight and the rumour was that in the event of a Russian attack our orders were to retreat as fast as our Bedford trucks would carry us to the other side of the Rhine. Occasionally we would exercise on the Lüneburg Heath, dig trenches and take part in mock attacks complete with thunder-flashes and blank ammunition. I did not find all this the greatest fun but it was substantially better than hanging around the barracks in Dortmund, where bored national servicemen marked off on the calendar the 'days to do' before demobilization and bombarded the British Forces Network with requests celebrating their day of release. *Happy Days Are Here Again* was easily the most popular radio request.

For the regular army I suspect that national service was also something of a disaster. When I went back to my old (by now twice amalgamated) regiment in 1985 I was impressed by how things had changed. Instead of unwilling conscripts I found soldiers who were there because they wanted to be there. Rather than talking about their leaving date they wanted to talk about how they could obtain the latest equipment. It was a professional army and a very good one, as has been shown time and time again over the last twenty years. The army I joined in the late 1950s also had that potential. There were good people who had had good wars and there were young regular officers coming in who by any standards were outstanding. But it was difficult to win enthusiasm from a conscript army. It had a dispiriting effect all round and sadly one or two of the officers who could remember better things responded by not so slowly drinking themselves to death. I remember one of my fellow subalterns arriving at Dortmund and being asked whether he would like to come out for a drink by his company commander. Feeling rather pleased at this invitation he accepted, even though it was still relatively early in the morning. He finally escaped from the cellar club in Dortmund sixteen hours and an uncountable number of drinks later.

A postscript to my national service was the most unlikely job I was ever given. The regiment had found that it made a lot of business sense to raise pigs, making use of the free cookhouse swill, and sell them on the open market. The result was that – until we were closed down on the grounds of unfair competition with German farmers – we had a fine herd of about seventy pigs. Two splendid soldiers from the farming parts of Essex were put in day-to-day charge, but obviously a unit of such importance required an officer. This job fell on the most junior subaltern who was me. As I went on my inspections I realized just how unsuited I was by knowledge or training to have anything sensible to say on the care and development of pigs. I then cheered up as I reflected that there was only one person more unsuited to this job than me and that was the man who had handed over this fine herd of swine – my immediate predecessor as regimental pig officer, Second Lieutenant Christopher Tugendhat.

So what effect did this odyssey from grammar school, to army, to Cambridge have upon me? It took time for all my ideas to form, but I ended up passionately in favour of a society where everyone has the opportunity to develop to the maximum of his or her ability. The greatest tragedy is to see talent unfulfilled. By 1960 we had come a long way from the pre-war years of unemployment and stifled opportunity, but even then Harold Macmillan could make a speech addressed purely to 'young men'. In the last thirty years we have made much more progress and today about half the students of law and medicine are women. But my strong feeling remains that we have a long way still to go. Women still do not have the same opportunities as men; children in tower blocks do not have the same chance as children in green suburbs; while the ethnic minorities, the unemployed and the disabled represent profound and urgent challenges.

I am also implacably opposed to divisions based on race, religion or class. Class is not simply an obsessive interest in school, university or regiment. It is about excluding people, sometimes on the basis of birth but sometimes because you are determined to preserve your own little patch. In my father's old company there was not only a division between shop floor and management, there were all kinds of divisions in management itself. My ideal company would be organized on the lines of the National Freight Company with its emphasis on employee involvement; or like Nissan in Sunderland where the managing director wears blue overalls like everyone else and all eat in the same (excellent) canteen. Working as a team is the most satisfying and potentially the most successful way of making progress in Britain.

By the same measure I hate hierarchies. My idea of hell would be working for some big nationalized industry where your future was entirely dependent upon the marking of superiors and where the only alternative would be to leave the industry altogether. I do not regard it as a contradiction to believe in keeping industry firmly in the private sector but with good public services to meet the nation's other needs. We cannot create opportunity without an excellent education system or without providing health care irrespective of wealth.

In the summer of 1961 I left Cambridge and in October I joined *The Times* in its old Victorian building opposite Blackfriars Station.

In the same month, three stops down the Underground line at Westminster, Margaret Thatcher was taking her first step on her ministerial career as Parliamentary Secretary at the Ministry of Pensions and National Insurance.

CHAPTER 3

Fleet Street

EVENINGS IN PRINTING HOUSE SQUARE
Lord Northcliffe: 'Help! Again I feel the demons of
Sensationalism rising in me. Hold me fast! Curb me,
if you love me!'

From the original watercolour by Sir Max Beerbohm
The Times

On Monday 5 June 1967, the Middle East war began with Israeli aircraft swooping down on Egyptian airfields. I heard the news on the radio in my flat at Regent's Park Terrace, north of Camden Town. By this stage in my journalistic career I was the Home Affairs Correspondent of *The Times*, covering all the policy areas of the Home Secretary from police and prisons to race relations and immigration. I was also unmarried. I rang my news editor to say that if the paper wanted volunteers to cover the war I was ready and available. I thought little more about it as I drove into the office. However, when I reached Printing House Square I was immediately called in and told to proceed to Beirut by the quickest possible means. In the best traditions of Evelyn Waugh's *Scoop*, I became Fleet Street's only Home Affairs Correspondent to be found on the road to Damascus covering the war from the Arab side.

Sadly, I had no time to gather together the cases of kit which accompanied William Boot. Instead I turned up at Heathrow Airport in what one of my colleagues unkindly described as my cocktail-party suit. There I found assembled the flower of Britain's war reporters, some of whom were decidedly dressed for action. Murray Sayle appeared to be wearing combat fatigues – a sight to unnerve the stoutest heart – and everyone else seemed to be in a state of greater readiness than myself. With some apprehension I peered at the map to see just where Beirut was and, more particularly, what its geographical relationship was to Cyprus where our special aircraft's journey ended.

A few hours later we arrived in Nicosia where we soon found that all flights and services by sea to anywhere near the war zone had been cancelled. The next day there came an unmistakable sign that the war was going well for Israel. A special Israeli aircraft arrived to fly in the correspondents reporting the war from the Israeli side. For understandable reasons, no similar friendly gesture came from any of the Arab states. Although we did not know it at the time, the air forces of Egypt and Jordan had been destroyed and for them the war was as good as lost. In Arab eyes the chief collaborators with Israel were the United States and Britain. If we waited for a lift into the Arab world we would be waiting a very long time.

I spent Tuesday 6 June scouring Cyprus for some other way of getting across the 120 miles of Mediterranean which separated us from Beirut. In the late afternoon I had an enormous stroke of luck. In Famagusta I found a small team of reporters and photographers from *Paris Match* who had managed to bribe a Cypriot sea captain to attempt the crossing. For £100 in cash I was welcome to join the party. A local bank opened especially for me to cash some cheques and the deal was struck. At dusk we set sail.

We chugged into an area of potential conflict in a small fishing vessel which would have sunk in a collision with a reasonably sturdy rowing boat. A quick inspection showed an almost total lack of lifebelts and our small group dozed uneasily on deck quietly praying that we would not meet anything equipped with guns. But as a bright dawn broke over the Mediterranean we were spotted by an armed launch – of goodness knows what nationality. It circled distantly for a minute or two and then sped away, having fortunately come to the conclusion that no sane combatants would set to sea in such a ludicrous ship. It was the only real alarm on our journey to Beirut, unless you counted a general suspicion that the whole boat might sink of its own accord.

In 1967, Beirut was regarded as an oasis of stability – so unlike its tragic fate today. It was an ideal listening-post for the whole of the Arab world and all the major newspapers had offices there. It was a cosmopolitan city with luxurious hotels like the Saint Georges and the Phoenicia. You thought nothing of walking through its streets and markets. But although Beirut had an urbane exterior it was important not to be deceived. At that moment the Lebanese no more liked the Americans and the British than anyone else.

When we landed, the journalists of *Paris Match* were allowed immediate entry, the French being regarded as sympathetic to the Arab cause even though the Israeli air force was equipped with French-built Mirage fighters. Then followed a debate about what to do with me and a colleague from the *Sunday Times*; at one point it looked as if we would be ordered back to Cyprus, but finally a compromise was reached. We were given entry visas that expired in one hour precisely – which must rank as two of the shortest visas on record but was just long enough to enable us to pick up a taxi and drive to the British Embassy. Embassy officials managed to extend the visas and there followed a stay in Beirut which was both fascinating and frustrating. Nicholas Herbert, *The Times'* regular Middle East Correspondent, was trapped by the war in Jerusalem. I took his place and endured the entirely new experience of trying to get copy past the official Lebanese censor.

This proved to be no easy matter. One story for London involved reporting on a big demonstration in favour of the Egyptian leader, President Nasser. I duly produced my copy. No, said the censor, it would not do. 'We do not have demonstrations in Beirut.' I tried to think of a word which meant roughly the same and came up with 'display'. My hope was that the sub-editors in London would change the word back to 'demonstration' again, but no such luck. The sub-editors on the foreign desk of *The Times* did not believe in changing the words of their correspondents actually on the ground. A better way of getting accurate messages through was by telephone, although the difficulty was that you could be cut off in mid-sentence by censors listening in on the line. Ever since the Six-Day War I have not had much time for anything that smacks of official censorship. Censorship can be imposed only if the case for it is overwhelming. In the main governments and politicians should fight it out with the media and not seek to suppress their right to report.

In Beirut the greatest difficulty was to obtain accurate news of the war's progress. Official Arab broadcasts were for the most part useless. The Egyptians, after all, had reported their disastrous first-day losses as a great triumph. So where did we turn? There was no doubt which broadcasting organization had the highest reputation. A picture which remains with me is of an American reporter anxiously trying to tune into the BBC World Service. It was acknowledged as the best and most objective news service in the world. In my view that is still the position. It is a great pity that over the years so many politicians (Conservative and Labour) have appeared to regard the BBC as some giant conspiracy against them. The trench warfare obscures its unparalleled international reputation.

The real trouble with Beirut in 1967, however, was that it was frustratingly distant from the real action. Every journalist stranded there wanted to get to Jordan where Israeli forces were having obvious success, but reaching Jordan meant travelling through Syria and the Syrian authorities would have none of it. My most determined effort to get through was on Sunday 11 June. The taxi was allowed through Lebanese Customs and we drove through the gorge of a no man's land to the Syrian border. At first the Syrians took us for French, but when I handed over my British passport their attitude changed. After much discussion they finally agreed to send a military message to Damascus. As we waited in a small office the radio poured out the usual mixture of news bulletins and military music, including some of the marches from the Brigade of Guards' repertoire normally heard at the Trooping of the Colour. Half an hour later the message came back that no foreigners were to be admitted. There was no arguing with the decision and, in particular, there was no arguing with the raffish civil militia who were standing by armed with their Czech-made rifles. For a visiting journalist armed men in uniform are bad enough, but at least there is the probability of a command structure. Armed men without uniform carry no such assurance and are to be avoided.

Five days later our luck suddenly changed. The Syrians announced that transit visas to Jordan would be made available and in a small convoy of Mercedes taxis we set off from Beirut once again. One of my taxi companions was Jon Akass, an admirable journalist who died in 1990 after a long and distinguished Fleet Street career. The idea was to drive straight through Damascus. With the war lost, Syrian radio for several days past had been calling for the destruction of everything British or American. To our consternation, however, our taxi driver had other ideas. He decided that he would stop in the very centre of Damascus for, of all things, a shave. It was not until his shave was successfully completed that he agreed to resume the journey. Damascus had been swarming with uniformed troops and as we travelled to the border with Jordan there were signs of war all around us. We passed burnt-out tanks, dug-in military vehicles and soldiers still digging foxholes. There was no sign that the Syrians regarded the emergency as over. Nevertheless, our obviously British party was treated correctly and courteously at each of the three road-blocks on the way to the Jordanian border.

We crossed to a nation in a state of shock. All the territory on the west bank of the River Jordan was now under Israeli control and the old city of Jerusalem had also been taken. Seeing King Hussein a few days later at a press conference, it was impossible not to be impressed by his dignity. Equally there was no doubt that his decision to join the war against Israel had been both totally wrong and also catastrophic in its effect upon his country. Not only had he lost half his kingdom but he also had now to deal with an influx of refugees from the occupied territories.

Estimates varied of the number of refugees who had fled from Israeli occupation to the east bank. By mid-June some were putting the figure at 100,000 and some considerably more. What was certain was that a high proportion were Palestinian refugees from the 1948 war which followed the creation of the State of Israel and that Jordan was entirely unprepared to deal with the new-comers. The day after I arrived in Amman I visited one of the makeshift refugee camps about thirty miles north of the city. The lucky ones had tents or primitive lean-tos but about 2,000 men, women and children were sleeping each night on the bare ground without any cover whatsoever. Food was short and sanitary arrangements non-existent.

The way across the River Jordan from the west to the east bank was by the old Allenby Bridge near Jericho which had been half-destroyed in the fighting. By chance I returned to the bridge on 20 June. My report of what I saw included the following:

Although the war has now been over for almost two weeks so far as Jordan is concerned, the refugees continue to pour across. Often carrying enormous bundles, they clamber down to the precarious makeshift plank path, with its single piece of holding wire, to join the crowd, including many anxious relatives, on the east side.

Into this already difficult situation some Israel troops supervising the crossing introduced a dangerous new element today by firing their sub-machine-guns over the heads of the struggling line of refugees. The first time was just before noon when an Israel soldier fired single shots into the air.

This immediately silenced the waiting crowd and some drew back from the edge of the bridge. A second and more serious incident occurred soon afterwards, when the path of planks was crowded with refugees together with a few Jordanians from their bank who were trying to help old women and children across.

Suddenly the Israel soldier on the plank path fired a burst from his sub-machine-gun into the air, then followed it with another. The crowd fell silent again, and even the babies stopped crying. Deliberately, the soldier made his way to the middle of the bridge and fired yet another burst dangerously low through the girders of the bridge to just above where I was standing with a group of Jordanians on the river bank.

This time he cleared the bridge of all but refugees, and a little later fired a few single shots. The disturbing feature is that there was no obvious point to this display of strength. The refugees were already bewildered enough and to risk causing panic among already frightened people borders on military lunacy. There is a real danger that if such firing continues a ricocheting bullet will kill a refugee or one of the crowd on the Jordan bank.

Back in Britain this was not a popular message. Public opinion was overwhelmingly with the Israelis, rightly condemning the Arab threat to wipe Israel off the map. (I still have a map of the Middle East bought in Beirut where the word 'Israel' has been erased in impenetrable black ink.) The Israeli victory was seen as the triumph of good over evil. But few political pictures are black and white and there were questions which needed to be answered. In occupying the West Bank had the Israelis also encouraged part of the refugee exodus? Had some Israeli troops been too rough with the people living in the land they now controlled?

The report doubtless irritated the Israeli authorities just as much as it did some of my Jewish friends in Britain. Today the position is better understood, but in 1967 such a report seemed almost incredible. Just exactly who was this journalist questioning the tactics of an army which had saved Israel from annihilation? And yet that was my role. The reporter has only one justification and one duty and that is to report honestly what he sees. Leader writers

Above left My father

Above right My mother

At the age of ten, and goalkeeper in the cup-winning Kings Road football team

Above left At the age of five

Above right At the age of sixteen

Lance-Corporal in the King Edward VI School Cadet Corps

Above left A National Service Second Lieutenant in the Essex Regiment in 1957

Above right With Harold Macmillan at Cambridge in 1960. John Gummer and Peter Viggers are in the background

With R. A. Butler at Cambridge in 1960

Speaking in the election campaign in Nottingham in 1970

My winning speech in Sutton Coldfield in February 1974

and, above all, politicians are there to argue about the whole picture. The reporter describes that part of the picture he sees. A politician is there to put his case and put it as effectively as he can. The reporter is there to say 'but'. Newspapers are there to expose; governments (and political parties) to persuade. The hope is that both roles are carried out with honesty, but journalists and politicians have different interests. The essential role of the journalist will inevitably set him at odds with the politician.

Publish and be damned can be the only policy of any self-respecting newspaper. Of course, that does not justify the invasions into personal privacy and the cameras perpetually trained at, for example, the Royal Family. What is also beyond doubt is that *not* publishing has its own consequences. Let me give a personal example. In my more usual role as Home Affairs Correspondent of *The Times* I had in September 1966 written a series of articles on Britain's prisons. I travelled to Strangeways, Leyhill, Parkhurst, Grendon Underwood and finally to the nation's best-known prison of all, Dartmoor. During my visit there I drove on to the moors near Princetown for a sandwich lunch. By the side of the narrow moor road there were one or two holiday-makers training their binoculars on the prison in search of a real inmate. Dartmoor, like Alcatraz, is one of the few prisons to rate as a tourist attraction. But what really attracted my notice was a giant of a man working alone in a field next to my parked car.

It was such an unusual sight that when I returned to the prison I mentioned my lunchtime companion. There were knowing looks. 'For goodness' sake don't report that,' one of the senior staff said. 'That's Frank Mitchell, the mad axeman. He has been in prison half his life and we think we are getting him to the point when he can be released.'

Mitchell had been sentenced to life imprisonment in 1958 for robbery with violence, but in the view of the officials at Dartmoor the fires had now burnt out. He was twenty-nine and had been under some form of restriction since the age of nine. As a reporter I had a straight choice. I could write a piece on how a convicted armed robber was working unsupervised on the moor with the certain result that the story would be followed by the rest of Fleet

Street and Mitchell would be put back behind the prison walls. Or I could trust the judgement of the prison authorities who knew him best. Their view was that unless he was released soon there was a severe danger he would become institutionalized and never be able to adapt to outside life again. I chose not to write the story.

Ten weeks later, on 12 December 1966, Mitchell escaped but even then not to freedom. Just before Christmas, on 20 December, he wrote a letter to *The Times* saying that he was willing to surrender if he were given a release date. The decision as to when to release a life sentence prisoner lies with the Home Secretary. A second letter arrived the next day and asked for 'some reason to hope'. Then there was silence. Three years later the Kray twins, Ronald and Reginald, their brother Charles and two others stood trial at the Old Bailey for Frank Mitchell's murder. The prosecution's case was that the Kray brothers had organized his escape from Dartmoor and had kept him under guard in a flat in the East End of London. Embarrassed by the hue and cry, they had then ordered his murder. At the end of the trial the Krays and the other defendants were found not guilty. Reginald Kray, however, was sentenced to five years' imprisonment for conspiring to effect the Dartmoor escape. No body was ever found but no one seriously doubts that Frank Mitchell is dead.

Should I have written the piece about Mitchell working outside the prison? According to what I had been told, it would have wrecked years of careful work at Dartmoor. Had I published, however, Mitchell would probably still be alive today. I took the view, on the evidence I had, that his rehabilitation came first. The totally detached journalist would have written the story and not concerned himself with the consequences. As it turned out, that last course would have been infinitely better for Frank Mitchell.

The Times I joined in 1961 was a unique newspaper. Our geographical position opposite Blackfriars Station already set us apart from the actual Fleet Street papers like the *Daily Telegraph*, the *Daily Express* and the *Daily Mail* but the differences went much deeper. Alone among national newspapers, our front page was devoted to seven columns of closely printed classified advertisements recording births and deaths, offering exotic holidays and expensive cars and, most important of all, the Personal Column. It was not until May 1966 that *The Times* went over to news on the front page and we reporters competed to get our pieces on the first one that rolled from the presses. As it happened, the paper led with the notably inaccurate prediction 'London to be the new HQ for NATO'. Four days later I had the lead with a story that the Home Secretary, Roy Jenkins, was to carry out a ten-day study tour of police forces and prisons in the United States. The story was accurate enough but the report was significant in another way. It came on the day when the rest of Fleet Street were leading with the life sentences given to Ian Brady and Myra Hindley for the moors murders. *The Times* of that period had news standards all of its own.

At a time when enormous bylines proclaimed Fleet Street stars like Noel Barber, Chapman Pincher and Logan Gourlay, the writers of *The Times* were virtually anonymous. Up to 1967, specialist writers like David Wood and Charles Douglas-Home were simply 'Our Political Correspondent' and 'Our Defence Correspondent'. Our foreign correspondents like Louis Heren and Fred Emery wrote under the description 'From Our Own Correspondent'. (The 'own' distinguished them from 'our correspondent' who was probably a local news agency paid on the basis of what appeared in the paper.) We reporters on the home news side wrote under the splendid title 'From Our Special Correspondent'.

The concept was that *The Times* was a newspaper of record. What mattered above all was accuracy. There was a 'corrections column' to put right mistakes and it was inadvisable for a reporter to appear there too regularly. There was even a *Times* style book which instructed staff on what words were allowed and what were not. 'Sophisticated' was on the banned list as an example of an all-purpose sloppy word which could be used to describe a smart lady or an advanced weapons system. As my Jordan report showed, the Six-Day War was being fought by 'Israel soldiers' not 'Israeli soldiers'. The correct took precedence over the easy. One of the most controversial proprietors of the paper had been Lord North-cliffe, between 1908 and 1922. He had (unjustly) accused *The Times* of living by the motto 'News, like wine, improves by keeping' and had waged war with the 'Greybeards' and 'Monks' of Printing

House Square. Yet in the end the old gang's impersonal form of journalism had prevailed over Northcliffe's sensationalism.

The Times I joined had nothing to do with the cult of personality. It had everything to do with providing accurate, balanced news and allowing the reader to make up his own mind. News was not to be slanted. Opinion came in the three leading articles and the one turnover article on the right-hand side of the letters. Columnists like Bernard Levin were a later invention. I was just in time to experience life in the old Victorian building which had housed *The Times* since 1874. Fires burnt in grates and an antiquated lift took you slowly to the upper floors. Over the building there was a massive coat of arms; inside an impressive oak-panelled waiting room. No modern manager would have approved of the layout for a moment. The reporters' room was a long walk down a number of narrow corridors from the news room. Only in cases of dire emergency or supreme irritation did the news editor appear among us. When we moved into the functional new building, erected around us on the same site, our independence was at last rumbled: the open-plan reporters' room was placed directly next to the news room.

I had graduated to the main paper via a so-called training period on special supplements. These were the advertising supplements which appeared in the middle of the paper and were, as was evident from any trip on the Underground, the most popularly dispensable part of the paper. Indeed unless you were fascinated by the personnel policy of J. Walter Thompson or the coke ovens of the Spencer Steelworks it was difficult to know just who read them. Admittedly they were highly profitable, and there was no shortage of companies wanting to take this prestigious form of institutional advertising. In truth, however, it was not much of a training. I learnt more in a month on the *Oxford Mail* than in six on special supplements. Nevertheless, for a twenty-three-year-old straight down from university it was a fantastic opportunity, for after twelve months on special supplements you were transferred to the main paper.

The first reporters' room I joined was home to a colourful array of characters and some outstanding writers. There was Philip Ure who had reported everything from the Second World War to the 1952 West Country flood disaster. Over coffee he would gaze round mournfully at what he invariably referred to as 'the worst canteen in Western Europe'. There was Basil Gingell who somehow managed to combine being both naval and ecclesiastical correspondent. There was Hugh Noyes, the son of the poet Alfred, who was once sent to write about a nudists' convention at Woburn, but only after a solemn warning from the editor that 'under no circumstances should Mr Noyes remove his clothes'. Outside London there were regional correspondents like Brian Priestley in Birmingham who was always willing to help a young reporter like myself. The inexhaustible Frank Roberts presided over the news room; Geoffrey Woolley ran the letters columns; and Geoffrey Smith wrote obituaries. John Grant was defence correspondent and when he moved on his place was taken by a former colonel called Alun Gwynne Jones, now Lord Chalfont. In the senior echelons William Haley was still editor and Maurice Green was his deputy; Oliver Woods, an assistant editor, went out of his way to encourage young newcomers like myself.

For me as a young reporter two points were abundantly clear about working for *The Times*. First, the status of the paper was high. Government departments rang back and most doors could be opened. Pay, on the other hand, was low. I joined the paper at £600 a year and my salary only went over £1,000 when I joined the main paper. That, incidentally, was not the result of managerial generosity but the result of an agreement with the National Union of Journalists on a minimum Fleet Street rate. At meetings of the central London branch of the NUJ *The Times* contingent were always keen to get any slight increase in the minimum rate, much to the disdain of the *Daily Mirror* staff who were all paid considerably more. As far as I was concerned the NUJ did me a good turn in those days and I have remained a member of the union ever since. Even on the Fleet Street minimum life was not that easy, but there was one way to circumvent the pay problem.

If you left Printing House Square on a story, the tradition was that appearances had to be kept up. You travelled first class and you stayed in the best hotels. Thus from about the middle of the month I was always anxious to cover anything which would take me out of London. A good reason to leave town was a by-election and best of all was a general election when we moved from constituency to constituency writing sketches as we went. In both 1964

and 1966 I covered the general elections in the Midlands, happily
based in hotels like the Midland in Birmingham, and picking up
tips on how to fight a parliamentary seat.

I interviewed Brian Walden who was fighting to retain his highly
marginal All Saints constituency in Birmingham for Labour. I
watched Peter Tapsell making a spirited open-air speech in the
square at Nottingham in an unavailing attempt to hold on for the
Conservatives in 1964. I listened to Alec Douglas-Home being
shouted down in the Birmingham Bull Ring and the same happening two years later to Harold Wilson in 1966. I went canvassing
with the Conservative Party's youngest candidate, the twenty-three
year-old Jonathan Aitken who was fighting Meriden near Coventry
and took the temperature in Wolverhampton where there was an
unusual all-woman contest between Renee Short and Miranda
Greenaway. Wolverhampton was unimpressed by this triumph for
feminism but as I was in town I took the opportunity of interviewing
another candidate, Enoch Powell, for an election diary we were
running. What, I asked, was the biggest issue on the doorstep? I
expected to be told something about the cost of living but not a
bit of it. 'Immigration,' replied Enoch. I duly phoned in my piece
but it was never used. After all, who in 1964 had ever heard of a
former Conservative Cabinet minister thinking that immigration
was an important political issue?

For any journalist there comes a moment of decision about the
future. Do you remain a general writer? Do you specialize? Or do
you seek to make your way up the editorial ladder? My ambitions
were still in politics and I thought my best plan was to build up
a particular knowledge. I had noticed that alone among the big
departments of Whitehall, the Home Office had no specialist correspondents. And yet no department was more in the news. There
were problems in the police with too many men leaving the service.
There was a prison crisis following the escapes of the train robber
Charles Wilson, the ill-fated Frank Mitchell and the spy George
Blake. Race relations and immigration policy were rapidly becoming matters of public debate and there were rumbles from
Northern Ireland which was then still a Home-Office responsibility. For a journalist it was a rich and extensive vein and
eventually *The Times* agreed that I should become Fleet Street's
first Home Affairs Correspondent.

Virtually everything that concerned the Home Office came my way, even the day in May 1967 when crime came to Printing House Square itself. At about 10.00 in the morning I had driven into the square in front of the main building to find that my way to the car park was barred by a chauffeur-driven Jaguar. Suddenly, four or five men ran out from the car park, bundled into the Jaguar and sped off into Queen Victoria Street. I had not the faintest idea what was happening but followed after them in what my journalistic colleagues were loyal enough to describe as a chase. In fact the chase was soon over as the Jaguar disappeared into the traffic and it was only when I returned that I found there had been a robbery. Two security guards had been injured and the gang had escaped with about £50,000 in cash.

My period as Home Affairs Correspondent gave me an insight into the workings of Whitehall and the approach of two Home Secretaries. When I first took over, Roy Jenkins was Home Secretary. He had a first-class mind and a determination to make a mark. He tackled many of the issues that needed to be tackled – like race relations and prison security – but he had one serious drawback. He was too grand by half. The son of a distinguished miners' union leader, he gives the impression of being the offspring of a rather disdainful aristocratic family. It is one of those fine ironies of British politics that three of the founders of the SDP – Jenkins, Owen and Rodgers – all adopt a loftier tone than any modern Tory would dare attempt. Jim Callaghan, who took over from Jenkins, was not as clever but his skills with people were in a different class, a point which was underlined when he went on a hugely successful tour of the Falls Road area of Belfast in August 1969. He had arrived at the Home Office shell-shocked and exhausted from an unsuccessful period as Chancellor, but he ended up as leader of his party and Prime Minister. Indeed, when the news came through that Callaghan was to succeed Wilson, none of us in the Shadow team – Margaret Thatcher included – welcomed it. Labour had picked the man who just could win them the next election.

My day-by-day relations were not with the ministers at the Home Office but with the press officers. Tom McCaffrey, who later followed Callaghan to Number 10 and into the Labour Party, was the excellent head of the office. One of his assistants was a young press officer called Terry Perks who also graduated to Number 10 as assistant to Bernard Ingham and by chance handled my resignation from the Cabinet in 1990. Newspapers continue to debate the role of the specialist reporter. The case against the specialist is that he can become a prisoner of the department. The case for is that the specialist acquires considerable background, knows the personalities and can foresee developments. But very, very rarely was a story simply handed to me by the Home Office. It happened once, when John Profumo, the Conservative Cabinet minister who had resigned in the Keeler affair, was made a prison visitor. The reason for this was to get the news out and to avoid further hounding of Profumo. I was happy to cooperate.

A particular bone of contention among journalists is the political lobby system. Here you have political correspondents given regular briefings by both Government and Opposition spokesmen on the basis that nothing they say will be attributed directly to them. It is all 'off the record'. Let me illustrate from my own experience. In August 1966, *The Times* had two admirable political correspondents, David Wood and George Clarke. The House of Commons was sitting into August and both had holidays booked. With assurances that 'nothing ever happens in August', I was drafted in to hold the fort. On Wednesday 10 August, Harold Wilson reshuffled his Cabinet: George Brown became Foreign Secretary, Dick Crossman Leader of the House of Commons and Michael Stewart Secretary of State for Economic Affairs. I was left with a big open space to fill on the front page.

A meeting of the lobby was called and with some difficulty I found my way to the Prime Minister's room in the House of Commons. For the next half-hour Harold Wilson himself took questions on the ministerial changes. Everyone in the room understood the terms of the briefing: the Prime Minister could not be quoted directly. Thus my report referred to 'Government circles' denying that there had been any kind of a deal at the time of George Brown's resignation threat a few months earlier.

I added a description of what was to become a familiar issue over the next twenty-five years:

At one stage in making the changes Mr Wilson apparently considered more drastic treatment for the Cabinet by roughly
halving the number of members. In the event, however, he
considered this impracticable – and possibly unpopular outside
Westminster – but still hopes that more work will now be carried
out by Cabinet committees. In this way it is hoped eventually to
reduce the number of Cabinet meetings.

Would it have made any difference had I named Wilson and
put his ruminations in quotes? Certainly I cannot see how it would
have altered the reader's understanding. I doubt, however, whether
Wilson would have been as frank in an open press conference as
he was at the briefing. The end result would have been less news
rather than more. I remain unpersuaded by those who advocate
the end of the lobby system and the institution of regular press
conferences with named press spokesmen. Our system is not the
same as the United States. For one thing, the Prime Minister
comes to the House of Commons twice a week for on-the-record
comments on government policy. If I were still a journalist I would
not complain about the system too much. The best political correspondents are the ones who sensibly use all opportunities –
including lobby briefings – as a basis for their enquiries.

As a journalist who became a politician, however, I formed
rather different views about the relations between government and
press. What shocked me when I was in government was the easy
way that information was deliberately leaked. Two of the biggest
problems I faced in my career came directly from leaks. The first
was the leak of the Central Policy Review Staff's report on the
future of the welfare state; the other was the disclosure of some
of the major proposals in my social security review two weeks
before publication. In both cases the reports were detailed and
obviously came from inside government itself. By the very nature
of leaks you never know precisely who is responsible, but the
explanation that they are the work of disgruntled civil servants is
only partly true. In many cases, the culprit is a politician.

We should not be dewy-eyed about leaks. They are almost never
carried out because of an altruistic belief in open government.
Leaks are the work of those with a case to pursue. I imagine
the theory on the CPRS report was that prior publication of the

proposals would cause a storm and ensure that they were never implemented. In fact the leak simply provided Labour with a stick to beat the Government. Leaks were a constant hazard of ministerial life right from the beginning of the Thatcher Government and provide one of the major reasons why many sensitive issues were considered, initially at least, by small groups of ministers. It was the only way that security could be ensured.

Even more insidious than leaks were the anonymous ministerial comments that inevitably came when you were in the middle of a crisis. This had nothing to do with Bernard Ingham's regular press briefings. I always found Bernard entirely straight with me and supportive. His priority was to protect Margaret Thatcher, but what else would you expect her chief press officer to do? And yet the gossip of one or two ministers over lunch, or an injudicious remark in the lobbies of the House of Commons, can have a frankly debilitating effect and always at the most difficult times. In the middle of a strike it is not encouraging to read in the press that an anonymous minister believes that you are 'not getting the case over' to the public.

Even in the comparatively short time I have been in politics the working relations between ministers and journalists have changed. These days, no self-respecting up-and-coming minister or shadow minister would be without a lunch diary crammed full of political correspondents. Sometimes the correspondents come singly; sometimes they come in twos and threes. Lunching politicians is now a major media operation and the same journalists who refuse to go to Downing Street's briefings will regularly entertain on an entirely non-attributable basis. Every newspaper does it for the very good reason that it has proved a rich source of news and political gossip.

The advantage for ministers and their shadows is less certain. One or two have made quite a reputation for themselves by floating (or perhaps I mean leaking) their plans to a newspaper just before the official announcement. They thus achieve two bites at the cherry and leave behind them a grateful correspondent or news room. But there is a subtle pressure to go on and perhaps say more than was intended when the smoked salmon first arrived. Politicians cannot be seen to be boring or, even worse, not in the know. It is a cosy relationship, but for the unsuspecting it has its dangers. A senior political correspondent, whom I had known long before on Fleet Street when we had door-stepped the same meetings, once confided to me that 'politicians and journalists cannot be total friends'. He was right. Roles are different. Ministers and their shadows are not being lunched for the pleasure of their company but in the hope that they may reveal information which can be published.

In my views of the media, I remain at heart an old *Times* man. I believe that fair and balanced reporting is what journalism is all about. On newspapers today I admire the diggers and consistent reporters. In broadcasting my heroes are the news correspondents – like Kate Adie and Martin Bell of the BBC – rather than the overglamorized presenters. They show that fair reporting can still be lively reporting. The acid test of the current affairs output of television is the strength of its news coverage. Too often, however, news is taken for granted and the broadcasting organizations are judged by magazine programmes like *Panorama* and *World in Action*. The trouble with such programmes is that they are constantly trying to find an original angle on the news – which can lead them into error – or are fighting to be noticed by deliberately courting controversy.

When William Haley finally retired from *The Times*, he made a farewell speech in the reporters' room. His warning was 'beware – the morons are taking over'. It was a warning directed against the just-arriving BBC Radio 1 complete with disc jockeys. Haley's comments were too patrician by half. He had been Director-General of the BBC and had taken his austere standards from Reith before him. My complaint about the media today is different. I regret that the good reporter seems to have taken second place to the columnist. It was always said (at least it was said by us at Printing House Square) that the motto of the *Guardian* was 'Views are free: News costs money'. Giving your opinion is a substantially easier operation than collecting news and presenting a rounded argument.

Even the leaders of *The Times* were sometimes prepared with a speed and lack of background knowledge that made them pretty valueless. The space has to be filled. The first leader that I ever wrote for the paper was about some dispute at the Chelsea Flower Show. I know nothing about horticulture and even less about the organization of the Chelsea Flower Show. Yet I was given the subject at about 4.30 p.m. and told to produce a leader by 6.00. It duly appeared and doubtless was eagerly pored over by the protagonists in the dispute. As I read some of the hostile comments over my time in government, I tried to remember the circumstances of my first leader.

However, two encouraging trends in the newspapers of today cannot be denied. Television news is infinitely better than when I first watched it over thirty years ago and the modern press is a substantial advance on the position when I was in Fleet Street. I am sometimes introduced at dinners with the comment that I worked for *The Times* – 'when *The Times* was really *The Times*'. Up to a point, Lord Copper. We probably had more influence then in Whitehall and with the Government of the day, and yet the advantages for the reader were not overwhelming. We covered the escape of George Blake from the not very distant Wormwood Scrubs almost entirely with news agency copy, whereas today I imagine that the editor would put a small team on to the story. Thanks particularly to the work of Charles Douglas-Home and Charles Wilson, *The Times* is now much more accessible than it was, while you can hardly complain about the standards of a newspaper that has writers like Philip Howard and political reporters like Robin Oakley.

Fleet Street itself may now have been turned over to the banks, but the press is in surprisingly good shape. In the 1980s the press fought the battles against restrictive practices that should have been fought when I was there in the 1960s. The emergence of the *Independent* has led to the renaissance of the *Daily Telegraph* and a deliberate attempt by *The Times* to re-establish its authority. In addition we have seen the dramatic recovery over the last decade of the *Daily Mail*; the launching of other newspapers like *Today*; and the consistent development of the *Sunday Times* and the *Financial Times*.

In February 1968 I crossed the Rubicon from newspapers to politics. I stayed at Printing House Square for another two and a half years, but my aims and ambitions were now elsewhere. Since leaving Cambridge I had kept up my involvement in politics. I spent a number of years on the editorial board of the Bow Group magazine *Crossbow* under the skilful editorship of Michael Wolff who was to go on to become Director-General of the Conservative Party before his premature death. I had also given a hand to Leon Brittan who in 1966 had been the Conservative candidate in North Kensington.

When I returned from the Six-Day War I decided to try to get on the official list of Conservative candidates. Leon was one of my main sponsors and I was interviewed by a committee at Conservative Central Office under Geoffrey Johnson Smith. I was successful, but getting your name on the list was only a first step. The selection of candidates was – as it remains – firmly in the hands of the constituencies. As an approved candidate you could apply for any seat where there was a vacancy. Whether you were interviewed or not depended entirely on the constituency. As I was soon to find out to my advantage, Conservative Central Office could not dictate the selection process.

The first seat I was interviewed for was Kettering in Northamptonshire, then held by Labour with a majority of over 11,000. No one thought we would win it, but it was a good place for an untried candidate to cut his political teeth. I duly went through a first group of interviews to the final where I was beaten into second place by a barrister, John Taylor. He did what every would-be candidate should try to achieve: he made the selection meeting laugh.

A week or two later I received a letter from an old Cambridge friend, Martin Suthers. Martin was an officer of the South Nottingham constituency and they were looking for a new candidate to replace their former member, William Clark, who had now been adopted in Surrey. It was a highly marginal seat with a Labour majority of just 317. Central Office were lobbying hard on behalf of a former speech-writer to both Alec Douglas-Home and Ted Heath called Nigel Lawson. Martin's view was that the support of the party machine would not remotely carry the day in fiercely independent Nottingham. He added that he was writing to one other mutual friend urging him to put his name forward – and that was Leon Brittan.

In putting together the list for interview, the selection committee of the association rejected unseen such unknown applicants as Norman Tebbit and Sally Oppenheim. About twenty went forward, including Lawson, Brittan and Fowler. Our interviews took place on the Saturday and the final was to be on the Monday. On the Saturday evening both Leon and I received calls that we were through to the final, but even more to our surprise we learned that Nigel Lawson had not been put forward – and nor had anyone else. The final was to be a two-man affair. I was to fight it out with the man who had been instrumental in getting me on to the candidates' list in the first place. Leon had every reason to expect that he would win. He had already fought a seat and had been going strong in Conservative politics since Cambridge. I, on the other hand, had stepped back to devote myself to *The Times*. Against the odds, however, the Nottingham South association chose me as their new candidate.

Being selected for a seat is the most difficult part of politics. There are two rules. The first is to be persistent and the other is to take the rough with the smooth. You lose when you should win; you win when you should lose. For some, the trauma of selection is such that competing candidates never speak to each other again. But that is a foolish attitude in such an up-and-down business as politics where fortunes change so rapidly. Four years later, on redistribution of my South Nottingham seat, I tried unsuccessfully to wrest Rushcliffe from Ken Clarke. Three years after that, Ken found himself my junior spokesman at social services. I am glad to say that in spite of the vicissitudes of politics, our victories, our defeats, our promotions, or lack of them, the Cambridge Mafia remain friends. It is the only sensible basis on which a political life can be pursued.

For the following two years I worked flat out. The advantage of a daily newspaper is that there is a Monday edition. I was thus able to organize my week so that I spent Sunday afternoon to Thursday at *The Times* and the rest of my time in Nottingham. I also got married. I had met Linda Christmas when she worked for the news editor of *The Times* and she had then wisely decided to pursue a journalistic and writing career of her own. Our marriage did not last – mainly because I was never able or prepared to devote a sensible amount of time to it. Keeping politics and journalism running together, and later being Member of Parliament for Nottingham South and candidate for Sutton Coldfield at the same time, became my entire life. Throughout these years Linda supported me wholeheartedly and the responsibility for the breakdown of our marriage was entirely mine. The only silver lining is that we remain friends to this day.

In June 1970, in faultless summer weather, Harold Wilson called a general election. The opinion polls consistently went his way, although on the streets of Nottingham we were not finding the same reaction. There was an enormous enthusiasm in the campaign as we raced from house to house pursued by my energetic campaign assistant, Peter Morrison – who twenty years later was to become Margaret Thatcher's Parliamentary Private Secretary. If this was losing I wondered what winning would be like. On election day itself the first opinion poll came out showing us ahead. I set up on Trent Bridge waving a copy of the *Evening Standard* and desperately urging the motorists returning to my stronghold of West Bridgford to vote. Fortunately they did, and the result was that I won South Nottingham from the Labour MP, George Perry, with a majority of 3,700. Throughout the country, the swing to the Conservatives was sufficient to give Ted Heath a thirty-seat majority.

Then I hit a major snag. As Home Secretary, Jim Callaghan should have implemented the proposals of the independent boundary commission which redraws parliamentary boundaries every ten years. In 1969 he had refused to do so, much to Conservative anger as our party would have been the overall beneficiary. At the opening of the new Parliament, the Queen's Speech made clear that the boundary proposals would now be implemented. The direct result of that was the abolition of the Nottingham South constituency I had just won. I would remain Member of Parliament until the next election but in the meantime would have to find a new seat. It was not the greatest beginning.

It would be pleasant to think that as I left Fleet Street my journalistic career was well recognized at Westminster. I fear that was not the case. It did me not the slightest good with either of the two leaders I served. When Ted Heath first appointed me to the Conservative front bench as spokesman for Home Affairs in 1974 I was called to his room in the House of Commons. We talked about the new job but rather more about the press photographers who had been following him after his second defeat. Sensing my interest, he asked: 'Are you interested in the press, then?'

Margaret Thatcher at least knew I had been a journalist, but she managed the ultimate insult of my Fleet Street career. Years later when she was Prime Minister I turned up as a Cabinet minister to an official lunch for a distinguished visiting group from Finland. 'Ah Norman,' she said, spying me. 'You know all about paper.' And then to the assembled group she added the dread words: 'He used to work for the *Manchester Guardian*.'

CHAPTER 4

Reshuffle

Guardian

In terms of experience Margaret Thatcher's first Shadow Cabinet in 1975 was a mixed bag. There were undoubted political giants like Quintin Hailsham, who had been a central player for as long as I had taken a serious interest in politics. There was Peter Thorneycroft, the new Chairman of the Party, who had resigned as Macmillan's Chancellor of the Exchequer in a clash over public spending, and there was Reggie Maudling who had himself contested the leadership against Ted Heath in 1965 when Alec Douglas-Home had resigned. There were men like Willie Whitelaw, Peter Carrington (Leader of the Party in the Lords), Geoffrey Howe and Jim Prior who had established themselves as public figures in the Heath Cabinet. And then there were the rest of us. Some had served in the 1970 Conservative Government and some had not. The press was decidedly underwhelmed at the prospect.

The Times, in those days under the editorship of William Rees-Mogg, was particularly scathing. Mrs Thatcher had exchanged Robert Carr, Peter Walker, Geoffrey Rippon, Nicholas Scott and Paul Channon for Nicholas Edwards, Airey Neave, George Younger, Sally Oppenheim and myself. 'If she were in football management,' *The Times* said, 'she would expect to receive a substantial transfer fee for making that swop.' Michael Heseltine must have fumed to be written off as not of 'the same weight' as the minister he was shadowing – of all people Tony Benn. Other papers were no more complimentary. Labour politicians often complain bitterly of the automatic press support given to the Tories. That was a long way from being so in the mid-1970s. Press sympathy was predominantly for the old team who had been displaced. Above all, there was no confidence that Margaret Thatcher had the clout to defeat Harold Wilson's experienced front bench. We all – Margaret Thatcher very much included – had to establish ourselves.

We were under immediate scrutiny – political, and to my surprise personal. As the newly appointed spokesman for social services, I found very quickly that as a member of the Shadow

Cabinet I was potential 'news'. A few days after my promotion I was sitting in my flat when I received a telephone call from a reporter on the William Hickey column of the *Daily Express.* They had discovered that I was now separated from my first wife, Linda. Until my entry to the Shadow Cabinet this had not rated a mention. Although there were a number of journalists who knew the position, they had taken the view that private lives were private lives. Indeed, even after my promotion, a reporter interviewing me from the much maligned BBC had gone to some trouble to avoid mention of the obvious fact that we had split up.

With Linda's agreement I decided that the only course was to make a brief press announcement to everyone. Inevitably the next day reports were carried by virtually every newspaper in the country. We did not like the process, as old photographs of happier days were dredged up, but, just as surely, twenty-four hours later the matter was no longer of general interest. Nevertheless, I felt a little apprehensive about addressing my women's branch in Sutton Coldfield the next day. I should not have worried. As I entered the room everyone got to their feet in an emotional standing ovation – which was symbolic of the personal support I have always received from my local party.

Politically, my immediate preoccupation was pensions. The great pension debate had swung to and fro for the best part of a decade. There had been Richard Crossman's pension scheme but this had perished with the incoming Conservative Government in 1970, and there had been the scheme of Keith Joseph which had lapsed with the incoming Labour Government of 1974. By this time the pensions industry was beside itself with frustration. They wanted some certainty. They felt strongly that an industry which necessarily had to make long-term investment decisions was being damaged by the very worst short-term politics. A third scheme had now been devised by Labour's Social Services Secretary, Barbara Castle, and more particularly by the Social Security Minister, Brian O'Malley.

By any standards O'Malley was an object lesson for a new shadow minister. He was a complete professional. Early on he told me his view of political life in the House of Commons. In debates he would give no quarter and take no prisoners, but once the debate was over he was happy to have a drink in the smoking room.

Everyone knew where they were. It was an enormous tragedy that twelve months later he collapsed at the dispatch box in the chamber of the House of Commons and died at the early age of forty-six, on the threshold of a Cabinet career.

With some ingenuity O'Malley and Castle put together a scheme which promised a second state pension for everyone but which at the same time allowed private occupational schemes to opt out of the state system provided their pensions met the government's requirements. This seemed to the pensions industry as good a deal as they would get and, bowing to their advice, Geoffrey Howe and Ken Clarke had already decided to allow the new bill through unopposed. Nevertheless it seemed to me that the debate on the Pensions Bill – which was to be my first front-bench speech on social services – would be one of the great Parliamentary occasions.

Over the next few weeks I applied myself entirely to pensions. I read everything there was comprehensible to read and met anyone in the industry who had anything to say. On Tuesday 18 March, the day arrived. With some trepidation I walked to the House of Commons from my flat and entered the chamber. Harold Wilson was ending a boisterous statement on the Common Market – boisterous because he was explaining why the Labour Government were now recommending a 'yes' vote in the forthcoming referendum to determine whether Britain stayed in Europe. The Labour Party was hopelessly split on this issue and a number of Wilson's Cabinet, including Barbara Castle, were totally opposed to the policy. The statement ended and as soon as the Prime Minister sat down the chamber almost entirely emptied.

Pensions are an acquired taste in the House of Commons. The real point about the day for most Members of Parliament was that an unopposed bill meant no vote and therefore no requirement even to be at Westminster. The decision about the future of our pensions system was taken with less than a dozen members out of a possible 635 present in the chamber. It was in these circumstances that the appallingly named State Earnings Related Pension was born. True to his word, Brian O'Malley tried to floor me early on with a couple of technical questions, but understanding that I too had done a little homework he allowed me to complete the rest of my speech uninterrupted. O'Malley was, after all, getting his bill without a division. Once the pensions debate was over, I

handed over the committee stage of the bill to Ken Clarke and
settled down to studying my inheritance.

Geoffrey Howe, who was now Shadow Chancellor, had
bequeathed me bundle after bundle of papers, each neatly contained by a barrister's pink ribbon, on subjects ranging from
hospital building to mental health and from child benefit to community care. The prospect was daunting and it was clear that there
was only one person who could do the hard slog to get on top of
it all – and that was me. In government there is a ready supply of
civil service experts able to take you through the most complex
areas. In Opposition you are basically on your own. You probably
have a research assistant but there is not the easy access to skilled
expertise which is the right of even the most junior of government
ministers. But knowledge was not my only concern.

It was rapidly becoming clear to me that there were going to be
no easy runs for us in social services. The conventional wisdom is
that in Opposition a party can promise everything. Nowhere is that
temptation greater than in policy areas like health, social security
and pensions. There is constant demand for improvement and
most often that is translated into requests for more cash. It would
have been easier and more comfortable to have given in to some
of those demands, but, rightly, this was not the Thatcher way.
Economic recovery and the control of public spending were central
to our new policies and Geoffrey Howe insisted that pledges for
new spending were to be avoided. We could not be in a position
of calling for restraint on public spending while at the same time
arguing for extra money on favoured projects.

By the same measure, it was difficult to attack any of the Labour
Government's public spending economies. Thus when Barbara
Castle cancelled the pensioners' £10 Christmas bonus, I was not
able to mount a full-scale bombardment. Later, after I had moved
on, my successor Patrick Jenkin felt similarly constrained when
Barbara Castle, under pressure from the Chancellor Denis
Healey, changed the whole basis of uprating old age pensions and
made a public spending saving of over £1 billion in present-day
monetary values. There never was such a responsible Opposition.
Imagine the howls of Labour anger there would have been if the
Thatcher Government had tried either of these devices. However,
our restraint did us no great harm. The public are rightly sceptical

about the financial promises of parties in Opposition. If they were not, in 1983 they would have elected Michael Foot who had promised more spending on more projects than any other Labour leader in post-war history. Our policy of caution over public spending did, however, have one real political consequence. It left me short of conventional ammunition in shadowing a department where a lack of resources is, and always has been, the characteristic complaint. But I had reckoned without Barbara Castle.

Barbara Castle had been a considerable politician while I was still at university and I came ready to be impressed. I was not. Right from the start we did not get on – which is more unusual than it may sound. Ministers and their shadows usually have some working relationship. With Barbara Castle I found no point of contact. She was like a political whale stranded on a beach. She was still fighting the battles of pre-war Britain. To her, the Tories were the 'enemy'. She appeared totally unaware that my generation of Tory MPs were not the offspring of mill owners but the products of the welfare state. On practically all the major issues of our time she was wrong – Europe, defence, nationalization – but the terrible irony was that on the one major issue that she got right she was defeated by her own party.

This was the issue of trade union reform. Her famous White Paper, *In Place of Strife*, set out a substantial part of the case for reforming union law. The White Paper was published at the beginning of 1969 and contained proposals for strike ballots, fines and conciliation pauses. After months of manoeuvring and mounting opposition Harold Wilson and his Cabinet abandoned the proposed legislation and settled for a worthless 'solemn and binding undertaking' from the TUC that they would do more to clean up their own house. It was a humiliating defeat. Faced with this position, many other ministers would have resigned. Barbara Castle not only stayed on, she tried to re-establish herself with her own particular constituency in the Labour Party – the left wing that had done so much to bring about the industrial chaos that *In Place of Strife* was designed to cure. Her rehabilitation campaign finally brought her to the health service where she managed to find an issue that combined irrelevance with loss of money. The issue was pay beds.

Anyone who believes that the Labour Party brings peace to the health service would do well to study this period. For over six months the press was full of stories of a health crisis and the villain was not a Conservative minister like Fowler or Clarke but the Labour Secretary of State, Mrs Castle. The presence of beds for fee-paying private patients in National Health Service hospitals dated back to the inception of the service in 1948. Compromises had to be reached and one of these was on pay beds. If private practice by hospital consultants was not to be outlawed, the question became where this private practice should take place.

The advantage of having a number of beds set aside for private practice in health service hospitals was twofold. First, it meant that consultants did not waste time travelling to a private hospital; second, it provided some extra resources for the health service itself which charged for the use of the facilities. In terms of the issues before the health service, pay beds were of little importance. Out of over 400,000 beds in health service hospitals, about 4,500 were designated pay beds. Nevertheless the beds produced about £30 million a year in income for the service and perhaps above all the opportunity for consultants to carry on some limited additional private practice. It was a facility that they prized and it was a safe bet that any attempt to end this arrangement would bring the Labour Government into direct conflict with the medical profession.

In the early months of 1975 there were frequent rumours about the Government's intentions and the health unions NUPE and COHSE (the National Union of Public Employees and the Confederation of Health Service Employees) started to make bellicose noises. On 5 May we forced a debate in the House of Commons and were rewarded by a statement from Mrs Castle. She made no secret of her motivation. The removal of pay beds, she said, has been 'part of our socialist policy for years'. The policy was to reduce immediately the number of pay beds; then to phase out the remainder; and finally to introduce a licensing system to prevent alternative private hospital provision being made above that which the Government thought fit. You did not need to be an expert to work out that a licensing system run by Mrs Castle with the friendly advice of the health unions might just result in one or two gaps in private provision. Having lit the touch-paper, Barbara Castle retired for a few months to prepare the consultative document and in August came back with a set of proposals which confirmed the medical profession's worst fears.

In the very first line of the document she set out her aim: 'The Government's policy is for the separation of private practice from National Health Service hospitals.' Pay beds were to go and even worse from the point of view of the medical profession a licensing system was to be set up which required controls both on the quality and the quantity of the private sector outside the health service. Ultimate power rested with the Secretary of State and the Department of Health, and if they decided there was no need for new facilities there would be none. The whole plan had an unmistakable 1940s ring to it and predictably the consultants were furious – while many commentators simply wondered whether the row was worth the political fall out. For pay beds were not the only problem that the health service faced. The junior doctors – the so-called training grade of hospital doctors who provide tomorrow's consultants – were angry about their new contract of employment. Rightly, they protested that the contract left a third of them financially worse off; but, wrongly, some took industrial action in pursuit of their cause. Other smouldering fires were the number of doctors emigrating and what proved to be justified concern that the Labour Government was about to cut the health service budget.

By November there was, according to the *Guardian*, 'the most serious crisis the NHS has faced in twenty-seven years'. Television ran special programmes on the issues; and the health service from the regional health chairmen downwards protested about low morale. This, let us remember, was not 1991 but 1975. Rows in the health service are politically impartial and any politician who pretends otherwise deceives both himself and the public. The row Mrs Castle had won for herself threatened to be monumental. Arrayed against her she had the might of the medical profession: the British Medical Association, the Royal College of Surgeons and the associations representing hospital consultants and junior doctors. A further complication was that the health unions were threatening retaliatory action against private patients if the consultants' threatened industrial action affected health service patients. As the crisis came to a head, the best help Mrs Castle received came from David Owen who was her number two on the health side of the Social Services department.

In the frequent Commons debates we had on health some of the best and most spirited defences of Labour policy came in David Owen's wind-up speeches. He knew his subject and managed to avoid the stridency of Mrs Castle. I thought then that he would win promotion to the Cabinet, although I was as surprised as everyone else when he was so rapidly elevated to Foreign Secretary. The future leader of the Social Democrats stoutly defended his left-wing boss but as it turned out her rescue came from a different quarter.

One of Harold Wilson's closest friends and best advisers outside the Government was the solicitor, Lord Goodman. Arnold Goodman has a presence both physical and intellectual. He is a big man – round and squat with thick bushy eyebrows – and resembles nothing more than the popular impression of a Hollywood producer. There is no doubt that he has a sense of theatre – he consistently kept Barbara Castle waiting for his entrance – but above all he has a razor-sharp mind. In November of 1975 he was retained by the Independent Hospital Group to fight the pay bed proposals. Although he soon resigned from this role, Arnold Goodman ended up as a mediator between the profession and the Government.

Government ministers, shadow ministers, chairmen and general secretaries all made the journey to his flat near the Temple. To Barbara Castle's ill-disguised fury, Lord Goodman took up a suggestion that I had made in a Commons debate, namely that the Prime Minister should convene a meeting with the medical profession's leaders. Mrs Castle felt (rightly) that such a meeting would imply no confidence in her negotiating and healing skills. Nevertheless, on Wednesday 3 December, the meeting took place at Downing Street and the outlines of an agreement were reached.

My advice to the consultants throughout had been that they could not justify industrial action, and that whatever they thought of the policy they could not pre-empt the decision of Parliament. The Opposition would fight the proposals in Parliament, and, although there was no guarantee of success, that was the only way a government bill could be contested. Lord Goodman now provided the consultants with something more tangible. He pointed out that the Government's line throughout the dispute was that they wanted private practice to continue but this would have to be outside the health service. He wanted the phasing out of pay beds to be related to the provision of private sector facilities; and he also wanted the decision to be in the hands, not of the department, but of an independent body.

Over the next few days the plan was finalized. Although a thousand pay beds were to go after the legislation reached the statute book, the remainder would be phased out on the decision of an independent board but *only* if there were reasonable alternative facilities. For Barbara Castle the result was a climb-down, but the true significance of the pay beds row only became clear several years later. When she started her campaign, private hospitals were relatively few. There were the long-established hospitals of the Nuffield Trust and there were one or two more expensive private hospitals like the Wellington in St John's Wood which took many of its patients from overseas. I remember being shown around the Wellington at the time, marvelling at how such expensive and well-equipped facilities could be afforded, and wondering whether there was any future for private hospitals at all. It was difficult to see how a private sector was going to become established in Britain. Any private hospital had to compete with an entirely free health service covering the whole of the country; while those who wanted private treatment could receive it in well-run and famous teaching hospitals.

All that was blown apart by Mrs Castle's assault on pay beds. As she struck nationally, the health unions attacked locally. Private patients found themselves treated as pariahs and deprived of even basic services. Private patients were not going to pay money to go to hospitals where some of the staff took pleasure in proving to them that they were unwelcome. The result was that private hospitals received the encouragement they required, and a separate private sector was born. Its creator was Barbara Castle.

The pay beds issue dominated the health debates at the autumn party conferences that year. As any politician will confirm, a party conference speech is a major test. It is true that you are speaking to your supporters but you are also being judged by them. In addition you have a large press and television audience only too ready to note successes and failures. Any politician puts effort and preparation into his conference speech. For me, Blackpool 1975 was my maiden speech from the platform – indeed I had only once before even spoken at the party conference.

Encouraged by Michael Heseltine – an undoubted master of the conference oration – I decided on an attacking speech. With some doubts I started with a joke. Barbara Castle, I recalled, was 'the Minister of Transport who couldn't drive – and she has taken the same degree of personal skill into every other government job she has ever had.' Fortunately, that got me off to a good start and I went on to dub her the 'midwife of chaos'. The speech was a success. In a subdued conference it was one of only three which received a standing ovation and back at Westminster I had unexpected confirmation that it had struck home. It was during an evening some days later at the House of Commons. I was walking along the corridor which runs beside the library. There were very few Members of Parliament about that night and the corridor was deserted. Suddenly, and from the other end, Barbara Castle appeared. We got steadily nearer and I prepared to say 'good evening'. Not a bit of it. She put her nose in the air and sailed past without a word.

The reaction elsewhere was more friendly. After I had spoken, Willie Whitelaw pushed through from the back of the Winter Gardens – the best political conference hall I know – to offer his congratulations; and during the evening, at a civic dinner, Margaret Thatcher sought me out to do the same. The press comment was to the effect that I had now established myself, and the *Daily Mail* went even further. Under the heading 'Bright Young Star Delights the Tories', their political staff, with what I regarded as a great perception, wrote:

A new star was born for the Tories last night – Norman Fowler, the youngest Shadow Cabinet member and the man who has to stand up to Social Services Secretary, Barbara Castle.

Young Norman's rise has been meteoric – a year ago he was a semi-obscure backbencher. But yesterday he was given a standing ovation by 2,000 wildly enthusiastic delegates.

I dwell on this not just to show off or even to embarrass the *Mail*'s unembarrassable political editor, Gordon Greig, but to make another point. In politics things are never as bad as they seem at the time. Crises pass; solutions are found for apparently insoluble problems. But by the same measure, things are never as good. By most political standards my star was high. My immediate future seemed assured. As we approached Christmas it became clear that Margaret Thatcher intended to make some changes to her Shadow Cabinet, probably in the early New Year. It was to be her first reshuffle. Speculation rose and over Christmas a number of political journalists sought my views on the impending changes, usually with the prefacing remark 'of course you will stay where you are'.

On the morning of Thursday 15 January, I received a message from the Chief Whip's Office asking me to see Margaret Thatcher in her office at 12.15. It was obviously about the reshuffle, but not having experienced a reshuffle before, my assumption was that probably everyone in the Shadow Cabinet was seen at such a time. I continued to write a press release about David Owen's failure to come to a sensible agreement on tobacco advertising and strolled over from my flat in John Islip Street to the House of Commons. I took a cup of coffee in the tea room and then made my way to Margaret's office. As soon as I entered her room I realized that something was wrong.

Sitting me down, Margaret immediately came to the point. 'Norman,' she said, 'I have something difficult to ask you to do. I want you to move to Transport.' She said that she knew this was a difficult move. In those days Transport was not an independent department but merely part of the Department of the Environment. Nevertheless she had taken a number two job under Robert Carr as Treasury spokesman, having been the number one spokesman on the Environment. She conceded that in my case there would be a difference. She had remained in the Shadow Cabinet. I would not. The Shadow Cabinet was already too big, with three members – Willie Whitelaw, Keith Joseph and Angus Maude – without specific departmental responsibilities. And the reason for my move? She said that I had done the social services job well, but she wanted to make room for John Biffen whom she intended to ask to take over as Energy spokesman. This left Patrick Jenkin without a Shadow Cabinet job, and she had no option but to ask me to move down. She would ensure that I did not lose out on the move.

It was in effect 'last in – first out' but that was not at all how I saw it at the time. I replied that I was now mastering the social services brief and all the work of the last twelve months would be wasted. I knew nothing of transport and I would want to consider returning to the back benches. Margaret said that she understood my reaction but she added that she too had been Shadow Transport Minister and it was a job which would enlarge my experience. I said that I needed time to think it over. Margaret agreed but said she wanted to announce all the changes at 5 p.m. that evening and would like to know my decision after the weekly session of business questions in the House of Commons. She wanted to keep the move secret but agreed that I could consult Ken Clarke and Gerry Vaughan as well as the Chief Whip, Humphrey Atkins. If I declined it would, of course, be announced that I had been offered another job.

As I left Margaret Thatcher's office I ran into Gerry Vaughan who was amazed at the news, but, after discussion, advised me to stay. Next I went to see Humphrey Atkins, in his office by the Members' Lobby. We had what can only be described as a deeply unsatisfactory conversation. In one of the least helpful interventions in the course of my political career, Humphrey Atkins made it clear that he had not supported my initial appointment. Whether this advice was intended to make me go or stay I have never quite worked out.

In fact I had no option but to stay. I was neither senior enough nor established enough in the party to attempt to throw my weight about. The likeliest result of resignation was a permanent career on the back benches. This, too, was the advice of Ken Clarke when I spoke to him on the telephone in his barristers' chambers in Birmingham. Ken's advice was that the party would take the view I had been roughly treated and that I would have their sympathy whether I went or stayed. If I stayed, however, I would have a debt in the bank to be repaid at some future date. At just after 4 p.m. I returned to Margaret's office.

Margaret stressed that the only motive was to make a place for John Biffen, whom she badly wanted on the front bench. Given later events – John was himself reshuffled out of office after the 1987 election – there is a certain irony in the position. Given the situation at the time it was an argument that was difficult to refute.

Having been opposed to many of Ted Heath's policies, John had served out the 1970 Parliament on the back benches where he had acquired for himself a position of undoubted influence and a formidable reputation as a debater. No Conservative politician more richly deserved promotion.

Finally I agreed to the move, but then we hit further snags. Patrick Jenkin was in the United States and did not know he was taking my job; the present Transport spokesman, Marcus Fox, was in the Middle East and could not be found to be told I was taking his. Marcus, in fact, became a Vice-Chairman of the Party.

The news soon spread around Westminster. Most people were surprised and most said so – including a whole range of political correspondents. Leon Brittan sent me an immediate note and one of my old social services team, Robert Boscowen, took me off to the smoking room for a drink. As I was coming out, I met Norman Tebbit who thought the whole thing was extraordinary. In the evening my friend David Walder took me off to the Cavalry Club and listened as I described at some length the injustices of political life. Little was I to know that it would prove to be one of the best decisions I ever made.

Over the next few days others came up to express their views. In the cloakroom I met Dennis Skinner, the Beast of Bolsover, who had already established a reputation for himself as the scourge of both front benches. He obviously regarded the move as some kind of plot and said that I had established myself in the last three or four months. 'They can't say you were no good because the party saw for themselves at the conference.' In the Members' Lobby, Michael Heseltine thought I was right not to resign. 'You may not be Chancellor by forty but you are years younger than the rest of us.' In the tea room Edward du Cann hoped that I was not down-hearted. 'Everyone gets kicked in the balls once in this game,' he said. 'When it happened to me I didn't recover for two months.' Edward had been removed from the party chairmanship by Ted Heath in 1967. Angus Maude, John Peyton and Airey Neave were among others who added their commiserations, while another member of the Shadow Cabinet sourly commented: 'If they were looking for volunteers I wish they had told me.'

As for the press, most attention was given naturally enough to the arrivals like John Biffen and to the departures like George

Younger – who for no sensible reason was moved out of his position as Defence spokesman but who triumphantly returned as
Secretary of State for Defence some ten years later. Of my own
position, *The Times* said that I should not be aggrieved and that it
was part of Margaret Thatcher's policy to give me more experience
before taking over my own department in government. The
Financial Times linked the move with my previous support
for Ted Heath. The *Daily Mail* described my move as 'surprising'
and the *Guardian*, not politically one of my closest supporters,
as 'sad'.

I have dwelt on the story of Margaret Thatcher's first reshuffle
because her reshuffles became such a regular feature of the
Thatcher years. Previous Prime Ministers had also made dramatic
changes. On becoming Prime Minister in 1976, Jim Callaghan
promptly sacked Barbara Castle and Ted Short; while in the night
of the long knives in 1962, Harold Macmillan sacked seven of his
Cabinet including Selwyn Lloyd, the Chancellor of the Exchequer.
But no political leader in recent years used the reshuffle more
regularly and methodically than Margaret Thatcher. When I finally
resigned from the Government in January 1990, the only survivors
from the first Shadow Cabinet were Geoffrey Howe and myself.
Only Geoffrey Howe had served uninterruptedly in both Shadow
Cabinet and Cabinet – but by November 1990 he too had
gone.

Reshuffles are an inevitable and necessary part of political life.
Any leader has a perfect right to change the team when it is clear
that the minister concerned is in substantial opposition to the
Government's policy. The sensible course for a minister who finds
himself in that position is to go before the axe falls. It should also
be recognized that party leaders, in Government and in Opposition, come under pressure to make changes. If things are going
badly, then the pressure from the press and party can become
intense. A change of cast can demonstrate that the party has not
run out of steam. Above all, the reshuffle is the only way that new
faces can be introduced. Regrettably, few politicians choose to go
when they should and have a prevailing attitude that they are good
for 'just one more job' or 'one or two more years'. The reshuffle
is the only way that this log-jam can be broken. Margaret
Thatcher's policy of annual changes meant that many young minis-

ters were allowed to show their paces in a government department. Had she pursued a less rigorous course, it is doubtful whether John Major, who was elected as a Member of Parliament only in 1979, could have progressed to 10 Downing Street by 1990.

Yet reshuffles also have their price. In the Thatcher years ministers often moved posts too quickly. The result was that at Cabinet level there have been no fewer than eight Transport Secretaries since 1979 and seven heads of the Department of Trade and Industry since June 1983. On occasions the changes took ministers from departments just as they had become established. In 1985 Leon Brittan was moved sideways from Home Secretary for no good reason; and in 1990 Ken Clarke and John MacGregor were moved from the Departments of Health and Education in the midst of taking through important reforms. Change is necessary, but the process of government would be helped if ministers as a general rule stayed with their departments for three or four years. Such a period gives them time to put their stamp on their departments and initiate and take through new policies.

For the reshuffled – whether they be Cabinet or junior ministers – change can be a bruising experience. I am lucky to have been on the receiving end only once, during my move from the Shadow Cabinet. But to me it was a hammer blow. I was knocked out, cast down and working at half speed for the next two weeks – and I was only being moved from one area to another and had been given all kinds of assurances. Imagine the impact upon a politician who has been told that he is out altogether and his career is at an end. And imagine the impact if the blow falls after months of debilitating speculation that he is destined for dismissal. By all means sympathize with the leader who has the difficult task of breaking the news and sometimes makes a lifelong enemy in the course of the interview. But above all spare a thought for the casualties of the reshuffle – some of whom never quite recover. Appalling letter writer that I am, I always try to write to those colleagues who are leaving office rather than to those who have just been promoted to it.

In 1976 I followed the political maxim: 'never resign'. This should perhaps be varied to 'never resign unless you mean it'. In politics you do not know what opportunities are just round the corner. I stayed and, as it happened, found in transport an area which I not only immensely enjoyed but where there was unlimited scope to make new policy. Even so, I made the decision to stay through gritted teeth and the only reality that meant anything to me was that, at almost thirty-eight, I had become the youngest *ex*-member of Margaret Thatcher's Shadow Cabinet.

CHAPTER 5

Shadow Minister

'Surely, sir, you won't leave us to risk going into Mrs Thatcher's Chamber of Horrors?'

Daily Express

A mere seven days after I was moved from social services I was in action in the House of Commons setting out the Conservative Party's policy on transport. The occasion was an all-day debate on the need for an 'integrated' transport policy which I soon found was code for Labour backbench demands for more railway investment and a policy of diverting both people and goods from road to rail. Many people wonder at the speed with which Government or Shadow ministers take up a new portfolio. Like me, they may have come without any previous experience or knowledge, but from the moment they are appointed they are fair game both in Parliament and outside. In the first weeks your fear is not so much that you will not know the answers, but that you simply will not understand the questions. You are desperately vulnerable. Your major hope is that your supposed political skills will see you through. As it happened this was no great problem in my first debate, thanks to the kindness of the MPs sponsored by the railway unions who never despair of making converts. It was they, as much as anybody, who lifted me out of the immediate gloom of the reshuffle. For here was a group of people who self-evidently considered transport to be of crucial importance. We may not have agreed on everything but on this central point they were obviously right.

As I examined my new portfolio over the following weeks my mood changed. No Conservative Transport Minister had made any major legislative changes since Ernest Marples went out of office with the Macmillan Government in 1964. Ted Heath's Transport Minister had been John Peyton but his proposals perished as a result of the February 1974 election defeat. As a policy area it was wide open, and luck was on my side in another respect. The position of the Transport Department within the Whitehall hierarchy changed. Neither John Peyton nor his Labour successors, Fred Mulley and John Gilbert, had a seat at the Cabinet table. To the frustration of Transport Ministers, ultimate policy authority rested with the Environment Secretary. Thus Labour's fascinating consultative paper – which to the

fury of the Left's transport establishment dismissed the integrated transport policy as a 'pipedream' – was written by
Anthony Crosland and not by John Gilbert. A few months after
Margaret Thatcher's reshuffle, the new Prime Minister, Jim
Callaghan, made the Transport Department self-standing under
the charge of a Cabinet minister, William Rodgers. Where the
Government led, the Opposition followed. I was also cut free
from Environment and for the rest of the Parliament
operated as Shadow Transport Minister entirely running my
own show.

There are two theories of opposition. The first is based on the
sensible belief that oppositions do not win elections, governments
lose them. The extreme followers of this doctrine take the view
that Shadow ministers have one role and one role alone and that
is to oppose. To reveal your own policy can only provide hostages
to fortune and is best avoided. Thus Labour would have done
better in 1990 simply to have attacked the community charge rather
than put forward plans of their own to institute a 'roof tax'.
There is, however, an alternative argument. The public are not
fools. They realize perfectly well that if an Opposition cannot
tell them what their policy is, it is because they have not worked
it out or are frightened to reveal it. Either way it sends up
warning signals to the electorate. Oppositions have to be credible
to be elected and the public have a right to know what they
intend to do. As a general election approaches, the media rightly
turn their attention to the policy positions of both the parties,
not just of the Government. The happy generalizations that
may get an Opposition by in mid-term can then be mercilessly
exposed.

The second theory of Opposition is that it provides an unprecedented opportunity to make a new policy. It is a curious breed of
politician who has no interest in developing policy. Opposition has
enough frustration. As a shadow minister you are constantly fighting in the press for just a few paragraphs to express your views.
Your usual fate is to respond to the announcements of government.
You have inadequate research facilities, inadequate support staff
and inadequate accommodation in the absurdly tiny rooms of the
Shadow Cabinet corridor in the House of Commons. You do,
however, have one advantage – the time to look, to stand back and

to make proposals. If you do not do that, then there is no point in being a shadow minister.

For the next three years I was left alone to get on with my job. Margaret Thatcher was often accused of interfering too much but I never found that either in Opposition or later in Government. She once announced to a group of ministers that 'Norman will always run a good department'. My colleagues were singularly unimpressed but it perhaps explained why for fifteen years she basically allowed me to develop my own plans without interference. Ultimately, most policies of any importance need to go to Cabinet or Shadow Cabinet. You would expect nothing less. It is highly unlikely that any party leader is going to allow one of the team to publish, say, a new strategy for social security without having a look at the proposals first. Michael Meacher, who was then Labour's Shadow Minister of Social Security, once tried just that in 1985 and was promptly ordered by his colleagues to disown them, which with some embarrassment and bluster he did. The general and sensible rule is that you have to persuade your colleagues that *your* proposals should now be adopted and become *their* policy.

Certainly at this stage, Margaret Thatcher put new policy proposals under stringent examination. She was interested in the effect of policies; she liked a good argument; and, as anyone who has served on her front bench knows, she had an instinct for picking out the weakest part of your case. Presenting a new policy could be trial by single combat. You did not survive if you did not know your case or if your case was fundamentally flawed.

In the early days of Margaret Thatcher's leadership in Opposition, there was a tendency on the part of one or two outside organizations to patronize her: 'Once you understand this area a little better, you will agree with us.' This was positively the very worst way of getting her on your side. I remember seeing a member of the British Rail board lectured for over an hour after an approach of this kind in the course of which Margaret demonstrated that she knew that particular industry only too well. Another approach doomed to failure is the one that goes: 'Well, those are my proposals, Margaret – but if you disagree, of course, I will change them.' That did not win her respect. She may have fallen out with equally strong personalities like Michael Heseltine and

Nigel Lawson on policy issues, but that certainly did not mean that she liked yes-men.

No minister – shadow or real – wins all his battles, but, in the words of one of my later private secretaries in the Department of Transport, I had a passing reputation for 'bringing back the bacon' in the proposals I put to Margaret Thatcher. That meant that I won more battles than I lost. My tactics were to prepare my case very, very carefully by doing everything possible to master the brief. I was not then easily dislodged. Edwina Currie, then my Parliamentary Secretary at the Department of Health, once came with me to a meeting at Number 10 Downing Street. On the agenda was the management of the health service. The questions, points, interruptions, suggestions came fast and furious. According to Edwina, it reminded her of a scene from one of those 1950s British films where eventually the captain brings his boat, battered but still floating, through the barrage.

I never resented this kind of examination. I always preferred such spirited cross-examination to the doubtful questioning of a colleague who was clearly reading the proposals for the first time as he spoke. Like everyone else, I was furious when my carefully worked and brilliantly honed proposals failed to make it – but then once or twice they did not deserve to. On other occasions I comforted myself with the reflection that if I could not get the proposals past Margaret Thatcher and my colleagues, I was unlikely to convince the public.

For me the years up to the general election of 1979 were my political salad days. My move had turned out to be a great stroke of good fortune. I was still outside Shadow Cabinet but I had access to it when transport issues came up. Not everyone in the Shadow Cabinet thought that was necessarily a bad deal. I missed the interminable discussions on devolution in Scotland and on Rhodesian sanctions but I was able to take to Shadow Cabinet any issue I chose. Thus when Labour supported legislation which would have had the effect of nationalizing the port of Felixstowe – the most successful private-sector port in the country – I was able to argue for the need to oppose it in the Commons and, more particularly, in the House of Lords. Although the Conservative Party had a clear majority in the Upper House, Peter Carrington rightly used it very sparingly and always needed to be persuaded that the decision of the elected chamber should be overturned.

My overriding concern, however, was to develop a transport policy for what I fervently hoped would be the next Conservative government. To help me do this, I gathered together a small group of Tory backbench MPs. Some, like Peter Viggers and Peter Temple-Morris, had been at Cambridge with me; others like Peter Fry and Roger Moate were already transport experts in their own right. We had the help of a young assistant from Conservative Research Department, Bruce Anderson, who later came to the conclusion that there was a brighter future for him as a journalist – a decision which proved to be spectacularly correct. Our small team met each week in my office in Abbey Gardens backing on to the lawns of Westminster School; in this cloistered calm, we looked at transport policy from scratch.

Like all Conservative policy-making of the mid-1970s, this had its difficulties. There were two quite opposite views about how the next election would be won. The first was epitomized by the Centre for Policy Studies under the direction of Alfred Sherman which favoured a deliberately radical approach. The Shermanites believed that the public was ready for fundamental change and that we should set out our policies fearlessly. They rejected with scorn the idea that fundamental reform might seriously alarm the electorate.

The alternative view was best expressed by politicians like Francis Pym and Jim Prior. The Pymites believed that although there may have been a change of leadership, nothing could erase the memory that Ted Heath had just fought an election on the issue of 'Who runs the country?' – and had lost. Conservatives needed to accept that there were some powerful institutions which the public did not believe could be suddenly and radically altered. The party might not like it, but the best that could be hoped for was a gradual step-by-step approach. We should aim to improve, not to transform. The trade unions produced the most obvious clash of approaches, and the extent and pace of industrial relations reform provided a passionate and continual debate inside the Conservative Party. But trade union reform was not the only issue where the two approaches came into conflict. We also needed to decide how we would tackle the most lasting legacy of the 1945 Labour Government, nationalization.

Transport in the 1970s was dominated by nationalized industries. The biggest of them all was British Rail. Although their workforce had fallen from almost half a million at the beginning of the 1960s, they still employed over 230,000 in 1976. There was the National Bus Company with a labour force of 68,000 and a fleet of some 20,000 buses and coaches. The British Transport Docks Board owned 19 ports, including Southampton, Hull and Cardiff, and accounted for about a quarter of the nation's ports business. Most intriguingly of all there was the National Freight Corporation, which ran a host of road-haulage and transport companies ranging from British Road Services to Pickfords, the removal people.

Losses and subsidies were the order of the day. British Rail had an operating subsidy of about £365 million a year – much of it spent not on passengers but on freight. The buses benefited from operating subsidies, grants for new buses and fuel rebates. Even the National Freight Corporation was losing money, mainly because of losses on its parcels business but also because of an ill-starred excursion into Europe. In the mid-1970s, only the British Transport Docks Board was making a reasonable return on the capital employed, although they could have done much better had they been able to operate free of the National Dock Labour Scheme, by then a notorious restrictive practice. This, then, was the public face of the nationalized transport industries. But as I got to know them better, a paradox became evident. Although the nationalized industries had a terrible public reputation, there were some undoubted industrial stars working in them.

You had chairmen like Peter Parker of British Rail. He had taken over the railways at a difficult time, with morale at rock bottom after the resignation in 1976 of the former chairman and Labour minister, Richard Marsh. One of his first priorities had been to restore the workforce's self-respect, and thanks to the bounce and energy that only Peter has, that is precisely what he did. At the chief executive level you had managers like Peter Thompson of National Freight who had already had a successful four years with British Road Services. One of his achievements had been to take on the Midlands transport-union baron Allan Law who had put a number of transport firms out of business. It was a famous victory, and while the dispute was on, NFC's competitors helped to move the company's strike-bound goods. When it was all over, however, none of the competitors who had gained so much from NFC's courageous stand returned the business. At the Docks Board you had Keith Stuart, who successfully took the company into the private sector; and at British Rail you had a number of good and totally dedicated managers, most notably Bob Reid. He was later to become chairman of the railways himself and deserves much more credit than he has received for the improvements that took place during the late 1980s. And on the main boards of the nationalized industries there were non-executive directors like Bobby Lawrence and Frank Law who would be an asset to any company.

So why were these important industries not enjoying more success? You did not have to be an unpaid member of Margaret Thatcher's front bench to come to the conclusion that the fault lay with nationalization itself. Whatever may have been the original aspirations, it had failed in practice. The ideal of involving people in the prosperity and direction of their business seems to me central, whatever your political belief, but 'public ownership' never fostered this commitment. Too often it led to a false sense of security – that a nationalized industry was immune from the normal commercial pressures that affected ordinary companies. At its worst, it led to a feeling that it did not really matter if the business succeeded or not because at the end of the day the Government would foot the bill.

For managers, nationalization was too often a course in frustration. Nationalization means that the business is owned by the Government. That has a number of inevitable consequences. Ministers are answerable in Parliament for the industries they sponsor with taxpayers' money. They do not want to be caught short with embarrassing losses to explain away, so they interfere. Civil servants do not want to be blamed for letting their minister down and therefore anxiously peer over the shoulders of senior managers. In practice, nationalization means outside interference in everything from major investment decisions to the chairman's salary. All of this was evident in the nationalized transport industries of the 1970s. As I examined them, I realized that there simply had to be a better way to run them. In spite of the difficulties, I wanted to explore the potential for denationalization – or, to use a word that was later to come into fashion, privatization.

Privatization was pioneered in the transport industries. It was not a policy which emanated from the Treasury or even the 'Shadow Treasury'. It is, of course, true that I wished to avoid unnecessary subsidies. There was no point in making losses that could be eliminated. Having come from shadowing social services, where I had seen the undoubted need for public spending, I was totally unsympathetic to the alleged social case for subsidizing the movement of goods and parcels. There seemed no sensible reason why the taxpayer should pick up the bill for such activities. At no stage, however, were any of us under the illusion that great profits were to be made by selling the transport undertakings to the public. Our view was that privatization offered a better and more effective way of running nationalized companies – particularly those competing with the private sector.

To me, the National Freight Corporation symbolized the issues we faced. What was the government accomplishing by moving goods and parcels from one part of the country to another? What great purpose was served by furniture removal being run by the state? The answer was none. The creation of the NFC had been a historical accident when the Wilson Labour Government had put together all the transport interests that happened still to be in state hands following the nationalization spree of the post-war Attlee Government. The corporation had been established by the 1968 Transport Act, the brainchild of none other than my old friend Mrs Castle. (It is one of the little ironies of my political career that I did virtually all the jobs that she did in government.) I could see no commercial logic for the arrangement nor any advantage to either the company or the workforce. But what really struck me was that here was a very good business trying to get out. NFC had its problems, particularly with the parcels services of National Carriers. In 1969 National Carriers, in the first year after it had been transferred from British Rail, achieved the unenviable distinction of making a £25 million loss on a £25 million turnover. But NFC also had its strengths in the general haulage area, in the fast-expanding truck rental business and in removals.

I decided that the NFC was the company which had most potential for privatization, but it was not a policy direction which immediately struck a sympathetic chord in the corporation itself.

There had been little denationalization for twenty years and no one knew how it would work out. The greatest fear was that it would lead to a period in which the company bounced in and out of public ownership. What business loathes most of all is uncertainty. NFC was struggling to recover from a £31 million loss in 1975. The last thing they wanted was a shadow minister causing concern to both their workforce and their customers alike. I was introduced at transport conferences with the hope that I would *not* be talking about 'all that privatization nonsense'. Dan Pettit, the chairman of NFC, and his deputy Victor Paige periodically lunched me to find out more about the new doctrine, and Frank Law, a main board director, was deputed to approach Margaret Thatcher to express concern at the damage that could be caused. I was asked to meet Frank and, although the meeting did not result in a change of policy, it marked for me the beginning of a close friendship.

I wanted to find a structure for the NFC that no one would want to change back – least of all the people working for it. That brought some reassurance, particularly as they needed no persuasion about the drawbacks of being a nationalized industry. Although I met him rarely at that stage, the chief executive of NFC, Peter Thompson, was coming to the same conclusions but from an entirely different standpoint. He had been a keen advocate of nationalization. He was not an armchair enthusiast but a man who had chosen to move his career from the private sector to a nationalized industry. Gradually, in what he terms 'the years of disillusionment', it became clear to him that nationalization was not working. A few years later we were able to work together not only to privatize the NFC but to create an altogether better way of running a business.

Privatization was not the only new course we followed in transport. In 1976 I spent five weeks in the United States looking at their transport systems and also taking in the Kansas City convention of the Republican Party at which Gerald Ford narrowly beat his brash, but more professional, challenger Ronald Reagan. As I crossed the United States there seemed relatively little that they could teach us. The train journey from San Francisco to Los Angeles was slow, long and tedious; bus services in a number of the cities were run down and on the point of collapse. But what the Americans did have was the good-value Greyhound coach services. For many people this was a reliable, low-cost alternative to air or rail. So why did we not have the same services in Britain? Of course we had *some* inter-city coach services but they were limited and appeared to adopt the lowest of low profiles.

The answer was the Traffic Commissioner system. This dated from the 1928 Royal Commission on Transport, which had faced the problem of an over-provision of bus services and unfettered competition. Bus services had been in steep decline since the end of the Second World War but the restrictions on new services continued. Commissioners, sitting rather like magistrates, would give a licence for a new service only if the operator could prove that there was a public need. Almost inevitably, a new operator wanting to run a coach service from, say, London to Birmingham would be opposed by any existing coach operator as well as by British Rail who would argue that the demand was already met. I could not see why this question should not be settled by the customer. If there was no demand for the service then the new operator would soon know. It all seemed glaringly obvious, but if privatization was controversial it was nothing compared to deregulation. Existing operators saw that it meant new competition; the unions (quite wrongly) predicted a threat to jobs; and experts in the industry saw their specialist knowledge of the intricate byways of Traffic Commissioner law becoming redundant at a stroke.

In October 1977, just in time for the Conservative Party Conference, I published our transport policy under the title *The Right Track*. We were heavily into 'right' ways at the time and my paper followed *The Right Approach* and *The Right Approach to the Economy*. I sought to set out a policy which met the needs not of the provider of transport but of the paying customer and the taxpayer. For the railways I did not reject state support, but I said that it must be identified with the services that were actually being supported. On roads I set out a policy which gave priority to economically important routes, like roads to the ports, and to bypasses. For the motorist I promised reform of the traffic laws and the introduction of a totting-up system which distinguished between the serious and less serious motoring offence. For coaches and buses I promised the reform of the Traffic Commissioner system together with minibus services and car sharing. Most important of all was the NFC where I was authorized by Shadow Cabinet to include a general pledge to introduce 'substantial private investment' into the corporation. At that stage my preference was for a joint private-public company like British Petroleum which would involve a change of ownership but would reassure the staff of NFC that we were not in the business of simply selling off the profitable parts.

It was most certainly a cautious start for privatization, which was to become probably the most distinctive feature of the later Thatcher years. Nevertheless, when I put my proposals to Shadow Cabinet I was much more concerned that they would be seen as going too far rather than not far enough. The prospect of privatization greatly concerned those in the party who were of a nervous disposition. They thought that it was merely the mirror-image of nationalization and would lead to inevitable strife in the industries concerned. Did we want to make promises that would be seen as confrontational and return to the industrial battlefield where we had been defeated? Fortunately for me, however, the future of the transport industries was not a preoccupation of the Shadow Cabinet and the policy went through without amendment.

Politically, my years as a Shadow minister had an important effect upon me. I was appalled by the high inflation of over 20 per cent we experienced in 1975 and 1976 and, in particular, its effect on retired people living on fixed incomes. I did not share the view that the all too slow and painful recovery had much to do with Labour's incomes policy, which simply led governments into battles where they could not determine the outcome. It seemed much likelier that the recovery of 1977 and 1978 had more to do with the intervention of the International Monetary Fund and their prescription of public spending controls and a sensible monetary policy. In spite of all the later criticism heaped upon us, the first of the monetarists was the Labour Chancellor, Denis Healey.

The other feature which particularly concerned me as a West Midlands Member of Parliament was Britain's continuing industrial decline. At one stage just before the war, Britain had had a motorcycle manufacturer for most letters in the alphabet: starting with AJS and BSA and going through to internationally famous names like Enfield, Norton and Triumph. By the mid-1970s we had virtually nothing and, worse, the West Midlands car industry seemed rapidly to be going the way of the motorcycle. Yet no one seemed to care. I remember seeing some strikers from the Austin Princess line who, to judge from their television interviews, thought that the world owed them a living irrespective of the doubtful quality of their product. They genuinely believed that Princess workers were the natural aristocrats of the car industry. Although customers were deserting British models in droves, the car workers refused to accept that it had anything to do with them.

There was no sudden moment of conversion, but over the years in Opposition I became convinced that radical action was necessary. I never became a Shermanite; they were always too unpolitical for me. They never seemed to understand the importance of taking middle England with us. I did, however, come to reject the cosy 1960s assumption that, given the difficulties, we had not done at all badly since the war. The *status quo* was not good enough. I wanted to see policies which brought inflation down and kept it down, and policies, like privatization, which promised industrial recovery. I also believed that the time had come to have a further serious attempt to reform the unions – a belief which was entirely confirmed by the events which started in the autumn of 1978.

The year had started well for Labour. Inflation had fallen and there was now even a prospect that it might edge below 10 per cent. The balance of payments had improved and in April Denis Healey was able to introduce a reflationary budget. Above all, the public had warmed to the reassuring presence of Jim Callaghan. The Liberals withdrew from their Parliamentary pact with Labour in June but by this stage Labour was through its critical years. The opinion polls showed a dramatic recovery from the black days when they lost by-elections in traditional Labour seats like Workington and Walsall. Everything seemed to be going Labour's way and an autumn election looked a certainty. I set off for a September holiday in France resigned to the fact that I would be called back. Instead, to my astonishment, I was telephoned to be told that Callaghan had gone on television to say that there would be no election and he intended to soldier on to 1979. It proved to be as disastrous a mistake for Callaghan as Ted Heath's delay in 1974 was for him.

When Callaghan postponed the election, he must have assumed that the unions would not rock the boat given the obvious imminence of a poll. He could not have been more wrong. The Government set down a 5 per cent ceiling on wage settlements, but this was immediately challenged. The crucial early action came from the workforce at Ford. The Government looked on helplessly as Ford conceded a 15 per cent increase; to add insult to injury, the Government then had its attempt to apply sanctions to the company defeated in the House of Commons – thanks to the abstentions of four left-wing Labour MPs. From December onwards Labour's authority went into spiralling decline. Tanker drivers and lorry drivers next challenged the incomes policy and for a while transport was at the centre of the stage. By this point I was back attending Shadow Cabinet each week, Margaret Thatcher having come to the conclusion that transport was too important an area to exclude. But the strikes soon moved on from transport to public services and there followed scenes which were a disgrace to any civilized twentieth-century European nation.

The immorality of the Winter of Discontent was the way that the public were singled out as the target. The dispute at Ford could at least be seen as a traditional battle between unions and employers. No such excuse could be made for the action in the health service. Public sector unions, notably the National Union of Public Employees, deliberately sought to act against the interests of some of the most vulnerable people in the country. Patients were singled out for abuse. The headlines during the first months of 1979 said it all:

> 1,100 Hospitals under Siege
> Pickets Vet Patients and Blockade Supplies
> Cancer Ward Sent Home
> Target for Today – Sick Children
> Mum Dies in 999 No-Go Row

In the north-west there was a strike of grave-diggers. Bodies awaiting burial were stored in warehouse mortuaries. A funeral cortège was pictured on television being turned back by pickets at a cemetery gates. In London, Labour's Health Secretary, David Ennals, himself became a target for action while a patient at Westminster Hospital. A shop steward explained the plan in words which are redolent of the times:

He is a legitimate target for industrial action. Ennals is now beginning to take his own medicine. . . . He won't get the little extras our members provide patients. He won't get his locker cleaned or the area around his bed tidied up. He won't get tea or soup.

With even hospital patients now a 'legitimate target', the reform of the unions became the central issue of political debate. Margaret Thatcher went on to the attack and perhaps for the first time sounded as though she was speaking for the ordinary people of Britain. The Government limped into March. Labour's only hope was to distance an election as far from the Winter of Discontent as possible, but even this plan was foiled. At the end of March a vote of censure was put down in the House of Commons, and for the first time since the defeat of Ramsay MacDonald's Government in 1924 a government in power was turned out. When the Opposition whips took the right-hand winning position in front of the Speaker it was clear that we had won – though only by the slenderest of slender majorities, 311 votes to 310. With some dignity Jim Callaghan got to his feet and told the House: 'Mr Speaker, now that the House of Commons has declared itself we shall take our case to the country.'

The major problem for any Opposition, particularly an Opposition led by an untried leader, is to persuade the public of your credentials. But in 1979 the Labour Government had none of the familiar defensive cards of ministerial experience and quiet success left to play. No one was going to believe a campaign which warned the public that the Tories would ruin the 'achievements' of the last five years. The Winter of Discontent had finally ended any lingering belief that only Labour could handle the unions. The public may not have believed that Margaret Thatcher would transform the position, but what had they left to lose?

For our part we ran a safe and rather dull campaign following a safe and rather dull manifesto. In spite of all our arguments about the direction of policy, our only manifesto commitment to privatization was the National Freight Corporation. In fact what we really needed was a doctor's mandate: the authority to take all the measures which were necessary for recovery. For one point was certain. There were going to be hard decisions to be taken.

The economy was weak, industry was run down and our industrial relations were the worst in Europe.

On Thursday 3 May, the country went to the polls. In Sutton Coldfield I found myself re-elected with an incredible majority of over 26,000. I had secured almost 70 per cent of the vote and Sutton Coldfield was now the safest Conservative seat in the country. Nationally our victory had also been decisive. The Conservatives had a clear majority of 43 over all other parties and Margaret Thatcher had been elected Prime Minister.

CHAPTER 6

The Month of May

W hat should a politician with hopes of appointment do following a victorious election? Not having been a minister before,
I had no idea. I had, of course, read the stories of politicians sitting
next to their phone for day after day waiting, usually in vain, for
the call from the Prime Minister. That seemed to me a dreadful
way of spending the next few days and I also harboured the naive
belief that appointments would be made in a rather more organized
way.

On the Friday afternoon after polling day I went round the
streets of Sutton Coldfield with my loudspeaker car thanking the
public for their support. I then caught an evening train from Birmingham International down to London. Rather than spend the
weekend waiting in my London flat, my plan was to collect Fiona
and Oliver (of whom more anon) and make a weekend of it in my
cottage in Sutton Coldfield, which was set in the country near the
Belfry golf course. We loaded up the car on Saturday morning and
set off north again – driving, incidentally, straight past the entrance
to the then deserted Downing Street.

On the motorway we were held up in a lengthy traffic jam and
it was not until 1 p.m. that we arrived at the cottage. Ten minutes
later the phone rang. It was my constituency chairman to tell me
that the Prime Minister's office had been trying to find me and
had been doing so since the previous evening. They must have
started ringing minutes after I had left the cottage. The message
was that I was to ring Downing Street urgently. I did.

The Downing Street official I spoke to was not amused. 'We
have been trying to get you for the past twelve hours,' he complained. The Prime Minister had wanted me to come to see her
at Number 10 that morning. That was clearly impossible and the
official was not at all sure what the Prime Minister would want to
do now. They would ring back. The clear implication was that it
had been very tiresome of me not to be sitting by my phone,
together with the unsettling hint that I would be lucky if plans had
not changed. The wait seemed interminable but in fact only lasted
a few minutes.

The Downing Street operator came back on the line: 'I have the Prime Minister for you.'

'I thought I had devised a fail-safe plan,' I mumbled.

'Fail-safe plans are designed to go wrong,' Margaret replied.

It did not really make sense but it was much better than the anonymous Downing Street official. The Prime Minister then got down to business. She wanted me to take over as Minister of Transport. I would become a Privy Counsellor and I would attend all Cabinet meetings. The point about 'attending' Cabinet and not 'joining' it was this. The size of the Cabinet is restricted by Act of Parliament to twenty-two members plus the Prime Minister. I was number twenty-three and therefore could not be a full member. Margaret said that I could speak on all the subjects in front of Cabinet, not just on transport, and that I would also be a member of a number of Cabinet committees. The only difference would be that I would be Minister of Transport and not Secretary of State for Transport. As far as I was concerned, that was a title that had been good enough for Ernest Marples and it was certainly good enough for me. I accepted with alacrity.

'Don't be too quick,' Margaret said. 'I must explain about the pay.'

The gist of this was that I would not receive the pay of a Cabinet minister but would be paid about £5,000 a year less at the level of the Chief Whip. Pay was hardly of great relevance at that moment, so I said that that sounded fine to me also.

Lastly, Margaret asked whether I could be sworn in as a Privy Counsellor that afternoon at 5 p.m. at Buckingham Palace. My heart dropped at the prospect of another journey down the motor-way but I said I could try. 'No,' she said, sensing the problem, 'you can be sworn in on Wednesday. Nick Edwards is in Wales and John Nott is down in Cornwall. I think the best thing is for you to go with them.' Cabinet would meet next week and she would see me then.

When I came off the telephone the person who was really impressed was six-year-old Oliver. For some reason he did not immediately understand the intricacies of my position as a minister in charge of a department, not officially in Cabinet but attending all Cabinet meetings, and paid at a rate between a Minister of State and a Secretary of State. He did, however, understand that no less than the Prime Minister had just rung up and obviously presented some good news.

To be frank, the offer exceeded my expectations. I now knew something about transport but I knew next to nothing about the workings of government. I had not held any government office before, and although I had reasonable expectations that I would be offered *some* job, it seemed unlikely that it would be heading a department. There were too many people already for the available number of senior slots. My hunch had been that Peter Walker would be brought back into the Cabinet and that Transport was exactly the kind of job he would be offered. Instead he was given Agriculture in place of the hapless John Peyton, who had slogged through the years of Opposition in Shadow Cabinet, latterly as Shadow Minister of Agriculture.

It showed another truth about politics. Trying to predict your future is a hopeless business as you never have all the pieces to make up the jigsaw. You never know who is being moved out – or for that matter who is moving himself out. However, it was now clear that the move to transport that had started so inauspiciously for me three years previously had in effect taken me into Cabinet in one move. At the age of forty-one I was the youngest of the team round the Cabinet table.

I had also managed to bypass all the usual stepping-stones to Cabinet office. There are broadly three ranks of minister. The most junior is the Parliamentary Secretary. That is the rank at which Margaret Thatcher, John Major and most of today's Cabinet began their ministerial career. Currently the Government has some thirty Parliamentary Secretaries divided between departments, with a big department like Environment having no fewer than four. The Parliamentary Secretary does everything his senior colleagues do not want to do. He answers a mountain of letters, and replies in the House of Commons to the late-night adjournment debates at the end of each day's business in which MPs can raise any constituency subject they want.

The next notch up is the Minister of State, of which there are currently twenty-nine. He is in effect the number two minister in the department and his hope is that his next and ultimate step will be to Secretary of State. The theory is that a minister acquires experience of government as he follows this course upwards. I have to confess that I have only ever replied to one adjournment debate and all my training as a Cabinet minister was on the job – thus explaining my doubtless many eccentricities in running government departments.

After the Prime Minister the next to telephone was the new Chief Whip, Michael Jopling. This too was a surprise appointment as Jack Weatherill had been Humphrey Atkins' deputy in Opposition, and on Humphrey's appointment to the Northern Ireland Office it was assumed he would have the job. Unusually in these circumstances, the arrangement worked out well for both men. Michael Jopling was one of the shrewdest Chief Whips the party has ever had; and Jack Weatherill went on to become Speaker of the House of Commons and one of the best-known politicians in the country.

The Chief Whip has a crucial role. He and his team of whips are responsible for delivering the votes in the House of Commons and ensuring that government business gets through, but they also have an important impact on who becomes a minister and who goes where. The final decision on appointments is that of the party leader, but the leader will almost invariably take the advice of the 'Chief'. Michael explained that the Transport Department was going to be a two-man affair – with just myself and a Parliamentary Secretary. He had a list of five possibles to take the number two spot and he ran through them. Every one of them went on to ministerial office and two went into the Cabinet. With no hesitation I chose one of the future Cabinet ministers, Kenneth Clarke.

In fact it was a surprise to me that Ken Clarke was on the market at all. After his spell as the party's social security spokesman he had been moved to industry with Keith Joseph and my assumption had been that he would become his deputy there. I put it to Michael that several of the other candidates for the transport job were too senior for me both in years and service and that Ken and I had worked well together in the past. Michael replied that he would see what he could do and some time later he rang back to say it had been arranged. Like me, Ken was not initially overjoyed at the move to transport. However, he very quickly forgot any (entirely justified) feeling that he should have been promoted higher and with typical energy threw himself wholeheartedly into the job. It was a partnership which was to last almost uninterrupted for the next five years.

Next on the telephone was Sir Peter Baldwin, the Permanent Secretary at the Department of Transport. Peter had already had a long career as a civil servant at the Treasury and was now gamekeeper turned poacher as head of one of the big-spending Whitehall departments. He congratulated me on the appointment but it was clear that he was concerned about my equivocal position in Cabinet. Having fought for independence for so long, no one in the Transport Department wanted to see that issue even half reopened. He was obviously troubled but nevertheless said that the next few months would be 'great fun'. Peter asked whether I wanted my first red box sent up to Sutton Coldfield by dispatch rider, but I replied that it was probably best if I returned to London and took delivery of it the next day.

An hour or two later we caught up with the news on television. The cameras at Downing Street showed Quintin Hailsham arriving on a bicycle; a jaunty Peter Walker rejoining the Cabinet; and George Younger walking up to the door of Number 10. One of the dramatic Conservative casualties in the election had been the Shadow Scottish Secretary, Teddy Taylor, who had lost his Glasgow seat; George Younger was now to take over the Scottish job. There were some new appointments like David Howell at Energy and Christopher Soames as Leader of the House of Lords. But for the most part it was the winning Shadow team. Margaret had given first preference to experience in Opposition. Geoffrey Howe was Chancellor, Jim Prior was at Employment, Michael Heseltine at Environment and Patrick Jenkin at Social Services. Most of the new appointments had written the policies for their new departments. If the promises did not make sense, they had no one to blame but themselves. On Sunday morning we returned to London.

My first red box was delivered to me in my Westminster flat a couple of hundred yards from my new headquarters at the Department of Transport. I was amused to see that on the very top there was a copy of *The Right Track*, the transport policy document I had written in Opposition. Viewed one way, this was a master-stroke of the civil service in the best traditions of Sir Humphrey of *Yes, Minister*: 'Of course we have read your little pamphlet, Minister.

Quite promising really.' But the episode was symbolic in a quite different way. It was the civil service saying 'this is your policy and we stand ready to put it into effect'. In countries like the United States, many senior public service appointments change with the administration, but the advantage of having a skilled and objective public service able to serve *any* elected government should not be underestimated.

Some ministers, both Labour and Conservative, have complained that the civil service has hindered their efforts to put their ideas into practice. I never found this in a substantial way in any of the three departments I headed. Of course there were battles and there were arguments. Civil servants are particularly sensitive about any ministerial proposal that one of their own functions should go to the private sector. Civil servants tell you the case that will be put against your policies and they give you their own views. It is important that they do, for they have more experience of working in the particular policy area than any minister. But in the end it is the minister who decides – and if he cannot win the argument with his own staff, then his chances of convincing the public are minimal. The only situation in which the civil service itself is likely to initiate change is when there is a policy vacuum because ministers are not clear about what they want to do. Whatever else, that was not a frequent complaint about the Thatcher Governments.

The British civil service is a Rolls-Royce machine which any minister with the slightest sense should use in the development of his policy. In Opposition I was scuttling around to find the facts; in Government I had them all at my fingertips. For any serious issue of policy I would call a meeting around the table in my office. In the debate everyone was encouraged to put their view and it was the quality of contribution which counted, not whether the contributor was a minister or a civil servant. Time spent talking policies through is always essential. Invariably, the major rows come when the policy announcement has been insufficiently prepared. At the end of the discussion, however, it is the minister in charge who decides. He may be in a minority of one but from the moment of the decision that policy becomes the policy of the department. At that point the internal debate ends. The civil servant's job is then to polish and defend the policy. It is a great tribute to the civil service that in eleven years I can think of only one occasion on which I was let down in this process.

I liked working with the civil service and admired the men and women in it. For them, ministers are passing ships. Some ministers may make a long voyage out of it; others move at such a speed that no one has time to get a really good sighting. Inevitably the attitude of the full-time civil servant must be: 'The Secretary of State is dead: long live the Secretary of State!' It is a way which has served the country well and I would propose only one amendment. I would allow Cabinet ministers to bring in more advisers from outside the civil service. Such advisers would move in with the minister and probably move out with him as well. In the meantime their role would be to progress, chase and initiate. The Secretary of State has a right to his own team and it is not a function which can be carried out by a single special adviser.

My first red box took me through all the major issues that faced the department in 1979. Different papers described the problems of British Rail; the need for a more ambitious road-building programme; and the mounting problems of financing bus services. There was a special section on what were called 'smouldering fires'. These were issues that could burst into public and political flames at any stage and ranged from the latest financial crisis at the Port of London to the delays being experienced by the public in booking driving tests. Up to that time I had not rated driving-test delays as much of an issue, but that was in Opposition. In Government I could not pick and choose my issues – they were all mine. I realized only too well that transport contained a range of subjects on which the public felt strongly and I vowed then to set the agenda myself rather than have it set for me by outside events.

On Monday 7 May, four days after the election, I went into the Transport Department for the first time. I was picked up at my flat by Peter Baldwin and by my new principal private secretary Genie Flanagan. It was at this point that I started to become conscious that I knew very little of the civil service world. I knew little about the role of the permanent secretary and even less about the role of the principal private secretary. *Yes Minister* achieved an important service here in helping public, *and* political, understanding. Peter Baldwin was Sir Humphrey, the most senior civil servant

in the department and in effect the chief executive. Each government department has its own permanent secretary and, like the
Cabinet of ministers, they also meet each week to review progress
and to give early warning of problems ahead. Genie Flanagan was
a female Bernard who kept my private office running with a small
and young team and was responsible for ensuring that everything
in my ministerial life went smoothly, from briefings for Cabinet to
ensuring that I turned up for lunch engagements on the right day
with the right speech. She also illustrated another truth about the
civil service, that there are within it a high proportion of very able
women. To the outsider this is one of its most impressive features.
The result should be that over the next ten to twenty years more
women will occupy the service's highest posts.

It was a pleasant early summer day as we walked down Marsham
Street. My new office was perched on the eighteenth floor of one
of the bleak, functional Marsham Street towers, rather ironically
inhabited by the Department of the Environment. Although the
departments had split up, ministers and civil servants still spread
indiscriminately through the three towers with Michael Heseltine
and his more numerous support staff occupying the floor below.
My office had one very substantial advantage and that was a magnificent panoramic view of Westminster Abbey and the Palace of
Westminster itself. Bill Rodgers, my Labour predecessor, had left
behind no pictures on the wall but a note wishing me luck and
saying that I had inherited a loyal team.

As it was a bank holiday the offices were almost deserted, but
nevertheless Peter Baldwin and I had judged it important to have
a preliminary talk. It was good that we did. For one thing was
clear: if I wanted to live up to the commitments in our election
manifesto, then the next months would be exceptionally busy.
Some politicians talk grandly about it not being their job to pass
bills. This is merely another way of saying they do not intend to
reform anything. Practically everything you change in Government
requires legislation. You require a bill just as much to take restrictions off and to denationalize as you do to put restrictions on and
nationalize.

The next forty-eight hours were spent settling in. As a minister,
the first thing you notice is the formal deference paid to you. Civil
servants may go away and confide to their mates 'Do you know

what old Fowler wants to do now?', but there is no question what they call you to your face. In all dealings for the first eighteen months at the Transport Department I was 'Minister'. Notes came through asking 'if the Minister is content' – an archetypal civil service phrase. Other enquiries are made in the same way. If Westminster had disappeared under a tidal wave I would have been invited to the window with the question: 'Minister, have you seen this?'

Inside the Transport Department, feelings about the new ministerial arrangements were mixed. The civil service knew only too well that they could have been reabsorbed into the Environment Department. But what irked them most was having a minister with a seat inside Cabinet but not officially on the list of Cabinet ministers. There was concern about my position, but there was also concern about the position of the department. In the Whitehall league Transport does not rank with the Home Office or the Treasury, but arguably it does come before Agriculture and Energy. With my appointment it had been unmistakably marked as the most junior of government departments.

Every effort, therefore, was made to strengthen my position, and in the battles of Whitehall none was more important than the size of my car. In those days, Secretaries of State were given big chauffeur-driven Rovers. Ministers of State had to make do with Austin Princesses. Should I have a Rover or an Austin Princess? The Department of Transport said that it should be a Rover; the Department of the Environment, which has the thankless task of arranging ministerial cars, thought a Princess would be more appropriate. No one will believe me, but I swear that I did not take part in the debate. From my point of view a chauffeur-driven anything beat the District Line from Fulham hands down. Finally the issue was resolved. The Transport Department won and my reward was a chocolate-coloured Rover. Over the next eleven years I had only two drivers – Len Welham and Ted Johnson – who successfully drove me through storms, snow and demonstrations without even a scratch.

A few days after my appointment, I had my first lesson in when and when not a ministerial car can be used. On the Sunday at the end of my first week in office I woke to hear on the news that there had been a fire at a nursing home in Sutton Coldfield and several people had been killed. I decided to go to the scene of the tragedy. There was nothing I could do but I wished to demonstrate that, although I was now a minister, I remained first and foremost the Member of Parliament for Sutton Coldfield. I consulted my office on how I could get there. The answer was that the official Rover could take me to Euston but after that it was constituency business and I was on my own – fire or no fire.

As a result I spent the next six hours on Sunday-service trains travelling to and from Sutton Coldfield. I make no complaint. In Britain you are both a minister and a constituency member at the same time. Long may that continue, for it gives you the independence to lay down ministerial office and still remain a Member of Parliament. It is quite unlike the American system where a Secretary of State who resigns or who is sacked goes into immediate oblivion. In this country the departing minister (even a departing Prime Minister) simply moves two or three rows back in the House of Commons.

In the first week of my ministerial life there was no question what was the most nerve-racking experience. That was being sworn in as a Privy Counsellor. Membership of the Privy Council entitles you to the prefix 'The Right Honourable' and in the House of Commons it also has a supremely practical advantage. When senior ministers go to the back benches they remain Privy Counsellors and as such are almost certain to be called to speak in debates. Every new MP knows the frustration of sitting through a debate waiting to give a speech and never being called. The speech is not given and the preparatory work is wasted. Privy Counsellors usually manage to avoid that fate, provided they do not abuse the privilege and seek to speak in every debate that is staged.

For the swearing-in ceremony we went to Buckingham Palace. As I learned in my National Service days, I am not notably skilled in remembering when to stand to attention, when to turn right, when to salute and the rest. Being sworn in is not quite as complicated as Trooping the Colour, but you are uneasily aware that all eyes are on you. You hope you do not stand up when you should be kneeling down or take the Bible in the wrong hand. Under the eyes of Christopher Soames and Norman St John-Stevas, I made no glaring mistakes and, for the first time but not for the last, I saw how the calm experience of the Queen herself managed to ensure that even her clumsiest subjects did not make fools of themselves.

The next day, Thursday 10 May, we met in Cabinet for the first time. The cameramen were out in force as one by one the Rovers drew up at the entrance to Number 10 Downing Street. Behind the deceptively modest black front door there is a world of offices and reception rooms. At its centre is the Cabinet room itself. The Cabinet table is coffin-shaped, so that theoretically every minister has a full view of proceedings and above all can catch the Prime Minister's eye if he or she wants to speak. But the fact is that some ministers do better than others. The Prime Minister sits at the centre of the table facing outwards on to Horseguards Parade. On her left in May 1979 sat her deputy, the Home Secretary Willie Whitelaw; on her immediate right was the Secretary to the Cabinet, Sir John Hunt, the Prime Minister's senior official adviser and the man who is also responsible for ensuring that the decisions of Cabinet are properly recorded. Directly opposite the Prime Minister was the Chancellor of the Exchequer, Geoffrey Howe; the Foreign Secretary, Peter Carrington; and the Lord Chancellor, Quintin Hailsham. Others with favourable positions facing the Prime Minister were Keith Joseph, the Industry Secretary; Francis Pym, now at Defence; and Jim Prior, the Employment Secretary.

The rest of the Cabinet were placed around the table on both sides. By common consent, the worst places, reserved for the most junior members of the Cabinet, are at the far ends of the table on the same side as the Prime Minister. I occupied the far-right seat at the table. As I learned over the next eighteen months, you had to lean right forwards and sometimes wave your hand urgently to get into the Cabinet debate. The placing did, however, have one advantage. At various stages over the next months volunteers were optimistically sought to make further public spending cuts or drop a cherished bill from the legislative programme. At that stage you could become practically invisible as you leaned back in your chair.

From the beginning, Margaret Thatcher adopted a business-like approach as the head of Cabinet. In Shadow Cabinet all proceedings were on Christian-name terms: 'Margaret, I agree with Geoffrey on this.' In Cabinet it was job titles only: 'Prime Minister, I support the argument of the Chancellor of the Exchequer.' It is

really a matter of taste, and the previous Labour Government had
stuck to Christian names, but it is remarkable how easily you slip
into the style. The only problem comes with some of the floating
titles of Cabinet. You should have no problem remembering who
is Chancellor of the Exchequer or Foreign Secretary, but who
happens to be Chancellor of the Duchy of Lancaster or the
Paymaster-General at any particular time can easily slip your
memory.

The first month of what is today seen as a radical government
was characterized by caution. At our first Cabinet meeting, we
were not going to rush into precipitate decisions – however obvious
they might now seem in retrospect. For example, we did not
immediately abolish the Standing Committee on Pay Compar-
ability but instead 'urgently considered' its future. We instituted a
freeze on new civil service recruitment and formally resolved to
reduce government circulars and the number of government-
appointed bodies (Quangos) that abounded at the time. Although
committed by our manifesto to a reduction in the size of the civil
service, we were not sure how quickly we should proceed. One
argument was that ministers should 'get their feet under the table'
before making any hard decisions. In the end that argument was
seen as a certain recipe for inaction and rejected.

At the second Cabinet meeting a week later, we came to the
area that was to give us more heartache during the first Thatcher
Government than any other – public expenditure. We had come
to power committed to lowering taxes, and this could be achieved
only by reducing government spending. Again, many reasons were
put forward why we should not act. No government department
likes to lose part of its budget, but at this stage in 1979 it was
difficult for anyone who had just fought the May election to argue
against the overall reduction of £1,365 million which we sought.
It did no more than bring spending down to the level reached in
1977/8 by the previous Labour Government.

Among the other issues to appear very early on were the Common Agricultural Policy, Rhodesia and the problem of refugees
from Hong Kong. There were already 32,000 boat people in camps
in Hong Kong and we had to decide whether to take another 900
aboard a ship in Hong Kong harbour. We agreed that it was right
to allow them to land but hoped, as we have been hoping

ever since, that some international solution would soon be reached.

The immediate test of the new Government was the Queen's Speech: the list of bills we intended to pass in the first session of Parliament. Our intentions would be judged by this programme. Our aim was to set out specific goals, not a collection of generalizations. On the evening of Monday 14 May, the whole ministerial team assembled at Number 10 for the eve-of-session dinner and to listen to the Cabinet Secretary reading the contents of the speech. Any Queen's Speech is couched in official language but, even so, the radical approach was clear to see. At the heart of the Government's thinking was the control of inflation through monetary and fiscal policies. By reducing the burden of direct taxation and restricting the claims of the public sector on the nation's resources, the Government would start to restore incentives, encourage efficiency and create a climate in which commerce and industry could flourish.

There followed promises to legislate to reform the law on picketing and the closed shop; to reduce state ownership and increase competition; and to give local authority tenants the right to buy their homes. Among the Labour Government laws to be repealed or amended was the legislation compelling local authorities to introduce comprehensive education; the Scotland Act and the Wales Act providing for devolution; and the legislation governing the interventionist National Enterprise Board. Every one of these measures was wildly controversial with the Opposition. It was clear that it was going to be an exciting, if bumpy, ride.

The theory is that all the real decisions of government go to Cabinet. But for the reasons that Harold Wilson had set out at his lobby briefing twenty years earlier, that is not practical. It would mean that Cabinet was in constant session and would reduce Cabinet ministers to the role of barristers with departmental briefs. The obvious solution is to set up subcommittees. Cabinet committees are intended to make the business of government manageable. Different ministers are on different subcommittees. The work is spread. Inevitably the result is that a whole range of subjects go nowhere near Cabinet itself. The vast majority are settled in the subcommittee to the satisfaction, or at least the agreement, of all parties concerned. A minister who finds his proposal rejected by the subcommittee has the right to take the issue to full Cabinet, but his chances of winning are generally slight. He can perhaps make it a resigning issue, although that card probably cannot be played more than once. His chances of reversing the decision of the Cabinet committee are particularly slim if the Prime Minister herself happens to have chaired it.

Cabinet committees, therefore, play a vital part in the life of ministers – but for some reason are still shrouded in secrecy. To her credit, Margaret Thatcher broke with precedent on 24 May 1979 and announced publicly that she was setting up four committees of Cabinet: Defence and Overseas Policy ('OD'), Economic Strategy ('E'), Home and Social Affairs ('H') and Legislation ('L'). I found myself a permanent member of 'H', which dealt with everything from the pensioners' Christmas bonus to future policy on Scotland, and a frequent attender at 'E' where any proposals on railway policy would be discussed. But the structure went wider than just the four principal committees. As the years went by, special 'Miscellaneous' committees (code-named MISC) were formed to look at particular subjects. For example, Margaret Thatcher herself chaired committees of ministers to consider major changes in social security, broadcasting, education, health and local government.

In effect, most of the Government's decisions on future policy were taken at committee level. All the proposals then went to full Cabinet, but it was difficult for anyone not on the relevant committee successfully to challenge the policy. The members of the committee had become expert in the months they had spent studying the area. They also developed a collective loyalty to the proposals made. I soon learned that in the everyday business of government nothing was more important to a minister than winning his battles in Cabinet committee.

The month of May started with Fiona and Oliver and it certainly ended with them. I should explain that Fiona was Fiona Poole and Oliver was her six-year-old son from her first marriage to David Poole. The House broke for the Whitsun recess on Friday 25 May, and the following Tuesday Fiona and I slipped off to the Chelsea Register Office to get married. For me it was quite simply the best day's work that I have ever done.

We had met years before, in the late 1960s, and I had seen Fiona from time to time since then in the House of Commons. In 1978 I had plucked up the courage to invite her to my fortieth birthday party. No one was more aware than me that my record up to this point had not been good. I had already been married once and, before that, had pursued a long on-off romance which had started in Cambridge. Both had collapsed and no one was to blame but myself. I was not at all confident that Fiona would accept my proposal. Happily for me – and after only the briefest hesitation – Fiona accepted.

I married an attractive, intelligent red-head and I acquired a lively young stepson. Even Andrew Roth in his *Parliamentary Profiles* is complimentary about Fiona. It was a marriage which gave my life stability and a purpose that it had not previously had. It also opened a window on to family life which as an only child I had not previously seen.

The advantages for Fiona were more doubtful. Although Oliver's grandfather had been the Chairman of the Conservative Party under Harold Macmillan, it was anything but a political family. Indeed I was something of an embarrassment. Since leaving Oxford, Fiona had worked in the research division of the House of Commons Library. As such she was a scrupulously independent civil servant and answered enquiries from MPs of any party. The last thing she needed was marriage to a party politician, but I am glad to say that no Member of Parliament as much as raised an eyebrow about the position.

We married on Tuesday 29 May and on Wednesday we set off for a brief three-day honeymoon in Venice. On the flight a small party developed, greatly helped by two first-class passengers, Michael and Anne Heseltine, who smuggled back free champagne to a growing number of friends and acquaintances. Arriving in Venice, we went by water to our hotel and there for the first time the social advantages and disadvantages of being a minister became apparent. It was only because a travel agent friend had been able to put together what I thought was a spectacularly good deal that we had been able to afford Venice, and certainly the internationally famous hotel where we were staying. As we entered the hotel the manager came forward. 'Welcome, Mr Minister,' he said kindly. 'It is a great privilege to have you staying at our hotel.' So far so good, but he had more. 'You will be glad to know that we have been able to change the rather modest room you booked for something rather more appropriate.' Somehow he failed to mention that it was also something rather more expensive.

Nevertheless, they were wonderfully sunny days in Venice and included a dinner with one of Fiona's oldest friends who drove several hundred miles to inspect me. All too quickly our time came to an end and we presented ourselves at the airport, only to be told that nothing was flying. There was a strike – not a British strike but an Italian strike. We would be taken to a hotel outside Venice for the night. A coach would then collect us at 4 a.m. the next morning so that we could catch an alternative plane from Milan. The May honeymoon was over.

CHAPTER 7

Family Silver

'But what makes you think that
Europe wants to get any closer to us?'

Daily Express

A few months after I joined the Department of Transport in 1979 I was presented with an issue which had baffled governments for well over a hundred years. I had called a meeting in my office, by now decorated with a number of pictures from the Government's own art collection including a marvellous study of the railway cutting at Acton by Lucien Pissarro. The subject of the meeting was the Channel Tunnel. The Channel Tunnel project had first been seriously mooted at the start of the nineteenth century. Over the years since then, the debate on whether it was better to cross the Channel by tunnel, bridge or ferry had raged to and fro.

Solutions had ranged from the ingenious to the bizarre. One Victorian scheme was for a tunnel lit by candles, where horses would draw passengers across in special vehicles, pausing only at an artificial island in the middle of the Channel for everyone to come up for air and water. Another project was for a submerged tube. Gothic turrets would provide ventilation shafts and the two ends would be marked by lighthouses. By 1876, planning had reached such a point that France and Britain signed a protocol laying down the basis of a treaty governing the construction of the tunnel and a start was made on either side of the Channel. It was not to be. Public and press opinion turned against the whole concept, with Queen Victoria pronouncing it 'objectionable' and *The Times* declaring that 'the silver streak is our safety'. For the next eighty years the argument that a tunnel under the silver streak of the Channel would pose a major security problem held sway, although a tunnel would have been of great advantage to Britain during the First World War.

As the twentieth century progressed the debate limped on, but it was not until the early 1960s that the tunnel became a serious prospect again. In 1961 the British and French governments agreed to set up a working group to consider the merits of the rival proposals and at the beginning of 1964 Ernest Marples, the British Transport Minister, and his French counterpart announced that the two governments would go ahead with a tunnel. In 1973 a start was actually made, but the following February the Heath Government fell. Labour inherited three major public spending projects: the third London airport to be built at Maplin, the supersonic Concorde aircraft and the Channel Tunnel. Labour wanted economies and the first project to perish was Maplin. But that was not enough for the new Chancellor, Denis Healey. In effect there was a choice between Concorde and the Channel Tunnel. Concorde (which was to be partly built in Bristol) benefited from a strong local lobby including a local MP, Tony Benn, who had now become a member of the Labour Cabinet. More to the point, it would cost more to cancel Concorde than the relatively paltry £17 million it would cost to go back on the Channel Tunnel. The result was that on 20 January 1975 Harold Wilson's Government, to the dismay of the French, formally cancelled the project and all work on the tunnel stopped.

In 1979 the issue came to me. It could scarcely have come at a worse time. No one was under any illusion that Margaret Thatcher was in the business of building expensive prestige projects – a category into which the Channel Tunnel was wrongly put. Public spending was being reined back and the Cabinet was getting down to the series of bruising public-spending battles which characterized our first few years of office. Nevertheless, Peter Parker and British Rail were anxious to get the project back on track and I strongly sympathized with their position. The tunnel was a long-overdue link with Europe as well as a new opportunity for the railways. But I also realized that I would be exceedingly lucky to keep my existing road and rail budgets, let alone add massive new expenditure.

At the first meeting in the department I did what every other Transport Minister appears to have done over the previous ten years: I hired Professor Sir Alec Cairncross to advise me. There was no question that a tunnel was technically feasible, but I wanted to know what the economics would be. What would be the likely traffic? What would be a sensible forecast of revenue? I particularly wanted to know Sir Alec's views now that British Rail had submitted a scaled-down plan. Poor old British Rail were between the devil and the deep blue sea. The Labour Government had cancelled their previous and more ambitious scheme for the tunnel and now the next Conservative Government was wondering if their current one was ambitious enough. Nevertheless, the questions were fundamental. The British Rail scheme would certainly cost less than the old plan as it now proposed a single-track tunnel, not a twin tunnel. This meant obvious limits on capacity and above all it meant no cars and no lorries which were the most lucrative traffic. It seemed too modest to be profitable.

What really concerned me was how to finance a tunnel project of any kind. I realized I would get no help from the Treasury and, indeed, I suspected that they could not understand why the department was wasting its time on this issue at all. In my view there was only one hope, and that was to build the tunnel using private venture capital. On Wednesday 5 March 1980, I explored the practicalities of this course at a meeting in the department and on 10 March I minuted the Prime Minister. I said that I believed it would now be right to give some indication of the Government's attitude to the building of a tunnel. I continued:

I see no advantage in adopting the Labour Government's negative stance and ruling out all possibility of a link being built. If private capital can be attracted – and I believe it could to the right project – it seems to me entirely right that we should do what we can as Government to create the right climate for a successful link to be built.

In essence I proposed that rather than having public investment we should substitute private investment without any Government guarantee. That basically meant that Government would not stand behind the project. We would do whatever Government had to do, like negotiate a treaty with the French, but we would not be financially responsible for the project. The policy was cleared over the next few days and on 19 March I told the House of Commons that

The cost of any scheme would be very large and I should make clear now that the Government cannot contemplate funding expenditure on this scale from public funds. However, if a scheme is commercially sound I see no reason why private risk capital should not be available.

The marks of the Treasury were all over my short statement of policy. They had conceded that the project could go ahead, but very few bets were being taken in Whitehall that the century-old logjam would be shifted. There was a general belief that our terms would not attract many takers and there was a suspicion that the Government did not really have its heart in the project in any event. Over the next months, rival consortia considered how to finance the new investment while at the Transport Department we could do little more than wait. Then, eighteen months later, we had an exceptional stroke of luck which entirely transformed the position.

In September 1981 the newly elected President Mitterrand came to London. He brought with him, among others, the new Communist Transport Minister, Charles Fiterman, whom I had met the previous week. We had talked over transport issues, including the tunnel. All the predictions were that the meeting at Downing Street between newly elected political opposites would be difficult. In fact it proved surprisingly genial and Margaret Thatcher's transparent ability (later to impress another political opposite, Mikhail Gorbachev) had its effect on François Mitterrand. There was, however, one problem. Pleasant as the round of meetings had been, there was next to nothing that could be agreed as a common objective for the final communiqué.

It was at this point that the Channel Tunnel at last came into its own. President Mitterrand shared the traditional French enthusiasm for the tunnel and, socialist or not, was prepared to concede private investment. Margaret Thatcher, too, realized the potential of having this major capital project financed by the private sector. It has been claimed that Margaret saw the tunnel as some sort of monument to her and her period of government. I never once heard her even hint at such a view. Her position as expressed to me was that if the private sector wanted to use its own money for the tunnel then we should certainly not stand in the way.

The result of the Downing Street meeting was an enthusiastic statement committing the two leaders to the project. It was the crucial turning-point because from that moment on the tunnel had not just the support of the Transport Department but the backing of Number 10. Cabinet ministers may be equal, but Prime Ministers are more equal than others. To get the backing of the British

Prime Minister and the French President was a good day's work.

Much of the debate today about the Channel crossing concentrates on the rail link on the British side. My involvement with the tunnel did not extend to the rail link which was decided after I had left the department. But that debate should not obscure the fact that private investment was the key that unlocked the Channel Tunnel door. The project had been cancelled by Labour for lack of public funds. Had we waited for the position to change, so that public investment or private investment with public guarantee could go ahead, we would still be waiting.

Yet the conventional wisdom in the transport world of the 1970s was that all progress depended on public investment, public controls and, of course, public ownership. Everywhere I looked the Government was involved. It even had a shot at controlling motorway service areas, provoking a debate which encapsulated many of the attitudes of the time. The service areas, with their awful tea and rubber sandwiches, had become a music hall joke. It seemed to me that although competition on site was difficult, it was at least possible to have competition between sites. To do that, however, you would have to allow the operators to advertise. There were already signs that told the motorist he was approaching, say, the Newport Pagnell or Watford Gap service areas. Surely there could be no objection to telling him in advance which areas were run by Trusthouse Forte and which by Granada?

Not a bit of it. One of my civil servants solemnly objected, arguing that such advertisements could present a potential safety risk. The theory was that on seeing the sign motorists would be so surprised that they might drive into the verge or the car in front. That policy was overturned in two minutes flat but it is worth remembering that it had held sway since the inception of the service areas fifteen years earlier.

Advertising, however, turned out to be only the tip of the iceberg. Although each site was controlled by the operator, they were supervised and inspected by the Department of Transport. That meant the Minister of Transport was answerable for them in the House of Commons. In Opposition we had had great fun pursuing Bill Rodgers on the standard of the baked beans and the quality of the fried cod. We hounded him to such effect that he responded in the classic 1970s way and set up no less than an official committee of inquiry to consider the whole position. The committee carried out a range of fascinating research and confirmed what the public knew already, namely that the ham sandwiches available in motorway cafeterias had a tendency to be 'thin, tasteless ham in soggy bread'.

Bill Rodgers having set up this committee, it now fell to me to decide what to do with their report. I had no intention of answering a Parliamentary question on soggy ham sandwiches and I could not see why Government was involved in the commercial operation at all. The obvious solution was to sell the leases to the operators and for them to decide what investment was required if they were to attract new business. When I put this to the operators there was an astonished silence. No one had previously considered this proposal and there was therefore no prepared group response. One or two operators immediately saw the attractions, but others still hankered after the old world. The meeting broke up with mixed feelings, but after a few days it became clear that we were in business. I put up for sale the service areas on new long leases, retaining some controls only to ensure that the areas were safe stopping places for motorway travellers.

My experience with motorway service areas confirmed my belief that far too much of transport was either in state hands or run under state control. Rather than concluding that I had been too radical in Opposition, I fast came to the view I had been too cautious. Everything I saw in Government suggested that the right place for the National Freight Corporation was in the private sector and that deregulation of the bus and coach services could provide great public benefits. But I now saw other opportunities.

The nineteen ports owned by the British Transport Docks Board were basically old railway ports and had come into Government control with the nationalization of the railways in 1946. The Docks Board was the biggest company in the ports industry and with its Southampton operations and its Humber and South Wales ports had secured about a quarter of the market. But nationalization had brought the board few obvious advantages. As part of the public sector it was subject to the usual Treasury controls on investment and borrowing, but it was also restricted in another way. Because it was publicly owned, its activities were restricted so that it did not compete unfairly with the private sector. The result was that the board was confined to the business of handling ships and cargo but required ministerial consent if, for example, it wished to develop the land attached to the sites.

The obvious solution was to give the board commercial freedom and control of its own destiny in the private sector. The board itself saw the advantage of this course but the chairman, Humphrey Browne, was worried that privatization would lead to a crippling strike. Personally I thought the fears overdone, but nevertheless I sought to find a way of transferring the operation to the private sector which would minimize the risk of industrial action. I proposed that the Government should initially retain a 51 per cent stake in the new company. In other words, the new company would start life structured in rather the same way as BP, with a Government shareholding but without the Government taking any part in the business. That stake was later sold and the privatization of the ports was completed without any industrial action and with many of the dockers buying shares in the new company.

British Rail's subsidiary companies, like the hotels and the cross-Channel ferry company, Sealink, were another area ripe for change. These companies had traditional links with the railways and their *raison d'être* had been that they were a natural extension of the business. They were there for the convenience of rail passengers. But times had changed. The railway connection no longer dominated the operation and most of the customers for both hotels and ferries came by road.

Both businesses had been starved of investment for more than thirty years. The hotels were dingy and British Transport Hotels had added only one new building to their stock since the end of the Second World War. The ferries were safe but too often they were outdated and uncomfortable. In part this was due to the public-sector controls on investment, but it was also because of the natural priorities that had operated year after year inside British Rail. What the public wanted was a good rail service and not surprisingly successive generations of British Rail managers put their major effort into achieving that. In competition for new investment, hotels and ferries came way behind the main business and these two potentially successful concerns were not getting the management or main board attention they deserved. Nor was there any reason to believe they would get it over the next thirty years, either. After talks with BR's Chairman, Peter Parker, we agreed that the sensible way forward was for a new company, British Rail Investments, to be formed and for the subsidiaries to be transferred to the private sector, with the proceeds going to British Rail.

In transport, then, Margaret Thatcher's first Government extended privatization far beyond what we had thought possible in Opposition, but there was no doubt what was the jewel in the crown. Some commentators and businessmen have suggested that the successful privatization of the National Freight Corporation was a foregone conclusion. It certainly did not seem that way at the time. We were not inundated with offers for the company from the private sector and our financial advisers doubted whether we could sell the business at all. The parcels side was still losing money heavily and by 1980 the world was running into recession. No country was worse hit than Britain, where an economic gale tore through companies which were already dangerously weak. Unemployment went up and investment came down. In the West Midlands you saw factories where the roofs had been removed to avoid rates on the empty building.

Among the industries affected, transport was badly hit. There was over-capacity in road haulage as the amount of goods to be transported went down and prices were cut. Even the inner-city property sites of National Carriers did not look very tempting once it became clear there was an abundance of that kind of property on offer. It was against this background that Peter Thompson, the chief executive of NFC, together with his chairman, Bobby Lawrence, came to see me in my small office on the Cabinet floor of the House of Commons on 18 May 1981.

At an earlier meeting, Bobby Lawrence had asked me for my initial reaction to the management buying the company. Peter Thompson now explained that he wanted to go beyond the concept of a management buy-out and to involve all the staff who wanted to buy shares. He feared that a management buy-out would leave things on the shop floor very much as before with the 'them' and 'us' of workers and managers. Employee ownership would open the door to involving all the staff in the company. My reaction was, if anything, more enthusiastic than before. It seemed the ideal way for the NFC to go into the private sector. Bad industrial relations had been the curse of the country for as long as I had taken any interest in politics; although the reform of trade union law was essential, further steps were also needed. I hoped that the NFC would be a pioneer not only in privatization but also in improving employee relations.

The 1980 Transport Act took all the action necessary to transfer the National Freight Corporation to the private sector and reform the Traffic Commissioner system so that new inter-city and commuter coach services could develop, together with other new services like car-sharing. With the momentum of privatization established, I was able to argue successfully for further legislation. The 1981 Transport Act enabled private investment to be introduced into the subsidiary companies of British Rail and effectively denationalized the British Transport Docks Board.

Of course, critics of privatization in transport abounded. Labour spokesmen competed with wild phrases about 'cut-throat competition' and 'rip-off'. But the most damaging criticism of the privatization process came some years later, and not from a Labour politician but from one of the most distinguished Conservative leaders since the war, Harold Macmillan. Macmillan likened the privatization programme to the reaction of individuals or estates when they run into difficulties. They dispose of 'all the nice furniture that used to be in the saloon and then the candelabra'. In short, they sell the family silver. Macmillan saw privatization as an ideological approach to the problems of industry motivated by a simple desire on the part of Government to make some quick money. I entirely dispute that.

The transport companies which have been denationalized are now successful and are trading profitably. This provides the best possible security for their workforces but it means something more in terms of the 'family silver'. Rather than paying out subsidies, the Government now receives substantial annual taxation receipts. Company profits mean income for the Government. Without that income, promises of better public services – that is, publicly financed services – are pure fantasy. To take just one example: Associated British Ports (the former British Transport Docks Board) has paid over £60 million in corporation tax over the last five years. The taxpayer received not only a capital sum when the companies were sold but now also receives a substantial annual dividend. Any estate owner who achieved this might be thought to have made a notable bargain.

There is no doubt that investment in the companies which have gone private has increased, sometimes substantially. Total investment in the NFC in the years since privatization has totalled almost £700 million, whereas in state ownership investment never exceeded £25 million a year. In Associated British Ports investment in the business approaches £200 million. In the motorway service areas, Trusthouse Forte alone have invested over £80 million since they were allowed to purchase their leases. The areas have visibly improved, with new restaurants and new hotels.

As for employee involvement, it is certainly greater than it ever was in the years of nationalization. The claim for nationalization was that public ownership would mean more commitment to those industries by the people who worked for them. It never worked out that way. Nationalization in the transport industries produced neither outstanding industrial relations nor employee commitment. Privatization has produced much more hopeful results. The NFC has been the outstanding example where for seven years the company was owned entirely by the workforce. Even now that the company has gone public, some 40 per cent of shares remain in the hands of staff or former staff. Annual General Meetings are attended by several thousand employee shareholders and (in contrast to the normally sedate company AGM in some discreet City hall) NFC has to take over the National Exhibition Centre in Birmingham or the Winter Gardens at Blackpool.

Privatization has also allowed good managers to manage and succeed. There are the well-known stars like Peter Thompson and James Watson of NFC, and Keith Stuart of Associated British Ports, who came with their companies from the public sector. But the process goes way beyond the top managers. It reaches right down into the companies themselves. As one senior manager said: 'Employees now expect managers to take decisions on a commercial basis and recognize that their interests as employees – and in many cases shareholders – demand it. This is in marked contrast to the position prior to privatization when the commercial objective was accepted by senior management but not by the bulk of employees.'

Above all, the result of privatization in transport has been a better service to the public. Coach services have increased and are provided in modern, comfortable vehicles at competitive prices. Commuting by coach has prospered. The hotels which used to belong to British Rail have improved substantially. Gleneagles, for example, is now open all the year round rather than just in summer and autumn following a major investment in all-weather sport and leisure facilities. At the motorway service areas petrol prices are now nearer the off-motorway prices and competition has benefited the motorist. As Rocco Forte said:

After the changes the consumer could see what he was buying before committing himself to leave the motorway. There was a real incentive for operators to provide a quality service which built consumer loyalty. In short, the consumer called the tune and the operators who prospered were those who best identified the needs of the consumers and met them at the right price.

Privatization has achieved better ways of running the transport industries and there is today no serious movement in any of them to return to state control. A similar position can be found in many of the later privatizations of the Thatcher Government. Certainly some, like British Telecommunications, gas, electricity and water, produced spectacular financial results, but the lasting impact has been on the businesses themselves. Privatization means giving businesses the chance to flourish; the process of deregulation means the Government getting out of the way. The Government provides the opportunity, but it cannot guarantee success. The most ministers can do is to argue the case for change and enable the changes to be made. The eventual success of the venture depends not upon ministers but upon the managers and the work-force in the companies themselves. The significant feature of privatization has been that the transformation has usually been carried out by broadly the same teams that had worked under nationalization. Throughout the privatized businesses, attitudes to the customer have improved and the bureaucracy of State industry has been removed. It is essentially for reasons like these that the governments of the new democracies of Eastern Europe look to privatization as a way forward.

It is for the same reasons that I would now support the denationalization of British Rail. Some argue that this is impossible, given that some rail services will be unprofitable. Yet there is no reason why Government cannot enter into contracts with privatized companies whether privatization is on a regional basis or takes place in some other way. Privatization would not mean the end of support for the railways. It would provide better value for both the taxpayer and the passenger. The potential gain from rail privatization would be a more commercial railway and a better service for the public.

When I was at the Transport Department, my aim was a good rail service for the public and as efficient a service as possible. That meant continuing to support British Rail financially while at the same time fighting to make the industry more productive. Manpower had come down over the years from 470,000 in 1960 to 215,000 twenty years later, but the business was still over-staffed. Everyone knew this, but we faced the same problems in increasing efficiency and productivity as in all the other traditional industries like coal and steel. Our challenge on the railways was to win change – but without, in Peter Parker's words, 'bringing the roof in'.

At the time, the two dominant rail union leaders were Sid Weighell of the National Union of Railwaymen and Ray Buckton of the drivers' union, ASLEF (the Associated Society of Locomotive Engineers and Firemen). They were a contrast in styles. Sid Weighell was tense and cautious. Negotiations were long and painful. He was always looking for the catch. When he agreed, however, the agreement stuck. Ray Buckton was a much more extrovert character. He was always available to the press for an instant comment and was a politician in his own right. On the other hand, he was extremely difficult to pin down to any conclusion. He gave the impression that he was constantly looking over his shoulder at his executive which contained some hard and prickly characters. One other point about the two union leaders was abundantly clear. Whenever they came to meetings at the department they sat at opposite ends of the table. Whatever reservations they had about dealing with me were as nothing compared to the reservations they had about dealing with each other.

On one point, however, they were united. They wanted to see a positive statement from the Government which demonstrated our commitment to the future of the railways. With the election of Margaret Thatcher, the assumption among some lobbyists had been that we would institute a new round of 'Beeching cuts'. In the early 1960s Dr Beeching, the chairman of the railways, had cut out some of the most unprofitable rail lines and the fear was that I would do the same. Indeed in November 1979 the *Guardian* had published a wholly imaginary story about 900 miles of railway being under the axe. For all its note of fantasy, however, the article was widely read and well timed. It appeared on the day that I was answering questions on transport on the floor of the House and there was a question on the future of railway services on the order paper. As I rose to answer there was a roar of laughter from the Labour benches. I looked behind me to see what appeared to be a solid forest of standing Tory MPs from county constituencies anxious to ask questions about their own particular rail lines. I repeated that I saw 'no case for a further round of Beeching cuts' and that there had been no secret talks or plans. The House settled back more or less reassured.

The only occasion when rail closures were raised in my time at the Transport Department was in the spring of 1981. The issue arose when I took to Cabinet committee my proposals on railway electrification. British Rail's diesel stock was coming up for replacement and we needed to decide whether to reinvest in diesel equipment or to invest in electrification. The overwhelming advantage of an electric railway was that it was cheaper to run and maintain. It would also reduce dependence on oil, which was a sensible strategic aim, and the regular orders for the British railway manufacturing industry could help to win more export orders for electrified systems overseas.

In February 1981 the Transport Department and British Rail published a joint report which concluded that a substantial programme of main-line electrification would be financially worthwhile: it would show a real return on capital of around 11 per cent and it would cut oil consumption. At the end of March, I circulated a paper which enthusiastically backed electrification.

A meeting was set for mid-April but, just before it, the whole policy was challenged by an adviser to the Government, Professor Alan Walters.

Walters had two main points. First, he argued that the railway system should be reduced. Many experts, he said, believed that we should aim for a smaller, more concentrated and more efficient network. Second, he challenged the forecasts on electrification and said that competition from cars, the newly deregulated coaches and the airlines could all erode rail traffic. The case for widespread electrification was not plausible, he thundered. It was based on assumptions which were not credible. I strongly disagreed with both arguments.

I did not believe that there were large savings to be made simply from reducing the size of the rail network. Over two-thirds of the cost of the railways was the cost of labour. The obvious policy to follow was one of improved productivity, and I proposed, with the agreement of British Rail, a reduction in the workforce of 38,000. With electrification I could achieve this goal. If I simply concentrated on reducing the network, I would involve myself in a long and profitless public, political and industrial row. There would be public inquiry after public inquiry – for the law ensured that no closure could be made without one – and many areas would be deprived of valued rail services. I believed the case for electrification to be overwhelming. And although my department and British Rail had produced a joint report, this did not mean we automatically accepted BR's views. We needed to be persuaded of the case and we had gone through the BR figures line by line.

When the case came to ministerial colleagues, it was these arguments that prevailed. There was no support for reducing the network and the position that I had set out in 1979 remained the Government's policy. The Central Policy Review Staff were asked to examine the case for electrification. In June 1981 the CPRS reported back that there was indeed a commercial case for electrification but that the programme should be endorsed route by route rather than in some all-embracing fashion. As far as I was concerned, that merely represented a different path to the same goal and so on 22 June I told the House of Commons that rail electrification was going ahead. On the same afternoon I met with the rail unions and (loyally supported by Peter Parker) put the position to them. Both Weighell and Buckton would have preferred more, but the statement persuaded them that the Government did have its heart in the future of the railway system. The scene was set for progress towards a modern network.

My chief regret in my stay at Transport was that we were not able to do more in combining private and public investment in partnership projects. In particular, we could have done more to use private investment in the road-building programme. We are all deeply schizophrenic about roads. Held up in a jam on, say, the M25 we curse the planners for not having the foresight to have built a five-lane motorway joining up to other five-lane motorways. Comfortably seated in a television studio or before a television set, we tend to forget that experience and offer pious hopes that public transport will improve to such an extent that in some miraculous way new roads will be unnecessary. At the beginning of the 1980s, road building was not a notably popular cause. You could usually win support for bypasses from unhappy communities who had been pounded by heavy traffic on roads quite inadequate for the purpose. But on some parts of the M25 we were more likely to be met by demonstrators protesting against the road itself. I cannot remember any public movement to get five lanes. At times I reckoned we were lucky to get three.

Delay was written into the whole system of road planning. The procedures took so long that much needed links were not built until years after they were required. The M40 motorway was a case in point. A motorway connecting Oxford (and thus London) to Birmingham and the Midlands road network had been needed for at least two decades. I went to see the proposed route of the M40 in my time as Transport Minister, but the full motorway was not opened until 1991. I had another serious battle getting approval for the M54 to Telford – the only road I know of finally settled at a full meeting of a Cabinet committee. Nor did the Government's means of analysing the need for roads always help very much. The Treasury had a system called COBA – cost-benefit analysis. Ken Clarke was my minister of roads and I remember him coming back on more than one occasion with steam coming out of his ears. The analysis had shown that the cheapest option was to build a particular road in a straight line.

The mere fact that this took the road through a school and a housing estate was of secondary interest.

When I took over, it was evident that the need for new roads vastly outstripped the likely supply. Could not private investment fill at least part of the gap? Toll roads were one solution but I was less keen on them than on another idea we developed in the Transport Department. The idea was that the private sector would build and finance a number of roads and the department would pay a rent for them on the basis of how much traffic used them. The Treasury did not like this plan at all. In their view it was nothing more than delayed public spending in instalments. Some might think a little delayed public spending on roads would not have been a bad idea at that time.

Nowhere has the failure to build much needed roads been more obvious than in our cities. The result is that the city environment has deteriorated. The number of cars has increased and the roads are all too often inadequate to take them. Birmingham is one of the few cities where any attempt at sensible provision has been made. London, however, is pounded by commuter traffic and the only policy option which promises relief is determined action to exclude or price out the one-driver commuter car. There is now no other course. We face the vastly increased traffic projections for the twenty-first century with roads adequate to deal with the conditions of the nineteenth. No road-building scheme can bring relief to London in the foreseeable future. Almost all of us value the freedom that the car gives, but life is about balancing freedoms. There should be no absolute freedom for any motorist to drive into the middle of already congested cities free of charge.

I spent my last months at the Transport Department preparing a third Transport Bill whose aim was to reform the traffic laws and to introduce the 'points' system for disqualification. This followed my 1981 legislation which had introduced the first road-safety measures for fifteen years and was used (as I knew it would be) to introduce compulsory seat-belts. But I now felt the time was coming to move on to another department. At the beginning of 1981 I had been promoted from Minister of Transport to Secretary of State. This meant very little to me apart from a salary increase and a move from my position at the extreme right of the Cabinet table to the extreme left. I took over the chair previously occupied by Angus Maude, who since 1979 had carried out the impossible job of overseeing Government information. When things are going wrong the Government's supporters call it a failure of presentation and everyone trots out the old excuse that 'we are not getting the message across'. In the wider political world outside transport that excuse was much in use in 1981.

CHAPTER 8

Turning Point

'These days that *is* her normal dress'

Mahood, *Punch*

O ne of Margaret Thatcher's most famous maxims was 'you don't have problems – you only have challenges'. In 1981 we had one challenge after another. In 1979 we had won the election with 44 per cent of the poll. By early 1981 our support had fallen to below 30 per cent and as the months went by it plummeted even further to reach 23 per cent at the end of the year. Even in the 'poll-tax' dominated months of 1990 we did not quite reach that point.

The Conservative Party was cast in gloom. For much of 1981 we were running not only behind Labour but also behind the alliance formed by the Liberals and the newly created Social Democratic Party of David Owen, Bill Rodgers, Shirley Williams and Roy Jenkins. The SDP's aim was to create a real third force in British politics and their hope was to take votes from both parties. They believed they could win votes in Sunderland just as surely as in Mid-Sussex. We Tory MPs were not so sure. The SDP were likely to be a far greater danger to us, as disgruntled ex-Conservative voters who would never have voted Labour in a million years turned to a cosy middle party. It had to be admitted that there was plenty for the voters to be disgruntled about. The country was in the middle of a world recession with unemployment well above two million and looking set to break the three million mark, a prospect that a few years before would have seemed unthinkable.

Inside the Government the gloom was widely shared. Cabinet was an unhappy place. There were leaks everywhere and well-reported battles between the so-called 'dries' who were the outright supporters of the Government's economic policies and the 'wets' who were the sceptics. In fact the grouping was never much more than a rough guide. It was certainly correct to put Jim Prior, Peter Walker and Ian Gilmour firmly in the 'wet' camp and Keith Joseph would go down as an undoubted 'dry', but for most of the rest of us our opinion depended upon the issue. Nevertheless, no one could claim that it was a united Cabinet and this was made worse as the everyday issues of government started to go wrong.

In February 1981 we were badly holed in a dispute with the

National Union of Mineworkers. The National Coal Board
wanted to close some uneconomic pits and their advice was that
this could be achieved by local talks. Although the NUM executive
had decided to recommend a ballot on industrial action, the board
thought that there was no need to panic and no prospect of an
immediate ballot while local negotiations continued. That was the
advice on Monday 16 February. On Tuesday, the NUM was not
only threatening strike action but taking it. On Wednesday David
Howell, the Energy Secretary, was forced to withdraw the threat
of pit closures and on Thursday we woke up to a dreadful press
accusing us of ignominious surrender.

Clearly there were comparisons with 1974, but the charge that
really hurt was that the Government had been caught unawares
(which we had) and was not in charge (which we were not). But
then the Government does not run the nationalized industries.
Any minister must rely on the operational advice he is given by
the managers on the ground. The fact was that the board got it
wrong and we took the blame. The choice for us was whether to
take a strike unprepared or to live to fight another day. Wisely,
Margaret Thatcher decided to withdraw. This hardly won instant
acclaim, but it was both a wise decision which in 1985 was fully
vindicated and the decision of a strong leader. Strength does not
mean joining every battle that comes along. As John Biffen
remarked on weekend television following the débâcle, 'I did not
come into politics to be a kamikaze pilot.'

Swiftly following on from coal there came trouble in the steel
industry. Again the issue was how to manage change in a
traditional industry. Demand for steel had slumped throughout
Europe and there was no way we could sustain the industry at
its existing size. The trouble was that to create a slimmer and
more efficient industry, the Chairman of British Steel, Ian
MacGregor, needed money to help with investment and redun-
dancies. It was a sensible policy, but it looked as if the Thatcher
Government had simply executed a U-turn and baled out a
loss-making nationalized industry. Labour joy was multiplied
when it fell to Keith Joseph, the Trade and Industry Secretary,
to make the rescue statement. He was greeted with massive and
ironic cheers from the Opposition and listened to in almost total
silence by our own benches. The press trumpeted another defeat

for the Government. No one could foresee that over the course
of the next few years the steel industry would be successfully
reorganized and taken into the private sector.

But if February was dreadful, it was as nothing compared with
March. On Tuesday 10 March at 10.30 a.m. we trooped into
the Cabinet room at Number 10 to be given a summary of that
afternoon's Budget. Geoffrey Howe's plan was to increase taxes
on petrol, alcohol and cigarettes; to raise national insurance contributions; and, worst of all, not to increase personal tax allowances,
so in effect increasing personal taxation. It is always difficult for a
Cabinet minister to know just how much to say before a Budget
statement. You have the privilege of knowing the contents several
hours before everyone else, but at this stage in the proceedings it
is too late to influence the outcome. Everyone is aware that the
Chancellor has a difficult ordeal to face a few hours later and no
one wants to make the occasion even worse.

However, there was no such self-denying restraint in 1981.
When the summary was finished, virtually everyone around the
table at Number 10 gave their view. These were faithfully reported
in the press a few days later so that readers knew the position
of every member of the Cabinet. Jim Prior considered it a
disastrous Budget which would do nothing to reduce unemployment. Ian Gilmour and Peter Walker were deeply unhappy. It
was even reported that Humphrey Atkins was the only Cabinet
member not to speak. The only point the press reports missed
was that Jim Prior was so unhappy that he almost threw in his
hand and resigned. To a number of us the crucial omission was
any help for industry, which was going through an appalling
time. I was not alone in wanting to get private investment into
public-sector industries.

It was an unhappy and tense discussion and can have done
absolutely nothing for Geoffrey Howe's morale as he prepared for
the afternoon. Not surprisingly, he came under intense fire in the
House of Commons. Michael Foot was not a good Leader of the
Opposition. He never had the substance for a leader and Labour
would have done much better with Denis Healey. But Michael
Foot was a formidable orator and on occasions he could coin a
phrase which captured the mood perfectly. It was, he said, a 'No
Hope Budget' – and so it appeared to many Conservative voters.

Over the next months we lost just about every election we contested. We lost the Greater London Council to Labour and
ultimately to Ken Livingstone, and we managed to lose safe Parliamentary seats at both Crosby and Croydon. There were few
predictions of a Tory victory at the next general election and even
some concern that the country might topple over into serious civil
strife. There were riots in Brixton in April and in Liverpool in
July. The inner cities came seriously on to the political agenda and
Michael Heseltine made a brave attempt to introduce new policies
to tackle the undoubted deprivation.

By this stage Labour should have been riding high. However,
they were preoccupied with their own internal squabbles and
Michael Foot was scoring low personal ratings in the opinion polls.
The beneficiary was the SDP–Liberal Alliance. The Warrington
by-election was held in mid-July, and that night I went with Neil
Kinnock and David Owen to BBC Television Centre to await the
result. We talked first about the Toxteth riots and then came the
declaration. It was a sensational result with Labour almost losing
one of their safest seats to the SDP leader, Roy Jenkins, who from
virtually nowhere secured an incredible 44 per cent of the poll.
Neil Kinnock advanced the extraordinarily lame and inaccurate
excuse that it was always difficult for Oppositions in mid-term, but
no one was really deceived. Labour had done very badly, though
we were in no position to gloat. Our vote had collapsed to a paltry
7 per cent and the alliance of the centre now seemed capable of
taking everything before it. By this stage in the Parliament we were
deeply unpopular and had allowed ourselves to be painted as a
government forcing through doctrinaire policies. Labour appeared
intent upon returning to fundamental socialism with the shadow
of Tony Benn hovering over the whole party. The political ground
could not have been better for a new middle party and many,
including myself, thought that they could well achieve the breakthrough they sought.

The political commentator Hugo Young identifies the nadir of
our fortunes as the Cabinet meeting on Thursday 23 July 1981
which he describes as 'perhaps the most memorable meeting of
the Cabinet in the whole decade of the Thatcher Government'. It
was unquestionably the worst Cabinet meeting that took place in
our first period of office. A major reason for that was the timing.

The oldest rule in the Westminster book is that you do not try to reach difficult decisions in the last week of July. Ministers, Members of Parliament, civil servants are hot, tired and exhausted of argument. They want to get away; they want to forget about politics; they want to reintroduce themselves to their families. If that was the argument in a normal year, it came in spades in 1981. Yet in spite of all this, a Treasury paper was circulated which sought further public spending cuts that would affect every government department. Not surprisingly there was a collective explosion. What would such a policy do for unemployment? What would it do to improve morale inside the party? Whenever these arguments showed signs of running out of steam, we turned to complain about the inadequacy of the supporting papers.

Geoffrey Howe wanted public spending economies. Vast subsidies were going to uneconomic nationalized industries and local government was heavily overspending. Far from reducing taxation, as we had been elected to do, we would have to raise it – and raise it at a time when local councils were already pushing up rates. But there was an additional argument. If the market took the view that the Government's determination to control public spending was weakening, then we would see the pound fall and inflation increase. To have had more public spending rather than less would have been disastrous. Higher taxes and higher inflation would have been a lethal combination both for the country and the Government, given that there was no prospect of improvements in employment either. The real lesson of the 23 July Cabinet meeting was that, in spite of all the doubts expressed, Margaret Thatcher and Geoffrey Howe stood firm and gave not an inch. The partnership between the two was never a comfortable one – as personalities they were chalk and cheese – but politically it was immensely successful and entirely crucial to the Government up to 1983.

Looking back at that period, the crucial difference in Conservative politicians was between those who thought that the last twenty or thirty years had not been too bad, and who were sceptical that anything better could be achieved, and those who hoped that something better could be won and saw the last quarter of a century as a slow but steady decline. Positions, of course, are never as black and white as that – consolidators have radical streaks; sensible reformers know when to consolidate. My own feeling in 1981 was that we should try to achieve something better and that just muddling through was not enough. You only had to go abroad to see how we were regarded. I remembered my five-week trip in 1976 to the United States. The Americans were friendly and polite, but there was no mistaking their view that Britain had gone downhill to the point that we had become an irrelevance. The position had improved slightly since then but there was a massive distance still to travel.

There were points of Government policy where I disagreed with the official line. I thought that private investment could have been used more imaginatively in the period of the 1980–1 recession and was not satisfied with the Treasury's replies. I also thought that our style did not try hard enough to persuade or unite. I have never believed that consensus is to be spurned. Fudge is to be spurned, but consensus can be a good goal. I have always wanted my policies to last. There is no point in making changes if the next government that comes in simply overturns them.

Above all, however, I wanted to see change and recovery. My stay in Government had not made me less radical but more so. If agreement cannot be reached, then decisions still need to be taken. No one looking back on 1981 would claim that there was consensus on the correct economic policy either in the Conservative Party or outside. No fewer than 364 economists signed a statement calling for a change of policy and traditional reflation. Their advice was ignored and the tough decisions taken in 1981 were to lead to the much praised Budget of the next year and, even more, to the economic recovery which took us through both the 1983 and 1987 general elections.

It was also during 1981 that Margaret Thatcher really showed her style of leadership. It was decisive and at times attracted public support because she seemed to be taking action which the public overwhelmingly thought was right but never thought any government would have the nerve to carry out. In May the SAS were sent in to storm the Iranian Embassy in London which had been taken over by armed gunmen. The following night, I was speaking at a transport dinner in London and found myself sitting two or three down from a general. Before I rose to speak, I was asked by the chairman to express to the general their admiration for the

SAS's action. The reaction from the audience almost took the roof off Grosvenor House.

Similarly, Margaret Thatcher's reaction to the Brixton and Toxteth riots captured the public mood far more than the analysis of the Opposition. The first priority was to restore order and she made it plain that she backed the police unequivocally in doing so. The time for examination was after order had been restored and, rightly, she rejected the simplistic connection between high unemployment and rioting. Rightly, because there was no easy link to be made and only a few years previously the best criminologists were explaining the increase in crime as an inevitable consequence of prosperity. Crime rose in line with the golden curve of affluence.

At the same time, other features of her style of leadership were becoming clear. None was more evident than her grasp of all the issues of Government as she answered questions twice a week in the House of Commons. It is one of the requirements of any British Prime Minister that every Tuesday and Thursday between 3.15 and 3.30 p.m. he or she should appear at the dispatch box and answer questions from MPs on any subject. No Prime Minister has enjoyed this twice-weekly brains trust – and Margaret Thatcher was no exception – but few Prime Ministers did it as well or as consistently. The secret of her approach was care in preparation, and woe betide the department that sent her into battle badly briefed or not briefed at all.

This happened once in my early months at the Department of Health and Social Security. During negotiations on public spending with the then Chief Secretary, Leon Brittan, I had agreed to change the way of assessing Housing Benefit. My Minister of State, Hugh Rossi, had announced the change during discussion of a social security bill in standing committee on Tuesday morning – the change is still unjustly called 'the Rossi Index' – and the Opposition had protested strongly. At Prime Minister's Questions in the afternoon Margaret Thatcher was challenged by a Labour MP, Jeff Rooker, on the change and although she managed to deflect the question it was clear she had not been briefed. It was entirely our responsibility and that evening to well past midnight Leon and I took her through the changes until she was satisfied that she knew the policy thoroughly. We only broke for the night on the promise of a further meeting next day together with social security officials. By the next Prime Minister's Questions on Thursday she knew the policy rather better than we did.

The feature that came through most clearly, however, even in those early days of government, was Margaret Thatcher's stamina. Even in the worst hours she never gave any public impression that she was on the ropes. At the centre of her life was her family. I remember a few months after my daughter Kate was born in 1981 receiving a call from Number 10. Some problem had blown up and the Prime Minister wanted to see me. It was a Friday evening and untypically I was in London – and even more untypically I was baby-sitting. My private office helped out on the baby-sitting very effectively but I am sure quite improperly. Eventually I arrived at Number 10 about an hour late. 'Don't worry,' said Margaret, 'when all this is over the only thing that matters is your family.' Those words uttered by some political leaders would sound banal and from one or two others downright phoney. For Margaret Thatcher they were a simple statement of her position.

In the glimpses I had of her personal life, one feature always came through. This was the support and affection given to Margaret by her family. Carol and Mark were ever loyal and proud of their mother, while Denis had a role which would have dismayed a weaker man. He was the husband of the first woman Prime Minister, but he will go down in history as a wise adviser and a kind man. Her family gave Margaret Thatcher a security which had an immeasurable impact upon her success and the success of her Governments.

On top of the intellectual stamina there was a physical stamina too. July 1981 was by any standards a trying and testing month. In the middle of the month George Thomas, the Speaker, brought all the Cabinet together for dinner. Margaret Thatcher had been up early that morning – early even by her standards – to visit Liverpool. She had had a gruelling day on top of a gruelling six months. By rights she should have been exhausted, but not a bit of it. It was only a vote in the Commons at 11 p.m. that brought the evening to an end and then she returned to Downing Street for a few hours' work on her boxes before turning in. In over ten years in her Government, I never heard a complaint that any paper was held up at Downing Street because the Prime Minister had been too pressed with work to get round to it.

July eventually ground to an end and the steam was taken out of that difficult month by an event which had nothing to do with politics. It was the wedding of Prince Charles and Lady Diana Spencer at St Paul's on the last Wednesday. There were memorable pictures: the beautiful Princess with her long train carried by the small page-boys; the debonair Prince; the members of royal families from all over Europe; the world's leaders and statesmen; the small but immaculate figure of Nancy Reagan. Yet by far the most moving part of the whole day was the reaction of the crowds which lined the streets. Fiona and I set off from Fulham in our car at about 9 a.m. By the time we got to Trafalgar Square the crowds were thick on the pavements and cheering anything that moved. You only had to wave to get a reaction. The crowd were good-humoured, enthusiastic and often young. Their spirit stretched right into the Cathedral. Around St Paul's large television screens had been erected. The result was that every crucial move made inside the Cathedral by the bride and groom – like the placing of the ring on the Princess's finger – was followed a second or two later by the most enormous cheer from outside.

As Parliament went into its long summer recess, it was quite clear that Margaret Thatcher was going to reshuffle the Cabinet and the betting was that the shuffle would be a major one. She felt that the appearance of a divided Cabinet was disastrous politics. And frankly it was. You cannot expect public support if you do not have the support of your own ministers. The assumption was that she would bring in a number of new people whose loyalty she could count on.

One night in late July I was taken out to supper by Ian Gow, the Prime Minister's Parliamentary Private Secretary. Ian was later murdered by a terrorist bomb but nothing can destroy the memory of a unique politician and man. He had principle, determination and humour. If you ever asked Ian to keep a debate going in committee (while the front bench caught up) he would do so to order and with a style I have never seen equalled. It was altogether typical of him that his unshakeable beliefs should prevent him continuing to serve in the Government once the Anglo-Irish agreement was signed. Personal position would not have entered into his calculations. Our supper in July 1981, however, was all about the personal positions of other people. I was asked my views on the reshuffle. I was also asked my views on the chairmanship of the party. Peter Thorneycroft had been a notably successful chairman but was now seventy-two. What did I think of the prospect of an up-and-coming Minister of State called Norman Tebbit taking over the job? What about Cecil Parkinson? Had I ever considered the prospect myself? Ian went away, pondering on my replies – but one thing was certain: major changes were in prospect.

In early September I went to the wedding of Geoffrey Howe's daughter, Amanda. Another guest that day was Patrick Jenkin, the Social Services Secretary. As we talked at the reception in the garden behind Downing Street, Patrick told me that, instead of a debate at the Party Conference next month, he and his ministerial team had been asked to answer questions from the floor. Unkindly, I laughed and told him that that sounded just about the worst idea I had heard for a very long time. The hall at Blackpool is ideally suited to rousing speeches but is totally wrong as the setting for a question-and-answer session – which proved to be just as appalling as I had feared. A week later I was called back to Downing Street by Margaret Thatcher and told that I was taking over the Department of Health and Social Security and also the question-and-answer session.

The Cabinet changes of September 1981 were as extensive as any made in the Thatcher years of Government. Norman Tebbit was made Employment Secretary and Nigel Lawson came in as Energy Secretary. Cecil Parkinson took over as Chairman of the Conservative Party in what proved to be an inspired appointment. Mark Carlisle, Christopher Soames and Ian Gilmour left the Cabinet and Jim Prior went to the one job which no politician can refuse, Northern Ireland Secretary. As he left Number 10, Ian Gilmour sourly summed up the changes by saying they were 'not much good if you are steering full-speed ahead for the rocks'. He left unexplained why, if that was his view, he had not gone under his own steam somewhat earlier. As for myself, I was back where I had begun in Opposition. Margaret Thatcher had kept her word given over five years before that I would not lose out by my enforced move to Transport and I was now in charge of the biggest spender and largest employer in Whitehall. Created in 1968 to give Dick Crossman a new and senior job, the Department of Health and Social Security was responsible for over 40 per cent of all public spending. It employed almost 100,000 staff directly, mainly in our social security offices, and was responsible for the National Health Service – which with almost a million staff was the largest employer in Europe.

Slowly, very slowly, our political position began to improve, but then came the event which was to transform the Government's public standing. On Thursday 1 April 1982, my day started early at the Cabinet Office, just round the corner from Downing Street in Whitehall. A meeting of the Public Sector Pay Committee had been called for 8.45 a.m. – a sure sign that it had been called by Geoffrey Howe who was consistently the earliest ministerial starter. There was much hilarity when Geoffrey steamed in ten minutes late pleading a mix-up in his diary. At the meeting I reported on the position of the gathering health service dispute and we then looked at a number of other pay issues. The Cabinet committee over, we went through the connecting doors to Number 10 itself and a meeting of the full Cabinet. The main item on the agenda was future policy in Ulster but it soon became clear that another issue had become dominant.

The Foreign Secretary, Peter Carrington, reported that the Argentinian fleet was steaming towards the Falkland Islands. Until then, the Falklands had been the concern of the Overseas and Defence Committee and had not featured strongly in discussions in full Cabinet. There had been the curious tale of the Argentinian scrap metal merchants who had landed on the island of South Georgia, where the United Kingdom had exercised sovereignty since it was discovered by Captain Cook in 1775. The story was that the party had landed to remove scrap metal from a former whaling station but their action seemed eccentric rather than threatening. It was now clear, however, that the position was becoming deadly serious.

The next morning a telephone call came through from Number 10 just before 8.30 a.m. calling a special Cabinet meeting at 9.45 to discuss the Falklands. Caught by surprise, we used whatever means of transport were available. I arrived in the family Metro; Quintin Hailsham by bicycle. Outside Number 10 itself there was

a solitary television camera crew. Inside most of the Cabinet had
made it, even though it was a Friday and the day most members
made for their constituencies. Only Peter Walker, George Younger
and Leon Brittan were absent. We were brought up to date – or
as up to date as it was possible to be. We were told that not only
had the Argentinian fleet continued on their route to the Falklands
but there was now every reason to believe that Argentinian troops
had landed. This was not confirmed by Port Stanley for the good
reason that we were no longer in contact with Port Stanley.
Humphrey Atkins, who was in effect deputy Foreign Secretary
and the chief Foreign Office spokesman in the Commons, was to
make a statement at 11 a.m. The question was what should he say?
Clearly he would have to tell Parliament as much as was known.
When Humphrey Atkins made his statement it was listened to with
concern but the response was subdued. The whole proceedings
lasted only twenty-three minutes and assurances were given that
the House would be kept informed.

During the late afternoon I received another call summoning a
further Cabinet meeting at 7.30 p.m. It was here that we received
confirmation that Argentinian troops had landed and had occupied
Port Stanley. The question now was whether a military task force
should set sail. It was estimated that it would take them two to
three weeks to get to the Falklands and therefore, theoretically, the
decision could be rescinded if there were some kind of diplomatic
breakthrough. Personally I thought this highly unlikely. Once the
task force had been committed, only the withdrawal of the
Argentinian troops would justify them carrying out some gigantic
U-turn in the middle of the South Atlantic. I confess my fears
were elsewhere. My thoughts went back to 1956 and Suez when
the shambles of lengthy invasion and precipitate withdrawal had
destroyed Anthony Eden's whole political career. That was the
kind of crisis the Government and in particular Margaret Thatcher
now faced.

I thought we had no option but to send the task force. The
public at home would have been rightly outraged had we not taken
this action, while the lessons that would have been drawn by other
countries overseas were incalculable. It was decided that Margaret
Thatcher would announce the dispatch of the task force next
morning in the House of Commons in a special Saturday morning

debate. As we left Number 10 that evening, Downing Street had
become thick with reporters and cameramen. I left with Quintin
Hailsham. A brave reporter thrust a microphone under his nose
and asked him for his comments. 'I wish you a very good evening,'
replied Quintin.

The Saturday morning debate on 3 April was the first Saturday
debate since Suez and was dreadful in every way. The morning's
press without exception had attacked us strongly. Everyone had
been caught unawares. There had been no sense of impending
crisis and few newspapers were seriously featuring the Falklands
situation prior to the invasion. The public mood was one of anger
and frustration and that mood was fully reflected in the House
of Commons. Margaret Thatcher rose to half-hearted shouts of
'resign' from the Labour benches. Her speech went as well as was
possible, given that it was being made on the stickiest of sticky
Parliamentary wickets. She was followed by Michael Foot who
made a strong attack on the Government and ended with the
devastating charge that the Falkland Islanders had been betrayed
and 'the whole responsibility for the betrayal rests with the Government'. From that point on the debate went from bad to worse. We
were lambasted by a bellicose Labour Party and an impressive SDP
in the shape of David Owen. But worst of all we were attacked by
our own side. Edward du Cann, Nigel Fisher and Patrick Cormack
were just three who inserted the knife. Enoch Powell, who
although no longer a Tory MP was closely listened to on the
Conservative side, recalled that Margaret Thatcher had been
called the 'Iron Lady' and rather liked the description. He added:
'In the next week or two this House, the nation and the Right
Honourable Lady herself will learn of what metal she is made.'

The one defender of the Government position, Ray Whitney, a
former Foreign Office diplomat, was virtually shouted down. But
the House reserved its worst treatment for the Defence Secretary,
John Nott. Something had gone wrong and the House wanted
blood. John Nott was not the Foreign Secretary, and therefore not
responsible for reading the international scene, but he was the
next best thing. He was one of the most accomplished debaters
in the Government but nothing would have saved him from the
mauling. He made his speech – or rather sought to make it –
against a barrage of noise and calls to resign from the Opposition

and was listened to in stony silence by the Government benches. It is one of the unappetizing features of politics that often when things go wrong a minister can find himself entirely isolated and without friends. One Cabinet colleague surveying the scene murmured to me: 'There is no way that I am going to grow old in the service of this House.'

Suddenly, amid the noise, the Speaker brought the proceedings to a close. There was no vote and the House of Commons stood adjourned. The agony of the debate was over – although both John Nott and Peter Carrington next had to appear in a committee room upstairs in front of an unhappy party meeting. At the end of the Saturday debate we were in more disarray than at any stage since either coming to power or Margaret Thatcher taking over the leadership.

The weekend press was again appalling. The call for resignations continued both from newspapers and politicians, including Conservative ones. On the Monday I tried to settle down to a meeting at Alexander Fleming House (the DHSS's headquarters at the Elephant and Castle) with Tony Newton who had joined the department as Parliamentary Secretary for Social Security. Tony and I embarked on a consideration of Child Benefit but before many minutes had gone by a note was sent in informing us that Peter Carrington had resigned. After a pause we continued, but in a few more minutes another note came through saying that further resignations were expected. At that point I abandoned the meeting and tried to find out what was happening. It transpired that Peter Carrington and his Foreign Office team of Humphrey Atkins and Richard Luce had all resigned, and a little later it was announced that Francis Pym was to take over as Foreign Secretary.

My first reaction to the resignations was that they were tantamount to an admission of guilt when, in fact, the Argentinians could have attacked at any time in the previous fifteen years. Peter Carrington was a major loss, and although I admired the loyalty of Humphrey Atkins and Richard Luce I thought their resignations unnecessary. I was wrong. The resignations defused an extremely difficult political situation. All attention could now be given to negotiation and to preparing for war rather than continuing the sterile debate on how it had all come about.

The change of mood was clear for everyone to see. The same

House which had torn into John Nott on the Saturday listened attentively to Francis Pym the following Wednesday. Francis spoke with force and authority and was able to make his speech entirely without interruption. As he ended, there was an enormous cheer on our side and I saw one of our backbenchers who had been particularly critical over the weekend waving his order paper in enthusiastic support. The wind-up speech for the Government was made by John Nott. In thirty minutes he substantially re-established his parliamentary position and announced a 200-mile naval exclusion zone around the Falklands. The immediate political crisis had been averted, but there was still a long, long way to go before we could claim victory.

Margaret Thatcher formed a small War Cabinet. It would have been impossible for the Falklands War to be prosecuted successfully with every decision coming to the full Cabinet of twenty-three members, a state of affairs that would have taken every other item off the agenda. Both diplomatically and militarily, it was necessary for the Government to respond speedily. Over the next weeks Alexander Haig, the American Secretary of State, shuttled to and fro seeking compromise. Yet all the signs were that this was going to be a fruitless exercise. In Argentina there appeared to be no one with whom Haig could reach agreement, for behind General Galtieri there was an array of powerful army, navy and air force chiefs. It was in any event difficult to see what compromise could satisfy both Buenos Aires and London. The only question was how long the talking could continue.

By the last week of April the task force was nearing the Falklands. The issue now was whether it should attempt to retake South Georgia. There were those who argued that such action would alienate world opinion and sabotage the chances of a diplomatic solution. That view was rejected and after a reconnaissance British forces took the island. Asked for her reaction, Margaret Thatcher gave vent to her feelings about the operation and also, I suspect, about what she saw as ever critical broadcasters who always found something to carp about even after an undoubted success. 'Rejoice,' she said, 'just rejoice.' Again she was nearer the mass of public opinion than the trendy commentators who criticized this old-fashioned way of expressing things. It has to be remembered just how perilous and unprecedented the operation

was. In 1956 the British forces had appeared to take an uncon-
scionable time to get from Cyprus to Port Said. Here was a task
force rapidly put together, travelling almost 7,000 miles and successfully taking an island without a casualty.

Elation, however, was short lived. On 4 May the news came
through that the *General Belgrano* had been sunk with over 350
Argentine sailors killed. There was no question that the Government's first duty was to preserve the safety of the task force but
the loss of life cast an enormous shadow. It had now been demonstrated beyond any doubt that this was real war and that any
prospect of retaking the Falklands as an uninterrupted triumphal
procession was illusory. This impression was tragically confirmed
a few hours later when news came through that HMS *Sheffield*
had been sunk. From then until the final Argentine surrender the
story was one of the skill and bravery of the British forces. The
San Carlos landing, the Battle of Goose Green and the final taking
of Port Stanley have all entered the history books. In purely military
terms it was an amazing success reflecting great credit on Britain's
small but all-professional armed forces – which were such a contrast to the much bigger conscript forces I remembered from the
1950s.

It was also an undoubted personal and political triumph for
Margaret Thatcher. Those who deny that have only to ask themselves who would have taken the responsibility had we failed. She
would have been held personally responsible and would almost
certainly have fallen from office. The stakes were that high; the
pressure on her was that great. The Falklands crisis tested her as
few leaders in recent times have been tested. Her success marked
an important and dramatic political turning-point for the Government. The conflict also showed features of her approach and style
which were later to become familiar. She was a good leader to go
to war with. She was decisive and she did not vacillate, and once
committed she intended to win. She distrusted the offer of talks
which had no other purpose than to string out negotiation. That
was her style in the Falklands and it remained her style in a number
of the confrontations that she faced over the next years.

I believe it is a hundred times better to have a leader who wants
to go forward rather than one who retreats towards the hills
when the going gets rough. The Falklands established Margaret

Thatcher as a leader of courage. That was clear from the outset, but what was perhaps not so clear was how professional a leader she had become, able to manage not only the immediate crisis but all the other issues of Government.

A few days after the Argentinian surrender, I saw her for a meeting on health service pay. I had put a point to the unions concerning long-term pay arrangements on which she had neither been informed nor consulted. My view was that it was enough to clear it with the Chancellor of the Exchequer and that she had a war to fight. After some spirited discussion Margaret agreed with the policy but pointed out with some feeling that she had been in the chair of every meeting of the Economic Committee throughout the Falklands crisis. War or no war, the Government's other business had not come to a halt.

At moments of crisis a nation needs a leader able to lead in the way Margaret Thatcher led then. In politics there are some very successful makers of deals and some very skilled negotiators. Those are valuable qualities, but as Enoch Powell suggested a leader needs more than that. The Falklands showed that Margaret Thatcher had the metal that leadership takes.

CHAPTER 9

The Health Strike

'In the unlikely event of Norman Fowler
needing a wisdom tooth operation, he can have
it . . . without an anaesthetic!'

Daily Mail

I began 1982 with a series of visits to look at the issues which were facing the health service. I went first to the Children's Hospital in Birmingham. The hospital had been built as a memorial to King Edward VII and it had seen better days. The wards were crowded and even in mid-winter very sick babies had to be wheeled out into the open air to get from one part of the hospital to another.

What really shocked me, however, was the sight of the babies in the intensive care unit. They were all about the same age as my daughter Kate, and three were fighting for their lives. They were the victims of whooping cough. Too young to have been inoculated themselves, the babies had caught the disease from their older brothers and sisters who could have been inoculated but had not been. Following newspaper and television coverage of the alleged dangers that went with inoculation, the vaccination rate had fallen sharply. In spite of the best efforts of the health service, we had been unable to persuade the public that by far the bigger danger was of children *not* being inoculated. The three little babies (one of whom later died) were the tragic proof of unsuccessful health promotion.

I went on to Birmingham's All Saints Hospital, which is cheek by jowl with Winson Green Prison. There, many of the patients were old and suffering from dementia. They sat in rows and watched television or simply stared into the distance. One old lady sitting upright, prim and wearing round National Health Service glasses, became agitated as I approached her chair. According to one of the staff, she believed that she was Queen Victoria and did not like anyone encroaching on the space around her throne. All Saints showed one of the major problems that the health service will face over the next years. With the increase in the number of the elderly, our demand for services and above all for devoted staff and volunteers will grow enormously.

The following week I went to Rampton Special Hospital which stands isolated in the countryside of north Nottinghamshire. Rampton began life as a criminal lunatic asylum in 1912 and today takes men and women who require treatment under special security conditions because of their dangerous, violent or criminal tendencies. For the visitor, it is scarcely credible that staff can work day after day with such clearly difficult patients. The noise, the abuse, the grimness are everyday parts of their working life. Many of the nurses are the sons and daughters and even grandsons and granddaughters of Rampton staff. Their role has changed from turnkey to nurse but many grew up with the expectation that Rampton would be their career. An enclosed community guards and cares for an enclosed community and we the public gladly subcontract this duty, hoping that it will be carried out unseen and unheard.

What I saw on my visits in 1982 illustrated just some of the health problems we faced. None of them was new. Only a party bigot would claim that they had somehow come in with the Conservative Government three years earlier. Every health minister faces the same central problem: it is not just a matter of putting right the deficiencies of the past; you also need to keep up with the ever-increasing demands of the present. Demand is created by medical advance itself. Hip replacements were once a rarity: now they can be carried out easily and the call for them has escalated. Somehow you have to provide for these additional demands, and many more, within the annual budget voted each year to the service.

It would be nice to believe that the Health Secretary spends all his time understanding the very latest developments in heart-lung transplants. Would that this was the case. Faced with a virtual infinity of demand, your role is to seek new resources and ensure that those resources are spent to best effect. You battle with the Treasury in public spending negotiations and you battle with the health service to make best use of the resources that are available. The health service has genuinely noble ideals: it provides excellent treatment irrespective of income. It also contains some of the most dedicated men and women I have ever met. Yet for all that, health provides just about the bloodiest battleground in British politics today.

When I took over at the Department of Health and Social Security, I was under no illusion about the difficulty of my job. Every one of my predecessors as Social Services Secretary – Dick

Crossman, Keith Joseph, Barbara Castle, David Ennals and Patrick Jenkin – had scars to show for their periods in that office.
And the scars of Labour ministers were just as plentiful as the
ones on Tory backs. I had watched Barbara Castle go through
contortions as she made massive social security savings. I had
watched her successor, David Ennals, come under withering
union fire for cutting back on the hospital building programme.
The central problem of the DHSS is that it is the biggest of the
big spenders among government departments. In any dispute about
public spending, you are in the front line.

I faced an additional problem with the health service. It is an
undesirable tradition of the service that complaint provides extra
cash and that any change proposed by Government is to be
opposed. The theory is that the only thing that has ever been wrong
with the health service is a lack of resources. If you demonstrate the
need, the Government irrespective of party will be forced to pay
up. I do not entirely decry such tactics. Sometimes it is necessary
to campaign for more resources by pointing out deficiencies. However, the shame is that for some health service insiders it has
become a way of life. They refuse to take credit for the undoubted
achievements of the service and retreat into such self-evident
absurdities as 'the health service is on the verge of collapse'. But
what I objected to most was the all too often blanket opposition to
change.

Soon after I went to the department I introduced a policy of
charging overseas patients for their medical care. If I, a British
citizen, fall ill in the United States I will have to pay for treatment.
It is important to be insured. I wanted to ensure that foreign
visitors who came to this country were also covered by insurance.
The policy caused great indignation in the health service. Apparently it was all right to receive money from the Treasury in neat
health authority allocations, but not for cheques or, worse still,
cash to appear over the hospital counter. Regrettably, this illogical
and antediluvian attitude still persists even when we are dealing
with nations substantially richer than ourselves. I simply do not
understand why Britain should provide a free international health
service or why the health service should not benefit from outside
contributions.

Too often, the health debate takes place amid generalized

allegations of 'cuts'. In reality the argument is all about whether
the government has increased the budget enough. The claims that
appear endlessly in newspaper columns are about whether the
government has taken proper account of the expected increase in
demand and costs. Only at times of crisis does the debate turn to
the *real* cause of cuts in patient care. Over the last twenty years
the starkest examples of operations cancelled, lives put at danger
and waiting lists increased have been the result of industrial disputes. Patients suffered in the Winter of Discontent in 1979. They
suffered in the 1989–90 ambulance dispute. And they were certainly the principal victims of the health dispute of 1982, which
proved to be Britain's longest industrial dispute for fifty years.

The 1982 dispute was my baptism of fire. About 70 per cent of
the costs of the health service are the costs of staff. The health
service is given a budget by the taxpayer which covers both the
pay of staff and the services provided. Unless some special addition
is made, the result of an over-budget pay settlement is a limit on
the expansion of new services. The only way to avoid that would
be for the Chancellor of the Exchequer to give the health service
an open-ended budget. No Chancellor of any party has ever done
that in the past and no Chancellor is ever likely to do so in the
future. You cannot run any service on the basis that 'it costs what
it costs'. At the heart of the 1982 dispute was a so-called pay factor
for public services of 4 per cent, which was intended as a marker
for pay rises to those working in all public services.

I had inherited my position from Patrick Jenkin. He would have
preferred a special health-service pay factor, but had to settle for
an above-average offer to the nurses, who most certainly were the
priority group, having fallen badly behind over the previous ten
years. On 8 March 1982 we provided an extra £82 million (mostly
from the Government's contingency reserve) and made an offer
to the nurses and some other professional groups of 6.4 per cent.
The offer made them a special case but by the same token was
condemned by other groups such as the ancillary workers, who
protested that they were offered only 4 per cent. A popular health-
service argument was that every one of the million or so
staff should get exactly the same percentage increase in pay – as
though the recruitment and retention position was the same for
all.

Arrayed against me I had both the TUC-affiliated unions and the Royal College of Nursing, the professional organization representing the nurses. With me I had the two Kens. The first Ken was Ken Clarke whom I had managed to bring over from the Transport Department. He illustrates the difficulty of trying to divide Conservative politicians into 'wets' and 'dries'. Many of his views categorize him as a wet – a European enthusiast; against capital punishment; and in favour of sensible abortion laws. But just as clearly he is a tough politician who speaks his mind sometimes in a blunt way. Once or twice we put these qualities to good use. An aggressive visiting delegation would be dusted down by Ken in his best James Cagney style, leaving me looking untypically reasonable and friendly in bringing the meeting to a conclusion. Ken Clarke is an exceptional man to have with you in a battle. He will not compromise to get an agreement he does not believe is justified and is not the least put out by demonstrations. In 1982 all these qualities looked as though they were going to be urgently required.

The second Ken was my Permanent Secretary, Sir Kenneth Stowe. In background he was very similar to my generation of politicians, although about ten years older. His school was the County High School at Dagenham and from there he had won a scholarship to Oxford. He came down with a First and started his civil service career in the humble surroundings of the National Assistance Board. His ability took him rapidly up the social security tree and to Number 10 as Jim Callaghan's Principal Private Secretary. Downing Street is a sure stepping-stone to becoming head of a department but the price that has to be paid is as exacting a life-style as can be found in Whitehall. With the new Conservative Government in 1979, Ken Stowe moved from Downing Street to become Permanent Secretary in the Northern Ireland Office – not exactly a rest cure – and in 1981 came back to the DHSS. He arrived a few weeks before me at the Elephant and retired just a few weeks before I left the department after the 1987 general election. For year after year he worked all hours serving different governments and different ministers. Like so many Permanent Secretaries, Ken was a substantial politician in his own right and knew every byway of Whitehall, in particular how to process decisions through the government machine. In short, he epitom-

ized the tremendous qualities of the British civil service –
undoubted ability coupled with unstinting hard work and independent judgement.

There are not many precedents for the same Secretary of State
and the same Permanent Secretary serving together for the best
part of six years. In the transient world of politics and government
such stability is exceptional, although in the world of business no
one would consider unusual such partnerships between a chairman
and chief executive. Since 1979 the other Cabinet ministers (Margaret Thatcher excepted) who have exceeded five years in one
department are Nicholas Edwards, the Secretary of State for Wales
between 1979 and 1987; George Younger, as Scottish Secretary;
Nigel Lawson, as Chancellor of the Exchequer; and Geoffrey
Howe, as Foreign Secretary. Under Labour, the best example is
Denis Healey who was Secretary of State for Defence from 1964
to 1970 and then Chancellor of the Exchequer from 1974 to 1979.
But we were very much the exceptions. Government would benefit
if, barring accidents, Secretaries of State remained with their
departments for longer.

The first months of the health dispute of 1982 coincided with
the Falklands War, but when the war ended public attention
returned to it. During hostilities, the health unions had called three
one-day strikes. They had also instituted a ban on anything other
than accident and emergency operations. In the hospitals, the
action was beginning to bite. Waiting lists started to lengthen as
operations were cancelled. The dispute had also moved against us
in another way. During the spring the recommendations of the
Top Salaries Review Board and the Doctors and Dentists Review
Body came to the Prime Minister. They had proposed astonishing
increases of 24.3 per cent for the judiciary and 19.4 per cent for
senior civil servants. A 9 per cent increase was proposed for doctors and dentists.

The review bodies are independent but Government has the
option of modifying their recommendations. I believed we should
do just that. With help from Norman Tebbit, then Employment
Secretary, I managed to get the awards reduced – but not by
enough. The judges still got 18.6 per cent and top civil servants
averaged 14.3 per cent. I did, however, manage to get the doctors
and dentists award down to 6 per cent. But the total package of

reductions convinced neither the public nor the unions. As we debated the awards in Government, various colleagues told me that my arguments for reductions were 'egalitarian' and that the pay increase for judges would in no way influence the expectations of the nurses and the ancillary workers.

The underlying fear was that if we accepted any connection we would be back to the world of incomes policy. I did not want that, but I believed that the top salary awards were *so* out of line with what we were proposing in the rest of the public sector that in the real world of industrial relations it made my job infinitely more difficult. And so it proved. The judges' pay increase was hung round the Government's neck like a heavy stone. The health unions and the nurses could see that others were doing better, and in addition to the top salaries group the miners and the firemen were settling appreciably above the public sector guideline of 4 per cent. Whatever the position three months earlier, our original offer to the health service could no longer stand. On 22 June we made a revised offer of 7.5 per cent for the nurses and 6 per cent for the ancillaries and administrative staff. The Royal College of Nursing agreed to recommend it to their members, but the health unions rejected it outright. The dispute began to intensify. The unions stepped up their industrial action and the waiting lists lengthened further. By the end of July we estimated that the industrial action had added 65,000 patients to the waiting lists in English hospitals alone. In addition 60,000 operations had been cancelled or postponed and 75,000 outpatient appointments had been cancelled.

There tends to be a Vietnam War factor about health strikes. During the Vietnam War the public became hardened and accustomed to the horrific scenes on television. In the health service the initial shock that patients can be denied treatment fades as the public becomes used to the fact that they are. Yet the impact of such action should never be underestimated. During July I went to St Thomas's Hospital in Lambeth. A strike of about twenty-five staff in the sterile supplies stores had dramatically reduced activity, which was already hampered by the union policy of refusing admission to any but emergency cases. About 1,000 operations had been postponed and even cancer patients were being delayed. A picket at the hospital claimed that 'emergency' services were being maintained. They doubtless were, but 'urgent' cases were being turned away.

August was even worse than July. As the dispute hardened, demonstrations became everyday affairs. Whenever I drove to a hospital my question would not be whether there was a demonstration but how big. There were demonstrations at Hammersmith; at Rugby where the most vociferous health worker turned out to be a school caretaker; at Bristol; and at Exeter where the demonstrators appeared to have gathered beforehand in the nearby public house. Throughout the dispute my technique was to go through the front door – I refused to be smuggled in – and then ask for a deputation of the demonstrators to come and talk to me. Usually that defused the demonstration and the visit could go ahead uninterrupted. Sometimes the police, however, had other ideas. At Cambridge, NUPE put a picket around the Union building where I was taking part in a debate and the police wanted to take me in by a side entrance. When I protested, they assured me that there would be no question of hiding me from the crowd. A week or two before they had got into trouble when Norman Tebbit had come to Cambridge and in the words of one of the policemen they had not 'shown him' to the demonstrators. They showed me quite successfully but the eggs and tomatoes missed.

Sometimes avoiding action did have to be taken. On one occasion I went to a hospital in south London to what the police reckoned would be a very rough demonstration. With a touching faith in our law-abiding qualities the demonstrators had gathered in large numbers with their eggs and tomatoes around the hospital entrance marked IN. Twenty yards down the road, however, there was an exit marked OUT through which we rapidly drove, successfully avoiding the missiles.

By the time I got to the Party Conference in October, I was under police guard. One Special Branch man said to me: 'There is only one other minister who has two police guards and that is Mr Tebbit – but we're armed and they're not.' As Frank Johnson commented in *The Times*, my appearance on the short walk between the Grand Hotel and the conference centre provoked uproar from the watching demonstrators. 'An ordinary hardworking citizen living quietly in the Cabinet' had become 'an object of hatred'.

You cannot entirely make light of such demonstrations. One day, I fear that a demonstration of the kind I faced in 1982 will go wrong and someone will get hurt. There *are* people out there who will use any excuse to cause trouble. I learned that when I went to a conference at Sheffield. As I left the railway station, the police warned me that there was a small demonstration against Norman Tebbit's recent industrial relations reforms. That was the plan, but the morning's press was full of extravagant reports of the 'cuts' I intended to make in health service manpower. 'Fowler' was inserted for 'Tebbit' on the placards and the demonstration went ahead with a degree of intimidation that made the front page of every national newspaper the next day.

It was not just street demonstrators who were assembled against us. The nastiest little attack we endured at this time came from, of all papers, the *Lancet*. An editorial alleged that the Government would welcome headlines saying that a patient had died because it would swing public opinion against the unions. It is a curiosity of medical politics that any charge, however gross, can be made against you. Unfortunately, not all health professionals take the objective standards of their medical training into their public and political comment.

During August I agreed to be interviewed by *World in Action* in Manchester. The format of the interview was that I was in a single chair placed to the side of a panel of six sitting in two rows. It was a classic Perry Mason prisoner-and-jury setting. In the jury were such well-known 'independent' commentators as Rodney Bickerstaffe of NUPE, a Regional Health Authority Chairman I had just replaced, a nurses' negotiator, a consultant who wanted more money for his hospital and an ancillary health worker. You will be amazed to know that these six good men and true found me guilty, although without the uproar that the producers had rather hoped for. Travelling back to London by train after the programme, I found that Rodney Bickerstaffe was a fellow passenger. We talked quietly together for half an hour but there was no point of contact. Bickerstaffe had taken over as General Secretary of NUPE from Alan Fisher who had been instrumental in the Winter of Discontent. He was determined to win where Fisher had failed and his members came first. I saw no prospect of any sensible compromise.

In mid-August I made the great mistake of seeking a four-day break from London to stay with friends in France. That was roundly attacked in the press and particularly the health press, even though I left Ken Clarke in charge. After my four days Ken was to set off on his own curtailed family holiday. As he flew out, I flew in. We changed over at Bordeaux airport. When we met in the lounge it rapidly became clear that he was not in his usual good humour. It transpired that the previous day he had been in Liverpool and given an interview to the *Daily Telegraph* which had been interpreted to mean that we were about to call in the troops. At the same time the press had been tipped off that the Health Minister was leaving the country on holiday from Heathrow and half a dozen photographers had literally chased on to the runway to photograph him. They were only prevented from boarding the plane when the aircraft's captain refused them permission. Not surprisingly, Ken was apprehensive about the position I might inherit when I touched down. Indeed the next hours after my return were spent explaining that we had no plans to use either troops or tanks and justifying what a BBC interviewer referred to as my 'controversial' four-day summer holiday. Ironically, a few years later Ken Clarke came under attack on the same issue.

I have never been able to understand this preoccupation with ministerial holidays. During the month of August ministers cover for other ministers. No one thinks twice if a minister retires to the country because his department can blandly assure all callers that the minister is 'working from home'. But woe betide any minister who does not possess a country seat and sets off across the Channel to 'abroad'. Even though air travel means that he can be rapidly recalled in an emergency, he is likely to be pilloried for dereliction of duty. The press scour whole countries for a sighting of the relaxing politician, and friends who might know where he is are propositioned with both money and arguments such as 'I am sure you will agree that it would be better for us to find him before the *Daily Mirror*'. There is no advantage in being governed by a collection of exhausted ministers doggedly sitting at their desks making bad decisions.

At the end of August, we suffered a major setback when the members of the Royal College of Nursing voted to reject our 7.5 per cent offer, despite their negotiators having initially accepted it.

The health unions were given the excuse to call a general one-day strike or 'national day of action' for 22 September. At the Elephant and Castle we looked yet again for a means of bringing the dispute to an end.

We had tried talking across the negotiating table and we had tried talking through the medium of Pat Lowry, the Chairman of ACAS. There was only one option left and that was for me to talk directly to Albert Spanswick, the Chairman of the TUC Health Services Committee. Albert Spanswick came from the old school of trade union leaders and I found him a more persuasive advocate for health service workers than Rodney Bickerstaffe. Industrial relations had not been good in the health service for many years and not all of that was the fault of the unions. Managers (where they existed) did too little to involve the workforce and there were often great 'them and us' divisions between the medical staff and the rest. In one demonstration my car was stopped at a hospital entrance but it soon became clear that much of the resentment was directed at what were seen as remote hospital authorities 'up there'.

My approach to Albert Spanswick led to a secret meeting at my house in Fulham just before the TUC Conference in September 1982. The meeting was friendly and Albert went off to Brighton where he roundly denounced me and all my works – without revealing that he was without his customary hat which he had forgotten and was hanging safely on a hook in my hall. The TUC Conference over, we had two further meetings at my home at which Albert agreed that a new two-year deal would be enough to get negotiations going again. I then had dinner with Trevor Clay, who had taken over at the Royal College of Nursing, and he also agreed that such an offer would be enough to bring them back into negotiation. The plan was that I would invite both the unions and the Royal College to the department on Thursday 16 September.

On the Thursday morning letters were sent inviting both the TUC and the Royal College in for talks. Trevor Clay immediately accepted but there was silence from the TUC. Eventually, just before 2 p.m., a small delegation arrived at the Elephant and Castle seeking clarification of what would be on offer. Albert as chairman asked me a number of questions to which he already knew the answers for the good reason that we had already gone over them in Fulham. The delegation left and we continued waiting until 6 p.m. when the news came through that the TUC were holding a press conference. They announced they were not even prepared to come in and talk. In the interviews afterwards I lost my temper for, I think, the first and last time in the dispute. It was clear that Albert had been overruled by his committee who had no intention of being deflected from the TUC's forthcoming national day of action.

The day of action on 22 September brought about 60,000 people on to the streets of London and, according to *The Times*, it was the 'biggest revolt for a decade'. Most of the pits and most of the ports came to a halt and the morning's newspapers also failed to appear. Nevertheless, behind the crowd scenes that so mesmerized television, the day did not prove an overwhelming success for the TUC. The vast majority of industry and of the health service went on working. Even more crucially, the TUC's tactics had turned the press against them and provoked the opposition of the nurses' negotiators. There was now over £1,000 million on the table and the unions had refused to discuss it. That was rightly seen as a ludicrously intransigent position.

The unions followed the national day of action with regional days but these were badly supported and attracted little attention. The TUC unions had shot their bolt. The *Guardian*'s cartoonist showed one health official saying to another: 'These regional days of action are so badly organized that Len Murray has to ring up Norman Fowler to ask where they are being held.' The health unions' refusal to return to the negotiating table proved a major mistake. Albert Spanswick had been right on that and the hard men of his committee quite wrong.

For the nurses, however, the negotiations proved to be a historic turning-point. For years nurses had wanted special pay arrangements which recognized that they did not take industrial action in pursuit of their pay claims. For years different governments had refused to give them. Inside government we examined a number of options. My first choice had always been a pay review body and the significant breakthrough came when Geoffrey Howe and Leon Brittan at the Treasury also backed this proposal. If the nurses accepted it, their pay would be determined in the same way as the doctors', by an independent review body. Although Government could alter the proposals, the presumption was that they would not. There was some scepticism about this solution – given that we had altered the recommendations for doctors and dentists – but it says a great deal for the good sense of the nurses that they accepted the plan. The result was that they received both a big two-year increase and a pay review body which has since been responsible for a further substantial increase in their salaries. On 15 December 1982 the health dispute collapsed and the unions eventually consented to a two-year agreement which could have been accepted months earlier. Their action had failed.

The 1982 dispute was an altogether typical example of industrial action in the health service. Any Health Minister faces a powerful coalition against him. He stands alone – as Kenneth Clarke or David Ennals will confirm – and he makes few friends. Nor can he always rely on the help of those who in any other industry or service you might expect to be on his side. I remember in June going to Brighton for a meeting of the National Association of Health Authorities. I was on time but kept waiting for a few minutes so that the assembled Health Authority Chairmen and administrators could pass a motion condemning the Government's offer as divisive. It is at least worth a footnote to any textbook on handling disputes that few employers have to contend with their management arm solemnly sitting down and condemning the negotiating strategy and then publicly relating their views to the press.

Even worse, we had the Chairmen of the Whitley Councils publicly giving the same message. The Whitley Councils are the means whereby pay negotiations take place in the health service. The Government may be the paymaster, but the actual negotiations are carried out by a team of health authority representatives who might be industrial relations experts but usually are not. Their concern in 1982 was not what was right but what was easiest. Had we taken their advice the nurses would never have received what has proved for them their biggest breakthrough since the war.

From the point of view of the economy, the outcome of the 1982 health dispute was immensely significant. As the *Daily Telegraph* said in a leader:

> The Government has won a very important victory. Apart from the huge expense of acceding to the health workers' demands, defeat for the Government would have brought in its train a series of demands from other workers which it would have found hard to resist. . . . It was an uncontrolled public sector which brought ruin on the previous two administrations.

This judgement was surely right. It was a clear part of the unions' pay tactics that groups with a claim to public sympathy, like the health workers, were put in front to establish a going rate. It was important that this strategy did not succeed and it was also important that the tactics of intimidation seen in 1979 did not win through in 1982. The 1982 health dispute served notice that the Government would not easily give way in a strike. That message was later underlined in the 1984–5 miners' strike. We had not been prepared to give way to health unions with much public support. The prospect of our surrendering to Mr Scargill and the NUM was remote.

Yet for all that, there is an additional conclusion. The health service over the last twenty years has been marred by periodic pay disputes which have disrupted patient services. The result has been to destroy much of the progress in health care over the years preceding each dispute. We should not abandon the search for a better way of determining pay for all health service staff. The best result of the 1982 pay dispute was the nurses' pay review body. Implicit in that arrangement is a non-strike pledge. Government recognized that nurses did not take strike action and believed that it was right to have a system of pay determination which meant that they did not lose by that policy. This arrangement could be extended to any group in the health service prepared to give a similar pledge. I accept, however, that trade unions see their function to negotiate and they (although I suspect not their members) would fight to prevent this function being supplanted and the strike weapon abolished.

An alternative course would be to introduce general legislation to protect the public interest when an essential service is threatened. Over the last twenty years in Britain industrial action has affected a whole range of essential services from water, electricity and fire-fighting to the Royal Mail, public transport and health.

In many cases a virtual monopoly service has been involved and the direct target has been the public.

In many other countries, action has already been taken to provide some protection. In the European Community, minimum periods of notice are often required before a strike in an essential service can take place and a minimum level of service is required during industrial action. In the United States, a ninety-day notice of a strike in health care is required and the President has the power to impose an eighty-day cooling-off period.

It would certainly be possible for a cooling-off period to be introduced in Britain. A cooling-off period of, say, six weeks could be imposed by application to the courts and this would allow negotiations and talks to continue. It would allow contingency plans to be made to protect the public and it would apply just as much to a series of one-day strikes as a set-piece conflict. It would allow second thoughts and permit (but not require) the parties to use ACAS or any other means to find a solution. A cooling-off period does not guarantee success, but it offers a degree of public protection which at present is entirely lacking.

Clearly if this question was easy to decide it would have been settled in the years of the Thatcher Governments. At various stages over the eleven years, statements were made promising action. The fear must be that if we leave the issue unresolved then there will be other health disputes in the future and, just as certainly, the people who suffer will again be the patients.

CHAPTER 10

Safe in Our Hands

"FORCEPS... SCALPEL... MORE MONEY!"

Daily Telegraph

On Thursday 9 September 1982, a paper from the Central Policy Review Staff, the Government's think-tank, came to Cabinet. Each year there is an annual debate between the Treasury and the different government departments on the size of their budgets, but the aim of this meeting was to go one stage further. Geoffrey Howe, the Chancellor of the Exchequer, and Leon Brittan, the Chief Secretary to the Treasury in overall charge of government spending, wanted to look at the longer-term trends and to see how public expenditure could be successfully controlled in the 1980s. Their fear was that taxes would not only have to remain high but might well have to increase.

The CPRS paper argued that if the Government were serious about reducing public expenditure, the time had come to consider some radical solutions. The paper looked at education and social security but the most explosive set of proposals concerned the health service. Basically the paper suggested that we should consider moving away from the tax-financed National Health Service to private health insurance. There would need to be rebates for low-income families and for long-stay patients but the idea was that the working population would be required by law to obtain health insurance. The paper also advocated increased charges for the health service and suggested further savings, like charging patients to visit the doctor.

As far as I was concerned the timing of the CPRS paper was disastrous. I was still in the middle of the longest health dispute since the war. By any standards it was a sensitive period and about the worst moment that anyone coud have chosen to circulate proposals of this kind. If the proposals leaked they would be dynamite inside the health service, and yet they had come round with only the routine 'confidential' security classification. My guess was that they would find their way into the press and would undermine our efforts to settle the health dispute.

My opposition was, however, much more fundamental than this. I did not believe that it was a sensible way of making policy. It may have been the job of the think-tank to think the unthinkable, but such discussion needed to be on the basis of informed examination. These proposals had come forward without any consultation with any health minister, and indeed without any of us knowing that such a study was taking place. This was entirely the wrong way to make policy and a cavalier way of dealing with a popular and effective service.

Worst of all, no one seemed to have remembered that we had already been round this particular course, decided the policy, and rejected compulsory private health insurance. My predecessor Patrick Jenkin had sensibly asked for an examination of the different ways that European countries financed their health care. This had been carried out inside the health department and had come up with findings that were easily predictable. Every country in Europe was facing an explosion in demand for health care; every country in Europe was spending substantial public resources upon health; and in many ways our centrally run, centrally financed system was the most effective in controlling costs. There was no inherent cost advantage in moving over to an entirely new financing system and it was also clear that whatever system was chosen, taxation would still have to finance a giant share of the service. The unemployed, the poor, the chronically sick and disabled and of course children would need to be covered by public money.

There were also endless practical questions about private insurance. The assumption was that insurance would be paid only by those who could afford it while those who could not afford to pay would be exempt. But where was the line to be drawn? Would the elderly with the equivalent of average earnings be exempt or not exempt? Everyone over retirement age is exempt from paying prescription charges and any deviation from the provision of free health care for the elderly would be wildly controversial. Would health insurance be income-related like National Insurance or would it be genuine private insurance like life insurance or house insurance? A sensible policy on exemptions and rebates would reduce the possible savings and my guess was that in the end you would achieve surprisingly little in public savings. The potential for a massive row like that over the community charge was immense.

Months before the CPRS report came to ministers, therefore, we had reviewed the options and indeed in July 1982 I had set out the Government's position, after consultation with the Treasury. In a Parliamentary reply I said: 'The Government have no plans to change the present system of financing the National Health Service largely from taxation and will continue to review the scope for introducing more cost consciousness and consumer choice and for increasing private provision which is already expanding.'

The agreed position of the Government was that we would not move over to private health insurance but would seek to make the health service as effective as possible. The private sector would remain separate and the public would have the right to be covered by it if they wished – having first paid their taxes to support the general service. My view (the view of a confirmed industrial privatizer) was that the National Health Service should remain at the centre of our health-care system and that politically we would reap the whirlwind if we could be portrayed as moving away from it. Change was certainly needed, but I favoured change which would improve the service and for which there was public support. It was clear that the public wanted above all the assurance that our system of health care guaranteed the best possible treatment irrespective of income. I did not think much of the CPRS blunderbuss which seemed to be aimed firmly at the Government's feet.

A week later my worst fears were confirmed. Some kindly soul leaked the contents of the CPRS report to the *Economist*. 'Thatcher's Holocaust,' said the *Economist*, not intending to understate their scoop: 'Thatcher's think-tank takes aim at the Welfare State.' Leaks were a constant hazard of the first 1979–83 Thatcher Government and none did us more damage than this. Yet the irony was that there was no support in Cabinet for the proposals and they had almost reached the point of rejection when the leak took place. All the leaker managed to do was to provoke a bogus political row.

It was useless for me to point out that the proposals were not those of the Government but of a group of advisers whose only power was to suggest. That was, however, the truth of the matter. The CPRS had been set up by Ted Heath to advise on long-term policy issues. Its first director was Lord Rothschild and its staff was drawn both from the civil service and from outside Whitehall. The 'tank' had been continued by the succeeding Labour Government during which they carried out their famous inquiry into the

Foreign Office which proposed fundamental changes in the organization of the Diplomatic Service, and they were retained by
Margaret Thatcher when she took power in 1979. Governments
were not bound by their proposals and past history – as when
Labour threw out the Foreign Office report – was ample proof of
this. Yet for all that, the charge eagerly made against us was that
the Government were set on abolishing the National Health Service and 'privatizing' health care. It was a charge that was to dog
us through both the 1983 and 1987 general elections, and which
did us more damage than any other health issue. Successive
Labour spokesmen tried to establish that the Thatcher Government did not have its heart in the health service. Yet the truth was
that the CPRS report was consigned to the dustbin within a couple
of weeks of its first appearing.

At the Cabinet meeting on 9 September, we did not discuss the
CPRS paper in any detail. The general attitude was entirely hostile
to the report and we certainly did not agree that on the basis of
the report the CPRS should undertake further studies. Outside
Cabinet Leon Brittan argued in a speech that the Government
must have the right to look at new ideas, although I suspect that
both Leon and Geoffrey Howe must have been appalled at the
way the issue had been handled. The next day, I countered with
a speech arguing that as far as the health service was concerned
the issue had been settled and that the Government's policy was
to continue to make the service as effective as possible.

The issue surfaced again at Cabinet on 30 September when I
warned colleagues that the leaking of the CPRS report had caused
us damage. I outlined what my message had been over the past
two weeks and would be at the Party Conference – that we stood
by the National Health Service and had no intention of moving
over to a new system of finance. At that meeting two of the Cabinet
heavyweights, Willie Whitelaw and Quintin Hailsham, intervened
to give me support. Quintin Hailsham told me later: 'When I first
read the report my hair stood on end, and at my age that takes
some doing.'

At the Conservative Party Conference two weeks later I set out
both the Government's position and my own feelings. I told the
conference that I had not come into politics to preside over the
destruction of the National Health Service and repeated

the Government's commitment to it. I added: 'The Government is committed to the health service because we want to ensure that everyone in need of treatment receives it. Taxation will remain, as now, the predominant way of financing it. . . . What this Government wants is partnership, not apartheid, between the private and the public sectors.' At the end of the conference Margaret Thatcher returned to the same theme. She had been on the platform for my speech but used distinctive words of her own. The guiding principle for the Government, she said, was that health care should be provided for all regardless of ability to pay: 'Let me make one thing absolutely clear. The National Health Service is safe with us.'

The issue was never raised again in the remaining five years I stayed at the Department of Health. Indeed the real significance of the Welfare State report was that it marked the beginning of the end not for the health service but for the CPRS. They were as much the victims of the leaking of the report as ministers. John Sparrow, the head of the think-tank, led an unquestionably bright team but their abilities were not being best used. They needed to be positioned inside departments' own policy units or inside Number 10 itself rather than stumbling around Whitehall in an unguided way. Immediately after the 1983 general election the CPRS was disbanded and I very much doubt it will ever be resurrected.

I see nothing to regret in this, not because new ideas should not be examined, but because it can be done better. Three years later I led a review of social security which was regarded as even more untouchable than the health service. We did it in an entirely different way. We were open about the review itself. We asked the public what they thought. We used independent experts on the review teams. We made it clear that what we wanted was a better social security system and not just a cheaper one. The CPRS way was the wrong way of doing it. The report was not an impressive document. It contained no fresh insights. It simply set out some crude ideas on how public spending could be reduced and suggested that ministers should have six months to come up with more refined views. It was entirely right that this method of policy-making was thrown out.

Nevertheless in the public debate on health we were saddled

with the CPRS report. Ministers had rejected the report but politically it took us the next two general elections to repair the damage.
In June 1983, Margaret Thatcher went to the polls for the second
time. It was almost a year before it was strictly necessary and at
the time there were voices advising delay. Unemployment was over
three million and one strong view was that we should wait until
the autumn when the economic recovery would be more apparent.
Like every other Cabinet minister, I was asked for my opinion.
Influenced by our strong local-government showing in Birmingham and the Midlands, I advised June and that was clearly the
majority view. I do remember, however, another Cabinet minister
remarking 'It doesn't matter when you go, Margaret, you will win.'
At the time I thought that was particularly unhelpful advice. In
retrospect I think it was no more than the truth. Clearly we were
helped by the Falklands factor but, even more, we were helped by
the Labour Party.

Michael Foot had put together a series of policies to keep his
party together. The trouble for him was that this manifesto – 'the
longest suicide note in history' – had also made his party entirely
unelectable. Labour candidates found themselves pledged to uni-
lateral disarmament, withdrawal from the European Community
and an economic policy that would have brought the country to
bankruptcy within weeks. The outcome was never seriously in
doubt, although our eventual majority of 144 seats substantially
overstated our support. Our total vote actually went down and in
areas hit by high unemployment, like my own constituency in the
West Midlands, there was a swing to the Alliance of David Steel
and David Owen. Many people suspended judgement and
throughout the West Midlands reduced polls saw Conservative
majorities cut.

In the campaign itself there was one awkward moment and that
was on the issue of private health. It showed just how powerful
the CPRS factor had become. On Saturday 4 June, I came in
from a morning's canvassing in Sutton Coldfield to find an urgent
message to call Conservative Central Office. I learnt that Roy
Hattersley and Gwyneth Dunwoody, who spoke for the Opposition on health, had claimed at Labour's morning press
conference that they had a 'leaked' copy of a secret Health Department report planning the privatization of the service. Leaks were

the flavour of the year in 1983, but the trouble was that neither Ken Clarke nor I had the first idea what report this was meant to be as there were no plans, secret or otherwise, for privatization. Slowly it became clear that what Labour had in mind was a circular we had sent out three months earlier to health authority chairmen for comment, entitled *Co-operation between the NHS and the private sector at district level.* The idea behind the circular was the exact opposite of what Labour alleged. It recognized that there was a National Health Service and a private sector and, rather than arguing that one should be taken over by the other, proposed sensible cooperation between them for the benefit of patients.

The document proposed that, to reduce waiting lists, health service patients should have the opportunity of treatment in private hospitals; and that health authorities should explore the potential of placing contracts with private nursing homes for the care of elderly patients, in order to free hospital beds for other patients. We also wanted health service patients to have access to underused 'high technology' equipment in the private sector. The aim was to make use of all available resources whether labelled public or private for the benefit of the patient who wanted treatment. By most standards this was a peculiarly non-threatening document but we were in the middle of a general election.

Michael Foot claimed the document established 'the most serious attack on the National Health Service since it was originally started'. Gwyneth Dunwoody stated that we were secretly dismantling the health service and Roy Hattersley muttered about contracting out old people like refuse collection. It was all the greatest nonsense but the scare ran for a couple of days. Once we finally identified the leaked document, we countered in the most conclusive way known in politics: we published it in its entirety. Journalists read it and the clamour quietened.

Throughout the election Gwyneth Dunwoody was my opponent. She adopted a hectoring tone and continually interrupted in debates. Our duels were not on the scale of the later Clarke versus Prescott battles, where in the 1987 general election I saw a television chairman leave his chair several times to restore order. Nevertheless I fear our debates were not much more edifying. During one television interview, with Dunwoody in London and myself in Nottingham, she again interrupted my replies. My patience snapped and I said: 'Do shut up and just listen for a moment.' It did me no good. The next day I was canvassing in Sutton Coldfield and a policeman came up to me. 'I am afraid you have lost my wife's vote,' he said. 'You should never tell a lady to shut up.' In fact my majority was healthy enough at almost 19,000. I was chased mercilessly about the streets by my campaign assistant, Simon Heffer, who is now the chief leader-writer of the *Daily Telegraph* but whom I knew in those days as a fellow (but younger) old boy from Chelmsford.

Four years later there was an important postscript to the CPRS affair. Following the 1987 general election, Margaret Thatcher set up and headed a small committee to examine the health service. It included my successor, John Moore, who early in his term of office made a speech which was interpreted as meaning that he was prepared to take a different stance towards the health service. The press was full of stories about fundamental change. The group also included Treasury ministers, who might be expected to support a change to private insurance if anyone would. The group went round the course for month after month but wisely came to the conclusion yet again that they did not intend to alter the basis of the health service.

The changes proposed were the ones that Ken Clarke and later William Waldegrave took through. As I know to my cost, any change in the health service is controversial. However, one charge that cannot reasonably be made against the Government is that they have privatized the service. The policy remains the policy that has been followed by successive health ministers from Iain Macleod and Enoch Powell through to Keith Joseph and myself – namely to make the health service as effective as possible. This is where the real debate is and where the Government have succeeded in taking the high ground.

Labour tend to regard the health service as some enormous trade union. They look at everything from the point of view of the provider and their only discernible policy is that they are against privatization. But that is not the issue. The real issue in health is how to continue to improve a good service for the benefit of the patient. The trouble with some of those who make much of their support for the health service is that they also oppose any measures taken to make it more effective. You can argue about the amount of resources devoted to health but what you cannot sensibly argue about is that the resources devoted to health care should be used to maximum effect.

The history of the past ten years has seen Labour consistently oppose any change inside the health service and, even more regrettably, has often seen groups inside it resist reform on the grounds that their vested interests are being challenged. Hardly ever do such groups consider the public good. My time at the DHSS showed that it was impossible to make any significant change without a fierce public and professional battle – even when improvement meant more resources for health care or put right long-standing problems.

In so many ways the health service of the 1980s was admirable and impressive. Of course there were loud-mouths – the sophisticated ones patronized you; the less sophisticated simply shouted. But these were the health service politicians and happily they were not typical. The vast majority from the most senior consultant to the most junior nurse worked long hours and responded to daily emergencies in a way that was an object lesson to us all. The question was whether their skill and dedication was matched by organization and management. I became convinced that with better management and a number of policy changes we could achieve a better service for the patient. Instead of privatizing the health service, I wanted to modernize it so that it could better tackle the problems of the 1980s and 1990s. By 1983 the health budget had increased from £9.5 billion in 1979 to £15.5 billion. I decided to examine some of the services that made up this massive total.

One of the areas I looked at first was the so-called ancillary services – that is cleaning, catering and laundry. By 1983 these services accounted for almost £1 billion of the annual budget and any savings made there could be transferred to the main activity of treating patients. It is the kind of argument that any businessman in charge of even a medium-sized company would recognize instantly. In no way did I wish to diminish the importance of these services or the importance of the people who worked in them. Any hospital needs to be kept clean and the patients need good food. Nevertheless, there was no reason why the health service should devote unnecessary resources to these jobs.

The first step was to check the cost of the in-house services against that which could be provided by private contractors. The health service does not have a monopoly in cleaning, catering and laundry skills in the same way that it does in the skills required to treat sick people. There are private companies who specialize in these services and who, incidentally, also have dedicated people working for them. In February 1983 I announced in the House of Commons that health authorities should put their ancillary services out to tender to see whether they would get best value from private or in-house organizations.

Six months later, in September, I followed this up with a circular to health authorities requiring them to put their services out to tender. They were not forced to use private contractors but they were required to make a judgement on the best value for their health authority. The policy was met with predictable howls of rage from unions like NUPE, and nor did every Health Authority throw their hats in the air with glee. It was easier for them to demand money from the Government than argue plans past their local unions. The health service has its fair share of people who want a quiet life and perhaps more than its fair share of Authority members who, for political reasons, opposed the policy itself. I suspect that even now there is the potential for greater savings. Nevertheless, this policy has now freed more than £100 million for use elsewhere in the National Health Service.

If I had trouble with the health unions on contracting out, it was nothing compared with my problems on manpower numbers. By 1983 the National Health Service was employing more than 800,000 staff – an increase of a quarter over the total in the early 1970s. With staff costs amounting to about 70 per cent of the annual budget, any moderately competent company would at least ask whether this proportion was justified.

As the Public Accounts Committee of the House of Commons had demonstrated, however, neither the Government nor the health authorities had accurate information on the exact numbers employed or any sensible means of controlling numbers. Nevertheless we made a start and asked the Regional Health Authorities to produce manpower plans for the next year. Their plans originally showed an increase of another 7,000 staff. At the beginning of October 1983 I announced that out of a total staff of 817,633 we would ask for a reduction of 4,837, which would save about £40

million. Again there was a furious row. This was the first time that
the health service had ever been asked to make staff economies.
Both Ken Clarke and my special adviser Nicholas True made it
clear that a good speech was 'needed' at the Party Conference in
Blackpool. Fortunately my 1983 conference speech went well and
the row started to calm down.

Perhaps the most intense of my health service battles of the
mid-1980s was over the selected list of drugs. For years ministers
had been urged to cut the heavy drugs bill. By 1984 the bill
had reached £1.4 billion and we were under both political and
professional pressure to reduce it. The only question was how.
Doctors wished to preserve their clinical freedom to prescribe what
drugs they themselves felt were necessary. The pharmaceutical
industry had a legitimate interest in seeing that their own branded
drugs were prescribed. They had devoted the resources to research
and development and they wanted a sensible return on that investment. As a Government, we wanted a good pharmaceutical
industry but we also wanted good value for the health service. I
found myself in the curious position of being the sponsor minister
of the industry and also the minister ultimately answerable for
health service spending. It was clear that some economies were
possible if more generic drugs were prescribed rather than
branded drugs.

Generic substitution could be achieved in a number of ways.
One suggestion was that discretion should be left to the doctors
and that they should tick a box if they wanted the generic drug.
This system, however, was uncertain in its effect. I was attracted
by another that I had discussed on a visit to Europe: certain
branded drugs would not be prescribed at all when entirely
adequate substitute generic drugs existed. We would not leave it
to the discretion of the doctors but, acting on the best medical
advice, set down what drugs could be prescribed and those that
could not. In theory it may sound radical to interfere with a doctor's
right to prescribe, although it was not the drug that was being
withdrawn, only the branded version. In practice those doubts melt
away when you realize just what drugs we had in mind.

Prior to the selected list, doctors could prescribe branded drugs
as cold remedies, laxatives, ordinary painkillers, antacids, vitamins,
bitters and tonics, tranquillizers and sedatives. The drugs in these

areas were not at the frontier of medical science and acceptable generic drugs existed. The new policy meant, however, that popular branded drugs like Mogadon, Valium, Librium, Dalmane and Benylin could not be prescribed under the health service – not to mention Beecham's Pills, Alka Seltzer, Andrew's Liver Salts, Vick's Vapour Rub and even more exotic preparations like Rock Salmon cough mixture and Male Gland Double Strength Supplement tablets. In retrospect it seems extraordinary that some of these could be prescribed in the first place.

On 9 November 1984 I set out for consultation a list of branded drugs which would no longer be prescribed under the health service. The reaction was instant. Predictably enough, the pharmaceutical industry fiercely opposed the proposals but, more surprisingly and entirely to their discredit, so too did the British Medical Association. There followed as fierce and nasty a little campaign as I can remember in the time I spent with the health service. The BMA and its Chairman, John Marks, refused even to come to the department to talk about the details of the scheme and vigorously campaigned against us. The pharmaceutical industry unwisely did the same and instituted an expensive advertising campaign. The free weekly magazines sent to doctors financed by drug advertisements joined in with a vengeance on the lines that 'Fowler's drug list ends prescribing freedom'. Seeing the way the debate was going, the health spokesmen of the Labour Party, Michael Meacher, and of the SDP, Mike Thomas, who had previously been urging me to make economies in the drugs bill, jumped overboard and joined the critics.

The result was that we were dangerously isolated with a strong coalition arrayed against us, but fortunately our opponents overplayed their hand. The BMA were criticized for their intransigence and the pharmaceutical industry's advertising was criticized for seeking to frighten patients. One company threatened that replies from MPs to their standard letter would be posted on surgery notice-boards in their constituencies. I am glad to say that these tactics backfired. Even in these days of lobbying, Members of Parliament will not be bullied in this way. When the issue was put to the vote in the House of Commons we had a majority of 127 and the campaign against us was left in ruins.

These, then, were some of the issues that took my time. However, as month after month went by, I became more and more convinced that the real problem with the health service was a lack of management. Over the previous twenty years we had become preoccupied with structural arguments about regions and areas when we should have been concerned about how the service was run. Compared with any major industry our methods appeared amateurish. Although we were the biggest employer in Britain, we had no serious employee-involvement policies. There was certainly a multitude of advisers but all too few people who took responsibility for action and for failure.

In early 1983, Roy Griffiths, the Chief Executive of Sainsbury's and one of the most successful managers in the country, agreed to head an inquiry into management in the health service. His report came six months later in an altogether typical form. Rather than some forbidding official document, his report consisted of a letter to me with the disclaimer that it was not intended to be a major addition to the already considerable library of the National Health Service. It was a plan of action. His diagnosis was clear:

If Florence Nightingale were carrying her lamp through the corridors of the National Health Service today, she would almost certainly be searching for the people in charge.

His solution was also plain. It was to push responsibility downwards so that, for example, day-to-day decisions in hospitals were taken in the hospitals themselves and not forever referred upwards to some 'higher authority'. For this to be effective there was a need for managers. The managers could be appointed from inside the service or taken in from outside. They could be professional managers or they could be doctors or nurses. The point was that they should be *managers* who took responsibility for securing the best service to the patient and could be held to account if there was failure.

In the summer of 1984 there was an event that tragically illustrated the Griffiths case. An outbreak of food poisoning at the Stanley Royd Hospital near Wakefield affected over half the 800 elderly patients and caused nineteen deaths. I appointed a public inquiry into the outbreak. The crucial message that came back was that we needed more hands-on management. In the hospital kitchen there was a gulf between those who were meant to be in charge and those who actually carried out the work. According to the report, the managers 'passed through rather than spent time in the kitchen'. They were punctilious in ensuring that new staff read the hygiene regulations, but the running of the kitchen itself was entirely left to those working there.

Yet in spite of its overwhelming logic, the Griffiths case was hotly disputed. The most infuriating charge was that the health service was different from business and therefore did not need the benefit of the techniques that had been developed in business and industry. Of course the delivery of health care is different from producing cars or selling food, but there are a large number of common problems that any manager shares. He must be concerned with the quality of service, the quality of the product and the productivity of his workforce. He must motivate and involve all his staff and he must live within and meet his budget. Regrettably, even today, there are a number of health service insiders who feel that they are an exception to these general rules and look down on the ways of industry with the patronizing assurance of those who know that 'we are different'. It goes without saying that the Labour front bench supported all of the most reactionary arguments that could be found to oppose the management reforms. Yet today no serious figure inside or outside the health service would argue that we should return to the old system.

The management of the health service is now infinitely better than it was and the trend to devolving responsibility downwards has continued apace. Even so, I found that a curious structure remained at the service's centre. It was rather like an old-fashioned nationalized industry where all lines led to the Secretary of State. It was as if the Secretary of State were directly running the railways himself, with no chairman or managing director between him and the service. We tried to solve this with management and supervisory boards based in the department but they were a long way from the boards of industry. When Victor Paige became the first general manager of the health service he found himself in a very different job from any that he or anyone else had occupied before. He was not the chief executive of a big corporation but in an uneasy no man's land between the department and the service. I regret that he resigned in 1986 but I have to admit that he had a point.

Since then the position has slowly improved but very much the same dilemma still remains. The health service is financed almost entirely by the taxpayer and will remain so. The Secretary of State is accountable to Parliament for that enormous budget – currently running at over £30 billion a year – and must remain so. The question is whether he can discharge that responsibility to Parliament without being in day-to-day charge. By the end of my stay in health, I had become convinced that it would be possible to create a health commission with its own chief executive or chairman.

Such a commission would have substantial advantages. Nothing will now take health out of politics but a commission could produce a more efficient service with the potential for advances in training, employee involvement and swifter decision-making. The advantage would be that ministers and civil servants would not be involved in day-to-day management. The commission would be given its objectives by the Government and would be accountable to it. I believe that this would lead to a better service and improved facilities for the public.

Our reforms to the health service in the 1980s went beyond the hospitals. The primary services – family doctors, dentists, pharmacists – are very much the front line of health care and in 1986 we published a Green Paper which was the first comprehensive review of the services for forty years. We estimated that on an average working day about 650,000 people saw their family doctor and another 300,000 went to the dentist. I approached the service from the point of view of the consumer, as we had already done to good effect with the opticians. In 1984 we had ended the opticians' monopoly and taken off the ridiculous restrictions on advertising which prevented the public from shopping around for the best value. The changes had met with howls of rage from the profession; a host of cartoons in the press; but above all a reduction in price for the consumer. We now went further, proposing changes in the way that doctors were paid so that the remuneration system much more clearly recognized the good doctors and the good practices. We also wanted to give the public more information about local health care and an easier means of changing doctors. These proposals and many more formed the basis of legislation following the 1987 general election – as too did the model report from Dame Mary Warnock that I commissioned into human fertilization and embryology.

So was the health service safe in our hands? My aim was to modernize the health service and I believe that the Government had significant success. We made better use of NHS resources than ever before. We raised extra resources for health from common-sense policies like contracting-out, selling surplus land (which alone raised over £1 billion) and controlling the drugs budget. We introduced modern management, probably the major advance during the 1980s. We built more hospitals and moved decisively away from the terrible stop-go years of the 1970s when capital budgets were slashed. Above all, we provided more care. It is always difficult to measure the exact outcome of health policy but some indicators give the picture. Between 1979 and 1987 the number of inpatients treated in English hospitals went up by a quarter and day cases by almost 60 per cent. Another figure I was delighted to see increase was the vaccination rate for whooping cough, which went up from 31 per cent to 73 per cent. So, yes, I believe the health service was safe with us. But that cannot mean that the process of change has ended. Commitment to the health service means constantly striving for better ways forward.

CHAPTER 11

Reforming the Welfare State

"Callous Mr Fowler has no compassion! He's refused Oliver Twist his ninth helping!"

Daily Express

Margaret Thatcher reshuffled the Cabinet in June 1983. After our election victory, Willie Whitelaw moved from the Home Office to become Leader of the House of Lords and his place was taken by Leon Brittan, who in a notable promotion became the youngest Home Secretary since Robert Peel. The Foreign Secretary, Francis Pym, who had always appeared a rather reluctant supporter of Thatcherite policies, was sacked and his place was taken by Geoffrey Howe. This left a crucial vacancy at the Treasury. Press speculation ran Patrick Jenkin as Howe's likeliest heir and not without reason. Patrick had been Chief Secretary to the Treasury in Ted Heath's Government and had been successful as Secretary of State for both Social Services and Trade and Industry. His dubious reward was to be given the Department of the Environment. The post of Chancellor of the Exchequer went to one of the most junior members of the previous Cabinet, the Energy Secretary Nigel Lawson.

According to his critics, Nigel was blunt in argument and had all the subtlety of a Chieftain tank. If he could roll you over he would. If he lost an engagement, he would simply regroup and try again. But such critics (of whom there were many both inside and outside Government) underestimated the new Chancellor. He was an undoubted intellectual heavyweight; he was a creative minister interested in political ideas; and, above all, he was entirely his own man. He invariably believed completely in his own case and pursued it relentlessly to the end. But there was no personal edge to his arguments. He was neither a plotter nor a courtier. As I was soon to find, he was a man you could like even when you were joined in battle with him.

From the start of his Chancellorship, Nigel Lawson made no secret of the fact that his ambitions were tax reform and lower taxes. Almost his first action was a post-election dawn raid in July 1983 on departmental budgets. The raid netted him £500 million and over the next few weeks he made his strategy clear. He believed that lower taxes were the route to higher growth and more jobs. His ambition was to reduce the standard rate of tax to 25p in the pound by the next election. But if this was to be achieved then public spending – as a proportion of national wealth – had to come down. Not surprisingly, given the increase in unemployment and the various crises in nationalized industries, public spending had increased between 1979 and 1983. Nigel was determined to have none of that during the next Parliament. All departments would be under close scrutiny, but none more than the Department of Health and Social Security, which was by far the biggest spender in Whitehall. It needed no great powers of prophecy to realize that Nigel and I were on a collision course.

At a meeting on 21 July the Cabinet approved the Chancellor's strategy. In the days following, press reports started to appear that I, and indeed Ken Clarke who as Minister of State for Health was still outside the Cabinet, were very unhappy about the new emphasis of policy. Both the *Daily Mail* and the *Daily Mirror* said that we might take our opposition to the point of resignation. I doubt if Ken's position was much different from my own but he must speak for himself. My position was this. I supported the move to reduce taxation. I shared the view that personal taxation was too high and that one way we could help industry was to reduce the tax burden upon it. It was, after all, only if this was done that there would be any wealth to distribute to services like health. But we needed a balanced approach. The reduction of taxation was not our *only* objective. We had other social policy commitments and we also needed to keep to those.

The difficulty of imposing spending cuts across the board was shown by social security. Benefits were divided into 'pledged' benefits like the retirement pension which the Government was committed to uprating each year according to inflation; and 'unpledged' benefits, like child benefit and supplementary benefit, where there was no such commitment and the Government decided each year whether to increase them or not. If we reduced by 5 per cent every unpledged benefit we would still, in 1984, have saved only £200 million. However, we would have provoked a huge political fracas and affected some of the poorest in the land.

I did *not* threaten to resign but I did make it clear that I would not endorse changes I could not justify. I took the view that the Cabinet and the Prime Minister should know my position. I was glad I did. There were hard fights over the next four years which

I do not resent. But the result was the balance I argued for. The Government did manage to bring down the rate of income tax, but at the same time we increased the annual budget for health between 1983 and 1987 from £15.5 billion to £20.7 billion and for social security from £36.7 billion to £48.7 billion. Yet securing a realistic budget was only one part of making policy in the DHSS. It was also important to ensure that the money was well spent. By the autumn of 1983 my plans for health were well under way. I next decided to set up a complete examination of the social security system.

My first step was the reform of pensions. In 1963 my father died at the age of sixty-one, four years short of his pensionable age. He had worked for the same engineering firm for thirty years and he had always set great store by the company pension. However, he made the great mistake of not living to collect it. There was no widow's pension – only a return of contributions. Fortunately my mother was able to return to teaching and to complete the final two or three years which qualified her for a pension of her own. In 1970 I left *The Times* on being elected to the House of Commons. I also had a company pension but I was what, in the pensions trade, is called an 'early leaver'. I was given a choice. I could have my own contributions returned or I could leave my pension where it was and draw it at the age of sixty-five. The only snag with this last course was that when the pension was paid out in 2003 it would still be at its 1970 value. It would have been frozen for over thirty years.

In the bustle of adapting to the new life of an MP at Westminster, it had occurred to me that I should look further at pensions. The only occasions on which I had seen them in operation they had failed lamentably. Like many people, however, I decided to leave it for another day. Pensions are hard to understand and surrounded by impenetrable jargon. Above all, a pension seems so far away when you are in your twenties and thirties. It is easy to postpone settling down to understand them. It is perhaps for that reason that the pensions industry had been able to get away with such arrangements for so long.

When I went to the DHSS I vowed to make time for a serious investigation into company pensions. The more I looked, the more concerned I became. The kind of company pensions then being offered were fine for those who joined a company in their twenties and worked through to the age of sixty-five. They were seriously deficient for people who moved jobs and, often, inadequate for widows. This was an area which cried out for reform. In September 1983 I called a conference on pensions at the DHSS headquarters. I invited the pensions establishment but I also brought in some of those who wanted change.

I opened the conference to the press and the large room was packed. When I spoke I made it clear that I intended to do something about the position of the 'early leavers' and that I thought it right that people should not suffer if they transferred their pension from one job to another. Some of the industry recognized that change was due and with various degrees of enthusiasm were prepared to go along with such proposals. What, however, caused almost universal consternation was my suggestion that we should go a stage further and see whether it was possible to introduce 'portable' pensions – pensions which you could take from one job to another. The industry was horrified. They saw this as a direct threat to their conventional final-salary pension schemes and a challenge to their whole way of life. Reform was one thing – but this was revolution. They were right. Company pensions were the golden handcuffs which chained staff to a company. Portable pensions could give the individual more freedom and end the penalty on changing jobs. At the end of November 1983, I announced that I was going to head an inquiry into occupational pensions. We faced a two-nation position. One nation had their own pension. The other nation relied entirely on the State. My view was that people wanted what they regarded as their own pension and my aim was to ensure an expansion in provision.

Pensions, however, were not the only area which cried out for reform. The social security system was the legacy of Lord Beveridge and the post-war Attlee Government. No one had carried out any overall review of the system since then. But that was not because anyone was very happy with it. In spite of the vast expenditure on pensions and benefits, the complaints flooded in. The system was seen as bureaucratic and ramshackle. It was certainly an improvement on the pre-war system, but I doubted whether the money was always reaching the people who most needed it.

An outstanding example was the Death Grant. The Death Grant

had been introduced before the war to help families who did not have enough money to bury their dead. But it was a universal grant, which meant that it went equally to the millionaire's widow and to the widow who had very little. Because it was universal, the cost of increasing it was very great. The result was that it had been increased only twice and now stood at the princely sum of £30. It was pathetically inadequate for the poor and totally irrelevant for everyone else. In terms of spending, it now cost £12 million to administer an annual expenditure of only £17 million on the grant. Why then had nothing been done to change this long-standing nonsense? Both Labour and Conservative Governments had taken the view that change would cause a fierce political storm, so no one did anything. At the outset of my investigation one of my civil servants said to me: 'My test of the review is whether you do anything about the Death Grant.' I knew what she meant. Like so much of the social security system it had become regarded as politically untouchable.

My experience with the pensions inquiry had already taught me one invaluable lesson. It is simply not necessary to make all policy behind closed doors. Indeed, obsessive secrecy can be entirely counterproductive for policy-makers. It creates suspicion and alienates the public. With pensions we had been open about holding an inquiry. We had taken evidence in public and given all the interested parties the chance to have their say. We had brought in respected experts from outside Whitehall like Mark Weinberg, Professor Alan Peacock, and Marshall Field of the Life Offices' Association to act as assessors. Our approach had changed the tone of the whole debate.

It was next to impossible for even the most reactionary supporter of the *status quo* to claim that Government should not even examine the pensions system. It meant that the industry had to justify, under cross-examination, its policies. Opponents of changing the rules on early leavers found it difficult to sustain their case. Rather than having the whole of the public and the press against us, we gained support. Letters flooded in from people who had often been cruelly affected by the system we were examining. Journalists like my old colleague Christopher Fildes became notable allies. Surely, I thought, if we can do this with pensions can we not do the same with social security? If the absurdity of the present position of the Death Grant were exposed to the public gaze, would not reform become easier? I recognized that all would not be plain sailing. Changing supplementary and housing benefit would be more contentious than reforming occupational pensions. Nevertheless, I felt that an open inquiry should be the aim.

My resolve to set up an inquiry into the social security system was strengthened by one other important factor. Like every other Secretary of State who has ever been in charge of social security, I was under pressure from the Treasury. The department took the largest slice of the Government's budget and each year the Treasury demanded economies. There was nothing remotely new in this. My predecessor, Patrick Jenkin, had been pressed for savings and so too had his Labour predecessors, David Ennals and Barbara Castle. The man in charge of controlling public spending is the Chief Secretary to the Treasury. In the time of the Labour Government the Chief Secretary had been Joel Barnett and it was he who had forced Barbara Castle into her major and controversial changes. During my time at the DHSS I met over the table with three Chief Secretaries and, I have to admit, had battles with them all.

My baptism of fire had been with Leon Brittan who was Chief Secretary until the 1983 general election. Friendship, I fear, counts for very little when the fur really begins to fly. Ken Clarke, having listened to one of our more heated exchanges, wondered if we would ever speak to each other again. I also had fierce battles with Peter Rees, while Peter's successor, John MacGregor, maintained that I was the only minister who almost walked out of one of his 'bilaterals'. I cannot remember that particular meeting – nor am I very proud of it – but the point illustrates the sometimes passionate disputes which can erupt during the annual public-spending negotiations.

No one should be too surprised at these clashes. It is an inevitable fact of ministerial life. The Treasury has responsibility for the health of the economy; the Social Services Department has responsibility for some of the poorest and most vulnerable people in the country. Certainly I did not regard it as my job to defend the departmental budget just because it was the departmental budget. On the other hand it most certainly was my job to prevent indefensible cuts. No one is going to thank you if you end up making changes which either cause real hardship or bring the political roof in – or manage to do both. It is, of course, a matter of judgement and your viewpoint will depend on what Cabinet seat you occupy. Former Chief Secretaries have been known to make spirited claims for additional resources when they move to a departmental job. Colleagues who one year lecture you at the Star Chamber on how you have more than enough money turn up the next asking for extra themselves.

It is, nevertheless, crucial that such debates should take place. A similar process happens each year in industry. No manager, in any half-decent company, is able to get away with claiming that he has made all the improvements it is possible to make. In the public-spending round of Government it is certainly true that departments overbid on the basis that when it comes to the crunch they can bring the bid down without damage. Yet it is equally true that the Treasury just as consistently suggest economies that they do not expect to achieve but which concentrate the minister's mind and preferably chill his blood. It is possible to make light of the process but, be under no illusion, it is a deadly serious affair.

If as Secretary of State you get it wrong, then you – and crucially the people you are serving – live with the consequences for the next twelve months and beyond. And once changes are agreed, they cease to be the adjustments of the Government. They become quite plainly your cuts – 'Fowler's cuts'. You are virtually on your own in defending them, so you had better be convinced of the case before you agree to them. It is for reasons like these that I crossed out the best part of two months each autumn to devote to the public-spending discussions. Almost invariably, I ended up each year in front of the Star Chamber of ministers who were set up under the chairmanship of Willie Whitelaw to try to sort out the differences which remained between ministers and the Chief Secretary.*

I announced the review of social security on Monday 2 April 1984. Most attention concentrated on the last sentence of my

* Following the 1987 general election, I found myself in the unaccustomed position of being one of the Star Chamber's judges rather than the perpetual prisoner before the bar.

statement which I had inserted just before I stood up in the House of Commons:

> Taken together the various reviews and studies I have set in hand constitute the most substantial examination of the social security system since the Beveridge report forty years ago.

It was no more than the truth. Since the war, governments had by and large ducked the issue. There had been a great deal of tinkering but no overall review. But equally it was true that the circumstances of my review were very different from those of Lord Beveridge. Beveridge had presented his report in 1942 at a time when it was overwhelmingly agreed that there should be no return to the conditions of the 1930s. Yet for all their persuasiveness, the Beveridge proposals had not been implemented. Beveridge wanted a system based on insurance, with the public making insurance contributions to finance benefits like the state pension. But Beveridge was not a member of the post-war Labour Government. No one was content to wait for insurance. Instead, the new system was introduced on the pay-as-you-go basis which has bedevilled social security finance ever since. Pay-as-you-go means that today's contributors pay for the pension of today's retired people – on the basis that the next generation will pick up the bill for today's contributors when they retire. There is no invested fund, only promises of how much future contributors will be prepared to pay.

I was reporting in a cold public-spending climate. Everywhere in the Western world social security budgets were under scrutiny, not to see if they were too meagre but to see if they could be reduced. British ministers returned from trips to other countries with tales (usually apocryphal) about how budgets were being trimmed. I had, however, one advantage that was denied to Beveridge. I was not only able to review social security, I had the opportunity as a politician of implementing the changes – always provided I could get the support of my colleagues, of course, and that was not going to be easy.

Right from the start, there were tensions with Nigel Lawson's Treasury team. What I wanted to do was to ensure that the social security budget was being spent to best effect. It was easy to become mesmerized by the size of the budget, but when you looked at it in detail you found that almost half went on pensions and other payments to the elderly; that 20 per cent went to families with children; 17 per cent went to the unemployed; and that 13 per cent went to the sick and disabled. The spending may have been great but it was not being devoted to thousands upon thousands of undeserving and feckless claimants.

My view was that we should examine whether the money was reaching those that most needed it and whether the priorities of the system laid down in 1945 were still the same. In the 1940s the elderly, often totally without pensions, were the first concern. More and more, I became convinced that the priority for the 1990s should be families with children. I believed that we should assess the future cost of the whole social security system, and make any necessary changes now. My immediate aim, however, was a cost-neutral reform – and that was going to be difficult enough. For if priorities are reordered without extra resources then inevitably there are losers as well as gainers. The conventional political wisdom is that you hear from the losers, not the gainers. Nevertheless, the Treasury were going to take some convincing that major savings in public spending were impossible. Their concern was that we should save money.

Of even greater strategic importance to the review was a condition set down by the Chancellor at the very beginning. Nigel Lawson was not prepared to contemplate any examination of the tax system. Tax policy may have a profound effect on those on low incomes, but constitutionally any changes are a matter for the Chancellor of the Exchequer. Hence the bulk of the Cabinet know only on the day of the Budget what changes are to be proposed in the afternoon. Nigel had absolutely no intention of giving up any of his rights, and thus an examination of social security and tax together was impossible. Inevitably this meant that the tax-credit system proposed by the Heath Government was not on the agenda and nor were some of the more ambitious income-guarantee schemes which inevitably required reform of taxation and social security being taken together.

By excluding taxation we missed an undoubted opportunity. Only if tax is taken into account can the overall position of any individual be seen. It is also not easy to say where social security begins and taxation ends. National Insurance is both a tax to finance current social-security spending and an entitlement to future benefit. Yet even without tax, a review of social security was eminently justified on its own account and long overdue. We paid out pensions to ten million people and Child Benefit to every family in the land. We employed over 90,000 staff. Whether tax was covered by the review or not, there were still decisions to be taken on such fundamental issues as the future of the pensions system, support for low-income families, and the special payments system which was breaking down. There was a mountain of work to be done.

For the next nine months my review teams took evidence. I continued to chair the inquiry into pensions and later took over family policy when the much liked Minister of State for Social Security, Rhodes Boyson, went off to be the number two in Northern Ireland. His place was taken by promoting Tony Newton, who was already in charge of the group looking at supplementary benefit. Tony was one of the undoubted stars of the review and became my invaluable right-hand man. No one knows social security better and no one has a greater social commitment.

As with the pensions inquiry, we recruited outside experts into the review teams like Jeremy Rowe, the deputy chairman of Abbey National, who took on Housing Benefit. The whole process was serviced and kept running by as exceptional a staff of civil servants as I ever worked with in over ten years as a Cabinet minister. We took evidence in public and this went without interruption or serious demonstration. It proved an invaluable way of putting issues on the table and encouraging serious debate. When a review of the health service was set up following the 1987 general election, it was claimed that our kind of public review would be too slow. In fact there was not much to choose between them. Our advantage, however, was that we allowed the public to have their say on possible changes *before* proposals were published.

My immediate personal priority was pensions. By June we had made sufficient progress for me to tell the House of Commons that we intended to move against the 'frozen' pension. We would require by law that the pension left behind by the early leaver should be either revalued each year or transferable to the leaver's new scheme. By July I was able to set out my proposals on personal pensions. The case put forward by the pensions industry was less than persuasive. I certainly did not want existing company schemes to collapse and saw no reason why this should happen. I did, however, want to provide the public with new options. Some people covered by the conventional company scheme might prefer a personal pension. Even more to the point, a new opportunity should be given to over 10 million people who were covered only by state provision. The essence of personal pensions was that it extended choice and encouraged personal saving. In the autumn of 1984 I introduced a bill to bring the first pension reforms into effect. So far so good – but this still left me with what was to prove the most controversial part of the whole social security review.

No sensible review of social security could avoid the fact that the State Earnings Related Pension Scheme (known by its unlovely acronym, SERPS) was stacking up an enormous future bill for the public. There were no funds building up. Everything depended on contributors picking up the bill in ten, twenty or thirty years. We had, in effect, written a post-dated cheque. Between 1985 and 2025 the number of pensioners was set to rise from 9 million to over 12 million; and the total cost of pensions for the public would rise from £17 billion a year to almost £36 billion if pensions were linked with prices and to a colossal £50 billion if they were linked, as Labour wanted, to the higher of either prices or earnings. The bill for the retired population would be borne by the working population, but the ratio of contributors to pensioners would slowly worsen so that by 2025 there would be only 1.8 contributors for each pensioner. Nor was this simply speculation. The higher number of births from the mid-1950s and through the 1960s inevitably meant more pensioners sixty years on.

That was one side of the case against SERPS. But there was also another. There was an overwhelming case for the State providing a basic pension but less of one for the State providing an additional pension as well. The second pension could be provided by an expanded pensions industry. My view was that most people would prefer a pension that was theirs by right rather than being dependent on the decisions of government. 'A pension of your own' could have the same kind of appeal as 'a house of your own'. The role of Government should be to ensure that such pensions met sensible regulation so that the public interest was protected.

These ideas were confirmed by a special Gallup Opinion Poll we commissioned for the review. Half those questioned had not heard of SERPS – which might not have been surprising had it not been that most were members of it. But the crucial finding was this. The sample was asked about the importance of having an occupational pension *additional* to the state provision. Almost 90 per cent who were in schemes, and two-thirds of those not in schemes, said it was important or 'very important'. As far as the industry was concerned, the case for SERPS was very simple. They had experienced the uncertainties of the 1960s and 1970s and they now wanted stability. Stability had not provided an increase in the number of occupational pensioners, but it had provided a secure environment for the lucky half of the nation who were covered. As for Labour, they liked SERPS mainly because it *was* state provision and they could see no reason to allow future governments the freedom to devote public spending to other areas.

In January 1985 all the review teams, the advisers and the civil servants withdrew for a snow-bound week at Wilton Park, a Foreign Office mansion deep in the Sussex countryside. Everybody was encouraged to have their say and the discussion was both productive and frank. But in the final analysis the decisions – and the responsibility – were mine.

I still have a note of the objectives for the review I set out at Wilton Park:

First I want to achieve a twin-pillar system – that is, explicit recognition that social security is not just the State alone. It also means individual contribution.

Second I want to encourage employment. Nothing is more important than that we should take down the barriers – like National Insurance and pensions – which stand in the way of new employment and job mobility.

Third I want to tackle real need. Our diagnosis of want shows that it is low-income families with children – the unemployed and low-wage earners – who are worst off.

Fourth I want to eliminate some of the complexity. The case is self-evident.

My wedding to Fiona in May 1979 together with my new stepson, Oliver

With Peter Parker, the Chairman of British Rail, in 1980

Kate being inoculated against whooping cough in front of the cameras in 1982

My team at the Department of Health and Social Security in 1983. *From left to right:* Ken Clarke, John Patten, Simon Glenarthur, Norman Fowler, Tony Newton and Rhodes Boyson

The DHSS team in 1986. *From left to right:* Tony Newton, Edwina Currie, Norman Fowler, John Major, Jean Trumpington and Nicholas Lyell

Leading the campaign against AIDS in 1986

Shaking hands with Ken Gifford, an AIDS sufferer, during a visit to San Francisco in 1987

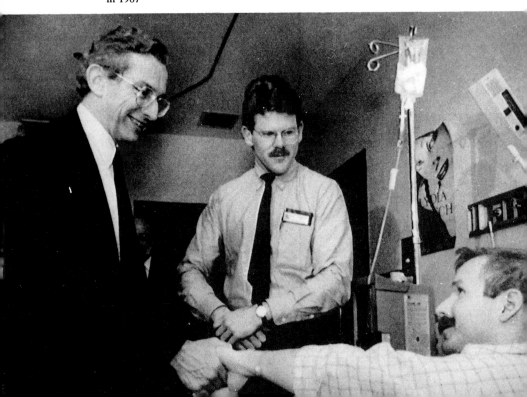

Showing a computer print-out of the hospital building programme at the Conservative Party Conference in 1986

Leaving Downing Street on the morning that the 1987 general election had been announced. *From left to right:* David Young, Paul Channon, Willie Whitelaw, Michael Jopling and Norman Fowler

A Cabinet Committee in progress at Number 10

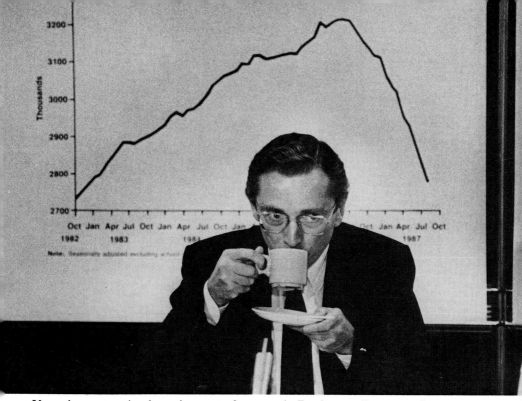

Unemployment coming down. A press conference at the Employment Department in 1987

Leaving Number 10 with Kenneth Clarke

With the children in Sutton Park in 1987

Margaret Thatcher visits Birmingham in 1987

Fifth I want to achieve a better delivery system – more co-operation with the tax system and better management.

It was against this background that the debate took place. By the end of the week the threads had been brought together and the outline of the report decided. Our proposals were that SERPS should be abolished and that the second pension should come from a variety of new options in the private sector which we would make available. Child Benefit was to stay and a new benefit, Family Credit, was to be introduced for low-income families in work so that people could no longer be worse off in work than on the dole. Supplementary Benefit was to give way to Income Support and the much-abused system of single payment was to be replaced by a Social Fund; Housing Benefit was to be reformed so that it did not discriminate against the low-paid in work; and the whole social security system was to be simplified. Among the benefits to be abolished was the Death Grant, to be replaced by a system which gave full help to families who needed it and none to those who did not.

Public spending savings mostly came from the abolition of SERPS. There were some comparatively small reductions to the Housing Benefit budget but the major savings – which ran into billions of pounds – were for the 1990s and the next century. They would allow invaluable policy options for future governments; they demonstrated that our Government looked much further ahead than the next two or three years. We had devised a new social security system which was intended to last. On leaving Wilton Park, I went to Sutton Coldfield to write up the Green Paper.

Back in London I had a foretaste of the conflicts that were to come. A special Cabinet committee under the chairmanship of Margaret Thatcher had been set up to review my proposals and effectively to decide whether they would become Government policy. Although the final decision was with Cabinet, it would be most unlikely that they would overturn the views of a committee which had spent a number of weeks going through the proposals almost line by line – particularly given that half the Cabinet were on the committee and the Prime Minister was in the chair. The decisions of the committee would be crucial in determining whether my proposals would be enacted.

Every paper to a Cabinet committee must be cleared by the Treasury. This is for the sensible reason that the last thing ministers want to do is to listen to an argument about figures being wrong. If the figures or the financial consequences are in dispute then that must be stated. The first meeting of the Social Security Committee was set for Wednesday 6 February. I needed to get my papers round before the weekend so that colleagues would have the opportunity to read them – the usual rule is that papers should be circulated to ministers seven days before a meeting. For a variety of reasons the rule is often breached, but there would be no excuse for missing the deadline with a report which had taken so long to prepare. First, however, I needed the Treasury to clear my paper – that is, to agree that it was an accurate description of the issues before the Government.

The draft went to the Treasury and on Thursday 31 January I went over to Downing Street for Cabinet. Both Norman Tebbit and John Wakeham were now back after the Grand Hotel blast and the opportunity had been taken to arrange a Cabinet photograph. Just before we were to go upstairs to be photographed, an agitated Nigel Lawson came up to me saying that he wanted a word. He had seen the draft. 'It won't do,' he said. I had made proposals on National Insurance but that, said Nigel, was a Budget matter. 'You have no authority to make proposals on National Insurance.' It was a head-on clash. There was no attempt to persuade and the result was that I blew up. I had, after all, been working on the review for the last year. I said that I had never heard anything more extraordinary. How could I make proposals on social security without mentioning National Insurance for which I had ministerial responsibility? No, said Nigel, it was not in the terms of reference. I replied that if colleagues agreed with him then we could forget about the whole review.

The argument continued up the stairs to Downing Street's reception rooms – where we paused to smile and be photographed – and all the way down again. As we sat down for Cabinet I told Nigel that we must meet afterwards. This we did – by which time we had both calmed down a little. Nigel changed tack and his tone became more accommodating. He said that he did not mind discussing changes to National Insurance with *me*, but he did not want to involve the whole Cabinet committee. I still found the argument extraordinary, but I also had to take into account the fact that if Nigel retained this stance then the committee meeting would have to be postponed and the whole exercise would get off to a terrible start.

In the end we compromised and deferred the issue for later discussion between us. As it happened that could not have worked out better. The aim of my proposals was to reduce the burden on the low paid. A few weeks later when it came to the 1985 Budget, Nigel set himself the same goal. We each had different schemes, but we shared a common purpose. It showed what could be achieved when the Treasury and the DHSS worked together.

The Cabinet's Social Security Committee met in the Downing Street Cabinet room for the first time on Wednesday 6 February 1985. Margaret Thatcher was in the chair. Nigel was conciliatory: although he would want to return to the question of public spending savings, he said that the report was a very thorough examination and also exceptionally well written. Even at this early stage it was clear that there was general sympathy for the proposition that SERPS should be phased out. The only question was what, if anything, should replace it. We here came to a central issue in all our discussions.

As SERPS was a pay-as-you-go scheme there were no immediate savings from its abolition. This is the essential dilemma (some would say dishonesty) of pay-as-you-go. SERPS consists of no more than a promise that future generations will pick up the bill. There are no reserves or investments to back these promises. If SERPS is abolished, future generations will certainly be relieved of a burden. The present generation, however, still has to finance the promises already made. The savings build up slowly – although over the years their total is immense. There is no altogether painless way of escaping from a pay-as-you-go scheme, particularly if you want people to make substitute provision. The one certainty, however, that confronted the Cabinet committee was demographic: if you left SERPS as it was then the eventual bill would become greater and greater as the proportion of contributors to pensioners declined.

My view was that we should bite the bullet, abolish SERPS and encourage substitute private pensions. In this I had the enthusiastic support of the Prime Minister who believed that the state scheme should be replaced by individual private pension provision with a minimum compulsory requirement. This took the issue a giant step forward. During the review I had been to Switzerland where I had seen a compulsory occupational scheme successfully in operation.

On Wednesday 13 February, we met for the second time with pensions as the agenda item. The only opposition to replacing SERPS with occupational or personal pension provision came from the Treasury on the grounds of cost. They were concerned about the cost of the increased tax relief which would inevitably result if the whole working population were covered by occupational pensions. The savings were major but they were in the future; the costs would arise now.

The prize, however, was that the whole working population would have a pension of their own. Personal savings would be increased and personal commitment improved. We had the opportunity to make a fundamental change, and I could not believe that we would allow that opportunity to slip away. That too was the conclusion of the special Cabinet committee and the decision was taken that SERPS should be replaced.

I now faced difficulties on another front. On Thursday 14 February the Cabinet had had its annual pre-Budget meeting when Nigel Lawson warned that public spending was still too high. Several voices were raised on the potential for savings in social security but no decision was taken. On 25 February, the special Cabinet committee turned its attention to the reform of supplementary benefit but the meeting was inconclusive. The next day I found out why. On 22 February the Chief Secretary to the Treasury, Peter Rees, had minuted the Prime Minister saying that the Chancellor and he had come to the conclusion that the Government should aim to save £2 billion from the social security review by 1987–8.

The minute stopped the Cabinet committee dead in its tracks – for the good reason that I was not prepared to go on. The disagreement was fundamental. The Chancellor wanted a promise of £2 billion in savings. I was not prepared to give it. If such a total were set down, it would blow the whole review out of the water. I saw no point in continuing until the point was settled. I spent the next few days talking to Cabinet colleagues – all of whom shared my view that the demand was preposterous – and then went to see the Prime Minister. My case was simple. If we accepted this entirely arbitrary target, the review would be seen merely as a cost-cutting exercise and not about the reform of social security. All our work of the last eighteen months would be destroyed. As at other stages of the review, Margaret Thatcher acted as mediator and the result of the meeting was that no £2 billion target was set down. The way was open for the Cabinet committee to get back to work.

Our next meeting did not take place until after the Budget in mid-March, but from then on the committee ran reasonably smoothly through to its seventh and last meeting at the start of April. At the end of this meeting I was where I wanted to be. The major changes – the replacement of SERPS, the introduction of Family Credit, Income Support and the Social Fund, and the reform of Housing Benefit – were all intact. The structure for the new social security system was there. It was as near a cost-neutral reform as was practical. We had certainly made some fully justified savings in Housing Benefit but these were a very long way from the £2 billion ambitions of the Treasury.

Outside Whitehall there was now intense speculation about what was to happen. In spite of the best endeavours of a range of correspondents, practically none of our plans had been leaked. Some of the speculation had been self-cancelling with newspapers predicting that the Government would take quite opposite courses. Much had been wrong. Our luck finally ran out on Thursday 18 April when the *Daily Telegraph* ran a lead story, not from their Social Services or Political Correspondent, but from their Economics Correspondent, Frances Williams. This predicted with remarkable accuracy that the Government had decided to scrap SERPS and that the task would be transferred to private schemes and companies.

It is idle to speculate on the source of leaks – that I did learn in my years in Government – but what was certain was that the *Telegraph* story could not have appeared at a worse time. The proposals were due to be considered by Cabinet ten days later and ministers do not like seeing what they are to discuss plastered all over the press beforehand. Even more to the point, a leak of this kind simply hands to the Opposition a weapon on a silver plate

and raises fears on your own benches. And so it was. Over the
next few days the press was busy reporting doubts about the
political wisdom of abolishing SERPS among 'ministers and Conservative MPs' while the Opposition tabled a censure motion
calling on the Government to withdraw its plans to abolish SERPS
and its 'callous dismantling of the Welfare State'.

I was in a hole. The leak was accurate and I was being forced
to the floor of the House of Commons to defend a policy before
it had been to Cabinet. I was also under no illusion that some
backbenchers on our side were nervous about the policy. The
forthcoming debate promised to be a highly uncomfortable
occasion with my defence alternating between 'no decisions have
been taken' and 'wait and see'. Neither defence was likely to go
down conspicuously well in a crowded House. At this crucial point
I was thrown a lifeline by, of all people, the Opposition Spokesman
on Social Services, Michael Meacher.

Michael Meacher had entered the House with me in 1970 and,
early on, earned a reputation as a conscientious, if rather dull,
expert in the social policy area. As the years had gone by, however,
his style had changed. He was forever denouncing me during
Parliamentary Questions in the most lurid terms but the denunci-
ations were invariably so protracted that even his own side lost
interest. Perhaps conscious that he had gained a megaphone reputation, Meacher had settled down to his own social security review.
His plan was to pre-empt my own and it is true that he was first
to publish some of his proposals. The only trouble was that under
questioning it became clear that one of his central aims was to
abolish mortgage tax relief. What was more, it was far from clear
whether the Shadow Cabinet actually supported, or indeed had
been consulted on, this proposal.

The result was the Commons debate became a debate on the
Meacher proposals, not the Fowler ones. Demonstrating that it is
not just Government ministers who get neurotic about the media,
Meacher desperately blamed 'malicious and fabricated press
reporting'. But the headlines the day after the debate said it all:
'Meacher defends benefit proposal.' 'Meacher gets a grilling.'
And even: 'Meacher says document is election winner.' This last
headline did not seem fully to express the collective view of the
Shadow Cabinet and the next instalments of the Meacher plans

for social security never appeared – much to our disappointment. But seeing off Michael Meacher proved substantially easier than seeing off the Chancellor of the Exchequer.

Cabinet consideration of the social security review was set for Thursday 25 April. The papers had been cleared by the Treasury and gone round to ministers. I had reported the results of the committee discussions and, unless an unexpected point was raised at the meeting, the outcome looked set fair. On the Tuesday night, however, my Private Secretary, Steve Godber, rang me at a dinner to tell me that at the eleventh hour Nigel Lawson had put round a minute which sought to reopen the whole issue of the replacement for SERPS. It was scarcely credible that this should happen at so late a stage and I asked the department to get the minute to me at once.

The Chancellor's minute maintained that the abolition of SERPS and the introduction of a new scheme would add to public spending. There would be the cost of additional tax relief and the extra costs for private industry and the public sector. If we made the scheme cover the self-employed, then their costs would increase too. Nigel Lawson then proposed we should either scrap SERPS and put nothing in its place or leave the whole issue until the next Parliament. But what most angered me was the last-minute timing of the intervention. Most of the points had been raised before and those which had not been raised most certainly could have been. With less than forty-eight hours before the crucial Cabinet meeting, the Chancellor of the Exchequer and the Social Services Secretary were in fundamental disagreement.

On Wednesday morning I did two things. First, I told the Cabinet Office I was not prepared to have my paper discussed with this division outstanding. Whatever the difficulties, I wanted the social security review off Thursday's Cabinet agenda. To continue would only mean chaos at the Cabinet meeting itself. Next I went to see Nigel. I have rarely been angrier than I was that day. I said that his action was indefensible and even 'unconstitutional'. By that I meant that the Treasury had cleared the papers for Cabinet and that agreement on the policy went back several months. Nigel saw my anger and was obviously surprised that I had taken the review off the Cabinet agenda. He nevertheless maintained that it would have been irresponsible of him to have gone forward without warning colleagues of his reservations. We had reached a position of stalemate – but a position which for the sake of the Government had to be settled.

This time the postponement of the ministerial discussion well and truly made the press. Accurately enough, the papers portrayed the battle as The Great Lawson v Fowler Row. The following Monday we met at Downing Street in an attempt to sort it all out. By this meeting Nigel had come up with a further solution: rather than abolish SERPS, he suggested that we modify it to the point that it could be afforded. This had always been the fall-back position, but at this late stage in the argument it cut no ice. The last person to reopen decisions already taken was Margaret Thatcher.

Over the next days we fine-tuned the scheme and made some useful improvements. The only basic concession we made to the Chancellor was to exclude the self-employed on the grounds that they were not covered by SERPS in any event. For the rest, the only changes were ones that made the scheme easier to introduce. Thus we agreed a way of phasing it in that reduced the cost of introduction but provided no disruption for those nearest retirement.

The social security review went to Cabinet in two instalments. On Thursday 2 May, I opened with a slide show which took the Cabinet through all the changes and complexities of the subject. Following this we approved most of the detailed proposals. The next Thursday, after still more work on pensions, we took the abolition of SERPS and its replacement by a compulsory occupational scheme to Cabinet. That was also agreed. The only thing that remained was to complete the writing of the Green Paper and the small matter of explaining the proposals to the House of Commons and the public. The debate in Government had taken longer than we anticipated. Nevertheless, I was determined that we would publish our Green Paper in time for a proper consultation and the preparation of legislation in the autumn. Over Whitsun we were on holiday on the Isle of Wight and I dictated the very last corrections to the Green Paper to one of my overworked social security team from a public phone box in Seaview. Publication was set for Monday 3 June.

The House was crowded for my statement. The atmosphere was more like the Budget than an announcement on social security.

Most of the Labour front bench, including Neil Kinnock, were in their places and the predictions were that I was in for a stormy time. Even stout warriors like Ken Clarke felt that all the rows, the leaks and the speculation were going to make my task difficult. Yet, as often happens in the House of Commons, the predictions of a major confrontation proved false. Making the statement, I was conscious of the silence in the House as it listened to the proposals. Then I heard the growls of support coming from our own side for proposals like Family Credit and the ending of SERPS. I sat down to a great Conservative cheer and then Michael Meacher had his opportunity. If ever a politician lost his audience with his first sentence it was Meacher. It was, he said, a 'new Victorian Poor Law' which would pave the way for the election of a Labour Government at the next election. From my side there were hoots of derision while the embarrassment on his own side was clear as Labour members found a sudden fascination in the detail of the Chamber's roof. It was game and set if not yet match.

For the next few weeks the debate on the reforms rolled on. Labour demanded that we publish illustrative figures on the effect of the changes on pensioners and claimants. This we did and, of course, the figures showed losers as well as gainers. There was nothing in the structure of the new scheme that meant there had to be losers. But dividing up the existing budget to reflect new priorities meant giving more in some areas and less in others. We could only have avoided that had we devoted some extra resources to the social security budget. I had not asked for that and, even if I had, my chances of obtaining them would have been zero.

The consultation period came to an end on 16 September and we then got down to work assessing the reaction. It is no weakness to take notice of what is being said in such a consultation. The press always urge you to do so – and then, when you do, immediately write it up as a U-turn. But there is every reason to try to get as much support for change as possible. For example, our original proposal was that Family Credit should be paid through the pay-packet. This had a number of advantages. It brought tax and benefit closer together, and putting family credit explicitly on the pay-slip showed total new earnings – demonstrating, among other things, the gap between take-home wages and unemployment pay. But a range of people inside and outside the House of Commons, including Emma Nicholson, then the women's Vice-Chairman of the Conservative Party, wanted payment to go direct to the mother. It was a policy aimed more towards the family than to employment, and I could see her point. With some regret we eventually changed our proposal so that Family Credit went straight to the mother.

There were other issues, like the Social Fund, but the big question remained pensions. I was becoming dangerously isolated. I had against me virtually the whole of the pensions industry. They were petrified that private pensions for all would mean a return to the years of political uncertainty. Over the previous eighteen months the pensions industry had had enough change thrust on them to last a lifetime. They regarded compulsory occupational pensions as several bridges too far and it was clear that they would continue to campaign against my proposals. Yet it was the industry which necessarily I had to rely on to deliver the goods. Even more ominously, both the CBI and the influential Engineering Employers' Federation had moved against me. They were concerned at the added costs they feared industry would have to bear. Yet even at this stage I would have proceeded had I been sure of my political support.

Margaret Thatcher remained totally stalwart in her support throughout, but not everybody took the same view. In particular, the events of the last six months had revealed the intractable opposition of the Treasury. Nigel Lawson had made no secret of the fact that he saw the proposals as financially prohibitive. The successful introduction of a national occupational pension scheme was by any standards a massive undertaking. There were bound to be administrative problems and questions to be ironed out. To embark on this course without the support of the providers of the pensions, of the companies who were going to help finance them or of the Treasury itself was an extremely doubtful venture. I could be tripped up at any stage.

As long as I live I will regret having to abandon our plans to give an occupational pension to every worker in the country. It was the worst decision that I had ever had to take in Government. That is not to say it was the wrong decision. Given the position in November 1985, there was no other decision for a politician to take. My Green Paper set out what I believed we should do. My White Paper six months later set out what I could guarantee to deliver. I had to get an already highly controversial bill through both Houses of Parliament and then introduce the new system without serious accident. It was going to be a major battle and there were plenty of press predictions that the radical changes would cost us the next general election. It is a good rule for a government entering a battle of that kind to be united. We were not. To have taken on the world in that state would have been political suicide. I was not paid to preside over disasters – however noble the cause. I had to think again.

One advantage of the Green-Paper debate was that the discussion had moved on. When I had started to examine pensions, many in the industry were opposed to any change in SERPS and almost everyone was opposed to personal pensions. Eighteen months later, personal pensions were accepted and the new consensus was that the Government should save money by reducing the benefits of SERPS rather than abolishing it. Just before Christmas 1985, I published the White Paper which set out the Government's new proposals for legislation. By a number of changes we reduced the emerging cost of SERPS by an eventual £13 billion, but the crucial part of the proposals were the new options we gave to the public. It was made easier for companies to set up their own schemes and for the first time everyone would be given the right of a personal pension of their own. Unit trusts, building societies and banks would be able to provide personal pensions and Nigel Lawson agreed that a 2 per cent National Insurance incentive should be given to those who joined the new schemes. The expansion of occupational and personal pensions remained a firm objective of the reforms.

The compromise was accepted by industry and the opposition melted away. There were fierce fights along the way – particularly in the House of Lords – but the concession on pensions took much of the wind out of the Opposition's sails. The legislation went on to the statute book in July 1986 and the new system was finally introduced in April 1988.

And what has been the effect of the reforms? Family Credit now provides double the spending power for low-income families than its predecessor scheme and more help is provided for children through the Income Support system. The Social Fund has been successfully introduced without all the problems nervously predicted by some of the experts. The unemployment trap has been substantially eased and the simplification of social security has had major effects. The whole system is now operating more efficiently. The time taken to process claims has been reduced; the error rate is down; and claimants are spending less time waiting. Social security is no longer a jungle of files and paper where only the skilled claimant triumphs. Yet in many ways the most spectacular success has been the new pension options. Over four million people have taken out personal pensions. Over 800,000 people are now covered by new occupational pension schemes. Contrary to the industry's predictions, existing company schemes have not collapsed. The public have been provided with more choices, and have shown that they want a pension which is theirs by right.

The social security review made some fundamental improvements, but that should not be the end of reform in this area. Very rarely can you finish the process of change in one step. The progressive stage-by-stage reform of trade union legislation shows a more useful model for modern government. The case for abolishing SERPS altogether and for second pensions to be provided by funded schemes in the private sector remains powerful. We need to make more progress in achieving a decade of retirement between the ages of sixty and seventy with men and women deciding for themselves when they want to retire. We need to provide a basic income guarantee for pensioners which will benefit existing pensioners who have retired without the benefit of today's occupational schemes. Above all, a new review should build on the improvements we made but correct the mistake of 1985 and consider social security and tax together.

According to Beveridge there were five giants on the road of national reconstruction in 1942: Disease, Ignorance, Squalor, Idleness and Want. By providing income, social security is the most effective means of tackling want. It may be technical and difficult to understand but no policy area is more important for poor people. Regular – and open – reviews of how we are meeting the challenge of want should be a feature of modern government.

CHAPTER 12

After Westland

Guardian

There comes a point in most ministerial careers when you consider resignation on an issue of policy. Doubtless in any government there are ministers sufficiently flexible to accept and defend any decision but they are fewer than popular legend would have it. Most ministers have sticking points and the determination to make a stand. Of course resignation is an exceptional course. Ministerial politics must have a give and take. There are disagreements and debates on any number of issues. A minister on the losing side of the argument will usually accept the majority decision. Only if that disagreement is fundamental to him would he consider resignation if he found himself in the minority. A minister who finds himself in the perpetual position of considering his position is in the wrong government or conceivably should not be in politics at all. Resignation is a serious matter both for the minister and for the government. The minister faces an indefinite career in the 'wilderness' away from office; the government can be seriously weakened if not wrecked by ministers deciding to leave. The early months of 1986 saw two resignations which shook the Thatcher Government to its foundations and it was in the immediate aftermath of these that I faced a crucial decision about my own future.

The Westland row had been smouldering for some months during the summer and autumn of 1985, but it was only as we approached the Christmas recess that press and political attention turned to it in a serious way. Up to then the issue seemed relatively small. The debate centred on a small helicopter company called Westland which was based in Yeovil with a workforce of about 7,000. It was Britain's only helicopter-maker but some way from being one of the nation's leading industrial companies. Faced with bankruptcy, the company in June had brought in a new chairman, Sir John Cuckney, a renowned trouble-shooter whom I had known when he had run the Port of London Authority. Cuckney's view was that there was no way in which Westland could survive on its own and the only chance of success lay in seeking an overseas partner. On 24 September Cuckney reported to the Government that, although talks were still continuing with prospective European partners, the most promising course seemed to be that the American company United Technologies should take a stake in Westland. One of the subsidiary companies of United Technologies was the Sikorsky helicopter company.

On 16 October, the ministers most involved with Westland – including Leon Brittan, the new Trade and Industry Secretary, and Michael Heseltine, the Defence Secretary – met under Margaret Thatcher's chairmanship. The decisions taken at this meeting laid down the course of the dispute. Most of the group felt that there were no overwhelming defence or industrial arguments why the Government should have a view on the ownership of Westland. Helicopters were not in the same class as the European fighter where co-operation between the European powers was essential. At the same time, however, Michael Heseltine was given the group's blessing to promote a rival European consortium. The prevailing attitude in the group at the time was that if he could bring that off then 'good luck to him'. The only stipulation was that the Government would remain neutral and the choice would remain firmly with the Westland board. In retrospect it seems a curious arrangement to allow a government minister to promote an alternative course but then not to advocate it.

When the same group of ministers met at the beginning of December there was still no definite European proposal on the table. They met twice, but inconclusively, and a full meeting of 'E' Committee, the Cabinet's Economic Committee, was then set for Monday 9 December under the chairmanship of Margaret Thatcher. By this stage there were unmistakable signs that a bid from a rival European consortium was likely to materialize and it was agreed that they should have until the end of the week to make definite proposals.

As the week progressed a European consortium of companies including British Aerospace did make a counter proposal to the Westland board. There now came one of the crucial points in the Westland saga. Michael Heseltine believed that the emergence of a definite European offer created a new situation and that there should be a further meeting of 'E' Committee on Friday 13 December. He believed that such a further meeting was necessary to enable the Government to reconsider its position of neutrality

and, what was more, that such a meeting had been promised by
Margaret Thatcher at the Monday meeting of 'E'. He regarded
the refusal to hold such a meeting as a denial of his right as a
Cabinet minister to put his case to his colleagues. Nevertheless
whatever the rights of that dispute, no further meeting of 'E' took
place and the Government's position remained one of neutrality.

A meeting which did take place on Friday 13 December was
that of the Westland board of directors who agreed to recommend
the offer they had received from United Technologies. Their
decision brought them smack into conflict with Michael Heseltine.
Michael's view was that the Government should continue its policy
of buying helicopters developed and manufactured in Europe.
Such a policy kept technology and jobs in Britain and allowed the
development of a European market comparable to the giant market
in the United States. He believed that Sikorsky's plan was quite
simply to extend the market for American helicopters and was
therefore entirely against his declared policy of encouraging European collaboration. As to the argument that the Government
should not intervene, his reply was that governments had always
taken a view on the ownership of defence companies. The Government was Westland's biggest customer.

Michael was jubilant, therefore, when on Friday 20 December a
new plan was unveiled by the European consortium which included
British Aerospace as well as Aerospatiale of France, MBB of West
Germany and Augusta of Italy. The bid was nicely judged and
analysts differed on which group now offered Westland the best
future – although the workforce favoured the Sikorsky bid. It was
clear that the commercial battle was going to be hard fought. The
assumption of most ministers like myself who were not involved
in the discussion was that politically the issue would also now be
settled. The future of a small West Country helicopter company
did not seem the stuff of which Government crises were made.
That happy belief, however, began to be shattered as newspaper
headlines like 'War of Words over Westland' and 'Heseltine's
Helicopter War' started to appear over the Christmas period. The
Government's official position was one of neutrality. Publicly, however, we appeared split with ministers taking strongly opposite
views on the final outcome.

Nevertheless, when I left for Washington and New York on

3 January for talks with both Government and industry leaders
there, I still could not believe that the Government was heading
for crisis. It was in Washington that I received a message that a
Cabinet meeting had been called for Thursday 9 January. Ostensibly the purpose was to clear Kenneth Baker's Green Paper on
the reform of the rates, but everyone also understood that it would
be used to reconcile the Westland affair. I arrived back at Heathrow at 10 p.m. on the Wednesday night and was briefed on the
car phone coming into London. This was to the effect that the
dispute remained unresolved and no one knew just how the next
day's Cabinet meeting was to proceed.

There had been various developments over the last few days.
The most important was a letter from the Solicitor-General, Sir
Patrick Mayhew, which had found its way into the press. The letter
appeared to suggest that on the Government's best legal advice
there had been 'material inaccuracies' in a letter Michael Heseltine
had sent to the bank representing the European consortium. During my time away the position had worsened and it was now taking
on the appearance of a bitter conflict between the Defence Secretary and the Prime Minister.

For Cabinet on Thursday morning, 9 January, I sat in my usual
place three or four down from the centre of the table facing the
Prime Minister. On my immediate right sat Michael Heseltine.
Although ending in unprecedented drama it was at no stage a
stormy meeting. Margaret Thatcher read out some of the newspaper headlines there had been over the past few days, illustrating
well enough the terrible press which the Government was receiving
as a result of the dispute. Everyone around the Cabinet table
agreed that the public debate had to be brought to an end.

There was also agreement that the decision on the future of
Westland was now a matter for the shareholders. Whatever may
have been the history of the row, the shareholders now had two
offers in front of them and it was up to them to choose. The
Cabinet, including Michael, agreed that there should be no
attempt to influence the Westland board one way or the other.

The break point came not on the substance of the Westland
issue – that had been decided – but on how press enquiries were
to be handled. On this Margaret proposed that all statements on
the issue should be cleared by the Cabinet Office. Michael took

the view that it was not practical for the Defence Department to defer to the Cabinet Office every time a newspaper rang up with a question. Michael was not prepared to submit to the suggested procedure; Margaret was not prepared to change course. The result was that to the stunned disbelief of the Cabinet Michael quietly closed his folder, said that he could not continue as a Cabinet member, and walked to the door.

The last act was played at such speed that I do not think anyone could have successfully prevented what took place. The standpoints were incompatible and certainly irreconcilable in the time we had at our disposal. Margaret Thatcher was certainly right that the division in the Government had to be brought to an end. We were in danger of becoming a laughing stock. No Government can conceivably command respect if ministers and departments squabble between themselves. On the other hand, Michael Heseltine was right to fear the outcome of a Cabinet meeting in which it had been decided that he and his own department could not speak to the press without first checking with the Cabinet Office. I had written on my pad 'Heseltine silenced' and there is no doubt that that is how it would have been seen. The press would have written stories about a humiliating defeat for the Defence Secretary.

Whether Michael was right to walk out or not is a matter of judgement, but he was right to fear the consequences of accepting what appeared to be becoming the conclusion of the Cabinet meeting. Still slightly jet-lagged, I was puzzling how this procedural row could be more satisfactorily resolved when Michael's folder closed and he left the table. But I doubt whether any intervention would have more than postponed the evil day. Relations between the two had broken down.

The result of Michael's departure was that the Government lost one of its most effective ministers and one of its best communicators. But it was not just the political loss that concerned me. I regretted the loss of a colleague whom I had enjoyed working with since 1975. At several crucial stages in my political career he had given me support. He offered encouragement at the time of my unsought 1976 reshuffle. He had supported my plans on privatization in transport when certainly some thought I was pushing too fast. He is criticized for being impetuous and that quality can hardly be denied. Against that there is another quality which receives little attention. You could talk to Michael in total confidence knowing that the contents of any conversation would not be revealed. As a politician he walks by himself and keeps his own counsel. Perhaps it was those very qualities which stopped him drumming up support from ministers like me who had not been on the Cabinet committee which looked at Westland. I was not alone among his friends in being totally unprepared for the dramatic developments of that morning. Michael's loss was bad enough but on both the political and personal fronts there was worse to come.

Cabinet continued in a rather shell-shocked way for another ninety minutes. The only unusual feature was that we were given an unprecedented coffee break after Geoffrey Howe had finished his report on international affairs. When we came back Margaret Thatcher announced that George Younger would take over Michael's job and one of the Government's brightest young stars, Malcolm Rifkind, would take over as Scottish Secretary. We completed a consideration of the local government Green Paper which was to lead to the introduction of the community charge and, as it happened, an even more serious political dispute than Westland. The Cabinet ended at just after midday. Michael's resignation had taken everyone, including the press, by surprise. He had left Downing Street with only a solitary photographer there to record the moment. By the time we emerged the press and television were there in force. There was also no doubt who was now the centre of attention. As we made for our cars the comments which were most sought were those of Leon Brittan.

When the House resumed on Monday 13 January it was Leon rather than the Prime Minister who had the thankless task of making the Westland statement. Yet the only trouble came when he was asked by Michael Heseltine, followed by others, whether he had received a letter from Sir Raymond Lygo, the Chief Executive of British Aerospace. His reply was that he had not, and most of us gave no more thought to the matter. Later in the evening a notice went up on the annunciator in the House of Commons that Leon was to make another statement at 10 p.m. that night.

Statements at 10 p.m. are very unusual and reserved for matters of only the greatest urgency. They are also extremely difficult to handle in the post-prandial atmosphere, as I had every reason to remember. In November 1984, I had been required to make a statement on a social security change which affected striking miners in the very midst of the coal strike. As I went to the dispatch box, the centre of the chamber was taken over by about thirty Labour MPs led by Eric Heffer and Tony Benn. My statement was torn from my hands by a Labour MP, Dave Nellist, and the sitting of the Commons was suspended, 'grave disorder having arisen' as Hansard records.

Leon fared better than that but only just. For what transpired was that a letter had been sent from British Aerospace but from the Chairman, Sir Austin Pearce, not the Chief Executive. It had also not gone to Leon but to the Prime Minister with the proviso that it was not being copied to anyone else. Leon had been told about the letter only minutes before going into the House to make the statement and took the view that he was precluded from mentioning a letter marked 'private and strictly confidential'.

He apologized, but as during the Falklands debate four years earlier the House wanted blood. The assumption was that the letter backed up Michael Heseltine's assertion that the Government, although officially neutral, had in fact told British Aerospace that they did not approve of their presence in the European consortium. The ever-patrician Roy Jenkins observed that whenever the Prime Minister and the Industry Secretary were together, 'we shall count our spoons quickly'. More damagingly, a Conservative, Patrick Cormack, intervened to ask Leon: 'Does he not feel that his inglorious part in this long and unhappy chapter should come to an end?' Leon's future seemed to depend on his performance in the Westland debate on Wednesday 15 January.

As it happened Leon made a strong speech and for a few days the clouds lifted. But any rejoicing was premature. On Thursday 23 January, Margaret Thatcher made a statement on the inquiry that had been set up to investigate how the Solicitor-General's letter had come to appear in the press. The answer was that – with the agreement of officials at Downing Street – the contents had been rung through to the Press Association by a press officer in the Department of Trade and Industry. The row started again with a new intensity.

I spent Friday morning defending Leon in a series of radio

interviews, but during my evening advice bureau in Sutton Coldfield the news came through that he had resigned. He had in effect
taken personal responsibility for everything that had taken place.
His departure represented another great blow for the Government
and a cruel personal setback for Leon. He should never have been
moved from his job as Home Secretary which he was carrying out
with genuine distinction. Had he been allowed to continue, he
would have gone down as a great reforming Home Secretary. Leon
was the most outstanding of our generation at Cambridge and
countless profiles remark on his intellectual strength. But what I
remember of him from the years at Cambridge and the period just
afterwards was a different quality. He was sought out for advice.
In the 1960s, if you ever went to his flat, the phone would be
ringing with yet more requests for guidance. His own generation
rated him very highly and most of us viewed his resignation with
a mixture of dismay and disbelief.

There was one more major scene. On the following Monday,
27 January, there was a short emergency debate. The predictions
were that Margaret Thatcher could well become the third victim
of the Westland affair and Margaret was herself under no illusion
that she was fighting for her political life. But as the debate progressed the danger receded. Neil Kinnock made a long, rambling
and ineffective attack which was generally counted a Parliamentary
disaster. Margaret Thatcher replied well and Leon Brittan
explained quietly and with dignity the reasons for his resignation.
Michael Heseltine ended his own speech in almost Party Conference mood:

> In what has been a difficult and stressful experience for the
> Conservative Party, let us understand clearly where we stand
> tonight. We shall be in the lobby together with one purpose –
> to maintain a Tory party in power in this country and to keep
> the Labour party out.

The one unexplained mystery of the Westland affair was why
Margaret Thatcher, a decisive leader if ever there was one, allowed
the crisis to develop. She could have headed it off by calling in
Michael to Downing Street to have it out with him face to face.
She did not do that and nor did she send a suggested letter to

Michael. Another course would have been to have had a meeting of 'E' Committee on Friday 13 December irrespective of whether it was promised or not, so that he could have put his case. Best of all would have been a full and early Cabinet discussion. As it was, we had the worst of every world. We lost two senior Cabinet ministers and the Government appeared both indecisive and divided.

A week after Westland ended, Leyland began. In terms of industrial importance the future of British Leyland's car, truck, van and bus company dwarfed Westland. The car business of Austin Rover produced 465,000 vehicles in 1985. They had some 18 per cent of the British car market and exported almost a quarter of their production. Altogether the company employed 67,000 in the United Kingdom.

Although it took its corporate name from the truck operations in Leyland, Lancashire, the company was entirely crucial to my own area of the West Midlands where it had many of its plants. Austin cars were made at Longbridge in Birmingham, and Jaguars at Coventry. Land Rovers were built on a 300-acre site about a mile from the National Exhibition Centre in Solihull and Freight Rover vans were produced at the Common Lane factory in Birmingham. In addition to this there were scores of component manufacturers dotted throughout the West Midlands. For every job in the vehicle assembly business, there were reckoned to be about three others with component makers and car dealers. Under any circumstances British Leyland was an important company to me, but in February 1986 it was doubly so. Nationally unemployment was over three million and the West Midlands was one of the worst hit areas with a rate of almost 16 per cent.

On Monday 3 February a front page story appeared in the *Daily Mail* under the headline 'Leyland Sell-Out Storm'. This was to the effect that the whole company was up for sale and that negotiations were at an advanced stage. General Motors was the favourite to take over the commercial vehicles business including Land Rover; and Honda was thought to be bidding for the cars. In the afternoon Paul Channon, who had taken over from Leon Brittan as Trade and Industry Secretary, was forced to make a statement in the Commons. He confirmed the General Motors' interest but revealed that, rather than Honda, it was Ford who were discussing taking over the car business.

As far as I was concerned, the publicly revealed position was totally unsatisfactory. I was a Cabinet member from the West Midlands whose constituency included many workers and managers who were either employed by Leyland or whose companies relied upon it. However, I had known nothing of this dramatic development of policy. I had not been consulted. I had not even been advised that such developments were in the offing. Yet it was becoming crystal clear that the strategy of sale had been approved by the Cabinet's Economic Committee.

I was a member of the Cabinet but I was also Member of Parliament for Sutton Coldfield. It was not my job to defend local interests irrespective of the commercial and industrial arguments. It was my job to evaluate the proposals on the basis of my local knowledge. After all, it was I who would have to defend the policies locally. I had been as exasperated as everyone else by the performance of the company in the 1970s, but that was before the company's dismal industrial relations performance was tackled. The steady transformation of Leyland symbolized one part of the Thatcher revolution. Yet here we were preparing to sell off the whole company lock, stock and barrel.

British Leyland had been formed in 1968 after a long line of mergers going back to the 1950s. Under its control were some of the best-known names in the British motor industry: Austin, Morris, Jaguar, Rover, Triumph. On occasions outstandingly innovative products like the Mini had come on to the market, but commercial success had eluded the company. There were far too many models in the range and the potential stars were not successfully developed. A tale is told that in the mid-1970s the chief engineer of Daimler-Benz saw the new Jaguar XJ 12 for the first time and exclaimed: 'Amazing, thank God you can't make it.' A combination of appalling industrial relations and weak management was bringing the company to its knees.

By the 1970s British Leyland was running into severe financial difficulties and in 1975 the Labour Government in effect nationalized the company. But nationalization did nothing to solve the crisis and in 1977 the company lost 250,000 cars through strike action of one kind or another. It was in that year that Michael Edwardes took over as chairman and the long slow recovery began. A determined Edwardes outfaced the militants on the shop floor and re-established the authority of the management. He changed the over-centralized structure of the business, devolved back to factory level and restored some of the pride in the product.

The company was not remotely out of the woods by 1986 but it had travelled a long way to recovery. Austin Bide, Edwardes' successor, had continued the turn round and now Graham Day stood in the wings ready to take over. I wanted to see the recovery continue. With difficulty the company had weathered the recession of the early 1980s and my feeling was that it could re-establish itself. If the Ford takeover went through then the whole British car industry would be owned by overseas companies. I did not agree with that on either industrial or political grounds.

The public had warmed to Michael Edwardes' efforts to restore the company to profitability. My guess was that they would not want to see Britain's last car manufacturer go into overseas ownership. To brand this as anti-American was absurd. The case for British Leyland not being sold as a job lot to Ford or General Motors had nothing to do with anti-Americanism nor indeed any other form of xenophobia. Leyland, after all, had pioneered a partnership arrangement with the Japanese company Honda which had proved notably successful. There was no reaction against that in the West Midlands.

The obvious difference between the new proposals and the link with Honda was that ownership passed. Decisions about the future of the British motor industry would be taken outside Britain. Competition would be reduced; dealers would be eliminated; and component manufacturers would be put at risk. At the time General Motors was under fire for its lack of commitment to British suppliers. I was all in favour of collaboration and alliances. In the modern motor industry it was difficult to see how companies could progress without them. But the case would have to be overwhelming for the whole company to be sold off. I noted that Germany, France and Italy still managed to have national motor industries.

On Wednesday 5 February the Labour Opposition forced a full-scale debate on the British Leyland position. The issues at stake had an uncomfortable resemblance to Westland – only this time no one could write off the row as a peripheral issue of industrial policy. For Paul Channon it was an uncomfortable beginning.

His strongest point in the debate was that the Government had already put £2.2 billion into British Leyland and were standing behind another £1.5 billion of additional obligations. By any measure these were substantial sums and there was no reason why the taxpayer should continue indefinitely to shoulder such a burden.

The Labour Party simply wanted the company to stay as a state-owned enterprise irrespective of the losses. Like most other Conservative MPs I wanted to see the company returned to the private sector, but I did not equate privatization with simply selling off the company to overseas buyers. That was also one of the unmistakable messages that came from the vote at the end of the debate. The Labour motion on Leyland was easily defeated by 129 votes, but when the House was asked to approve the Government amendment that endorsed the principle of a merger between the commercial vehicle activities of BL and General Motors the majority fell to 86. The missing votes indicated Conservative abstentions and the prospect of another damaging political storm.

On the Wednesday evening I was told by John Wakeham, the Chief Whip, that there were 'rumbles' in the lobbies that I and Peter Walker (who represented another West Midlands constituency, Worcester) would ride to British Leyland's rescue. I replied that I had talked to neither Peter nor the press. I did, however, intend to raise the subject at Cabinet the next day. I felt strongly that Cabinet ministers with a clear interest should be at least kept in the picture and not hear the news for the first time through the papers.

Early on Thursday morning, I received a telephone call inviting me to join the discussion of 'E' Committee on British Leyland which would follow Cabinet. I was happy to do that, but I still felt that the issue should also be discussed at full Cabinet. Accordingly at our meeting at 10.30 a.m. I raised what was rapidly becoming the Leyland row. My first point was that I believed that Cabinet members with a special regional interest should be brought into discussions of this kind. If that was not done, they were left in the impossible position of having to either accept or reject a decision already taken. Margaret Thatcher immediately accepted my point. The result was a declared policy from Margaret that Cabinet ministers with an important departmental, constituency or regional interest in matters like the future of British Leyland should be kept in touch and should not hear of developments for the first time when they appeared in the press. That has remained the policy of Government ever since.

Next I raised the central issue of the talks themselves and in particular the position of Ford. I argued that we should recognize the great improvement in industrial relations and productivity that had taken place over the last few years at British Leyland and predicted that we would have very substantial political problems seeing a Ford takeover through. As we went around the table it became evident that there was little support for the sale post Westland. The discussion at Cabinet was short, given that all the major players had now been invited to the 'E' Committee following.

At 'E' the decision was taken to break off talks with Ford. Whatever may have been the Committee's original view, the majority now clearly thought that a sale to Ford was either the wrong policy or not feasible. Even some of those who were sympathetic to the sale considered it 'a bridge too far' in the political aftermath of Westland. There was nothing to be gained in pursuing talks which the majority of the Committee felt were doomed to failure. Rather than allow the row to run on, it was decided to bring the negotiations to an end.

Three hours after ministers had reached their decision, it was announced in the House of Commons by Paul Channon. Labour's Industry spokesman, John Smith, spluttered with some rage that his fox had been shot. By the same token, there was relief on our benches that we had not continued with what to many seemed an unwinnable policy. It was, however, not the end of the Leyland story.

We still had to decide General Motors' bid for British Leyland's commercial vehicles. At first sight the issues here seemed easier, but that belief was soon dispelled. The commercial vehicle business consisted of Leyland trucks, Freight Rover vans, and, most controversially of all, Land Rover. Financially, trucks were in heavy loss. On a turnover of about £284 million they were making a loss before tax of £63 million. On the other hand, both Land Rover and Freight Rover were profitable.

Founded just after the Second World War, Land Rover had been for a time the world leader in its class. But it had frittered away that lead. It had suffered from being a small part of a big corporation determined to remain a mass car producer. Land Rover had been starved of investment and had not been developed to meet its potential. Remorselessly, the Japanese had taken over and properly exploited the four-wheel-drive market. Nevertheless Land Rover remained a world-famous marque. It employed 8,400 people and had a turnover of £380 million. The outlook for the four-wheel-drive market was good and the potential for the development of the business immense. Sensibly enough, General Motors was prepared to take the trucks as part of the price of gaining control of Land Rover.

There was, however, another part of the General Motors agenda. The Birmingham-based Freight Rover made Sherpa vans and was to be part of the sale. The management and workforce at Freight Rover had shown just what could be done in turning round a company. Until 1980, Freight Rover was part of the volume car business and had no separate identity. That was given to it by Michael Edwardes. By 1982 it was out of loss and by 1985 was making a healthy profit. Freight Rover had done everything that we the Government had wanted. It had shed staff, raised productivity and turned losses into profits. Its reward threatened to be closure. For the prospect was that after a short interval Freight Rover in Birmingham would be closed down and the operations moved to the Bedford plant in Luton. Bedford was already owned by General Motors but it was struggling to survive.

Anyone who believed that American or any other overseas ownership was an automatic recipe for success had only to look at the General Motors van and truck operation at Luton. Their financial results were disastrous. In spite of new investment they had made hefty pre-tax losses in both of the last two years put to us. In 1983 they had made a loss of £52 million on a turnover of £340 million; and in 1984 a loss of £62 million on a turnover of £335 million. It was not then surprising that what General Motors wanted was to take over the successful van business of Freight Rover and rebadge the vans as Bedfords.

During February General Motors pressed hard for the deal to be completed. In the last week of the month a new Cabinet committee was formed specifically to look at BL's commercial business. This time I was a member, as was Peter Walker, and the group was chaired by Margaret Thatcher. We were presented with an ultimatum from General Motors. They had been invited by the Department of Trade and Industry to explore the prospects of rationalizing the British commercial vehicle sector as long ago as 1984. Not surprisingly, they were becoming impatient. From their point of view negotiations had been dragging on too long and they now wanted a decision. Their proposition was that they should have exclusive negotiating rights with British Leyland and that an agreement should be reached by Easter. They also made it crystal clear that they wanted Land Rover and were not interested in any sale which did not give them that.

By now, however, General Motors had other competitors in the takeover battle. As the position had become public, other groups expressed interest. One of the most serious of the counter bids came from a management buy-out team led by David Andrews, the BL director responsible for Land Rover, and advised by Schroeders. Like the other bidders, however, they suffered from one drawback. Although the bid covered Land Rover (including the upmarket Range Rover) and Freight Rover, it did not extend to Leyland trucks. If we were interested in an outright sale of all the businesses as one, General Motors was the clear leader.

In early March we had a series of meetings in which we went through the options. As far as the British Leyland business was concerned, the profit forecasts for 1986 showed Land Rover and Freight Rover with good profits but with Leyland Trucks still showing a big loss. Whatever solution was adopted it was clear that the position of the truck business would have to be tackled and job losses would result. As for the General Motors plan, public opinion was running strongly against Land Rover going into overseas ownership. Personally I remained very concerned about the Freight Rover position. It seemed clear that by 1990 Freight Rover's factory in Birmingham would be closed and production centred on Luton.

Behind the scenes there was great lobbying by the rival camps but the dilemma remained the same. General Motors had the resources to develop the commercial vehicle business but no great track record of success. If we went that way then ownership of the business would also pass overseas. At the other extreme there was the management buy-out proposal which kept the business in the country but which did not have the resources necessary to develop

Land Rover and Freight Rover, let alone take on the ailing truck business. It all led to a most uncomfortable conclusion: namely that none of the proposals so far on the table provided the solution to the problem of British Leyland's commercial vehicles operation.

On Tuesday 18 March, the Leyland committee met for the fourth time. Paul Channon reported that he was to see David Andrews and that negotiations were continuing with General Motors. There was no further meeting that week but three days later, on the Friday, the press once again intervened. *The Times* led the paper with a story that 'a compromise deal' had been put to General Motors which would give them 49 per cent of British Leyland's commercial vehicles business. A similar piece appeared in the *Financial Times*. Theories varied on what would happen to the other 51 per cent but the likeliest seemed that it would be eventually sold too. It appeared not unlike the course I had chosen back in 1981 to take the British Transport Docks Board into the private sector. My course had been an irrevocable step to privatization. This seemed to be an equally irrevocable step to control and ownership passing to General Motors.

On the Friday morning I was both in London and in my office. I immediately sent off a minute to Margaret Thatcher expressing my concern. My minute to the Prime Minister said:

BRITISH LEYLAND

I would like briefly to register my concern at the reports in *The Times*, *Financial Times* and other papers today. I am concerned that the kind of arrangements outlined in these papers will mean – and will be seen to mean – that control will have passed to General Motors. It is open to debate whether such a move would be in the interests of Land Rover but it is difficult to see how it can be in the interests of Freight Rover. I do not know of course how accurate these reports are but I hope that we can seek to avoid fresh newspaper stories over the weekend prior to any discussion we may have next week.

I also took one further action. I ensured that a message was transmitted to Number 10 that I would have to consider my position in the Government if the plan set out in the press went through. I had never threatened resignation before, although at times I had been engaged in fierce rows. On this occasion, however, industrial, political and crucial local interests all came together for me. I accepted that not all the arguments went one way. Although there were many in the Midlands and elsewhere who agreed with me, there were others who thought that an alliance with General Motors was the way forward. It is not my purpose to argue that case again. I simply record that I was in fundamental disagreement and in those circumstances I felt that any self-respecting minister should go. To underline my concern I sent a further message to Number 10 on Friday afternoon just before I left for my constituency.

As it happened I occupied a strong political position. The Government had already lost two Cabinet ministers because of Westland. To have lost a third two months later would have been counted a political disaster. But such thoughts were a very long way from my mind at the time. The future of British Leyland was not an issue I had wanted to confront in the aftermath of Westland. The threat of resignation was not a step lightly taken. I did not weigh up whether I would win or not. I sought to make a judgement on a position which vitally affected the interests of the region I represented in Parliament. It was an issue I could not avoid. I would not have forgiven myself had the deal gone through with my silent acquiescence.

As the weekend came, events once more moved very quickly. By now Paul Channon had an impossible task. General Motors wanted control of Land Rover as well as the van and truck business but such a step would force me out of the Government. On Saturday I was rung by the press to be told that the deal had broken down and the General Motors negotiators were returning to the United States. And so it proved. General Motors had stuck to their guns and wanted immediate and undoubted control. They were not interested in a sale which excluded Land Rover. There was no ground for compromise.

On the following Monday, 24 March, there was a further meeting of the Leyland committee when Paul Channon reported the outcome of his talks. The next day the issue came to Cabinet. There were some ministers who were badly disappointed at the outcome and there was one suggestion that negotiations should be reopened. The prospect, however, of a fresh approach being made

to General Motors was resisted. It was by no means certain, in
any event, that General Motors would want to resume talks. I had
not known that they had been invited to produce plans for the
rationalization of British Leyland's commercial vehicles but I could
well appreciate their frustration. They had already spent months
on what had proved to be an entirely fruitless task.

On Tuesday afternoon Paul Channon made a further statement
in the House of Commons announcing that 'the talks have been
ended'. He explained:

> General Motors wished to have effective control of the company
> from the outset and an assurance of full ownership and control
> within a relatively short period, and it became clear that it was
> not able to compromise on these points.

I had been dealing with Social Service questions that afternoon
and remained on the front bench to hear Paul's statement. This
time it was the turn of Bedfordshire Members of Parliament, like
David Madel and Graham Bright, to complain at what they saw
as a missed opportunity to establish Luton as the centre of General
Motors' European operations. They obviously felt that the Midlands had had more than its fair share of influence in the decision.
Margaret Thatcher, who was sitting a few places away from me,
turned to me to say, 'You won, Norman. Next time we will have
some Luton members in the Cabinet.'

Five years later I remain unrepentant about my role. It may not
have endeared me to all my colleagues but I would certainly do
the same again presented with the same facts. I was conscious of
the impact on my own area in the West Midlands but I also
believed that the issues went far beyond a regional dispute. It
concerned the nature of British industry itself. Had we agreed to
a Ford takeover of cars and a General Motors takeover of commercial vehicles then the decisions about the future development of
one of our most important industries would have been ultimately
made outside Britain. The British motor industry could not stand
alone and aloof, but there was a world of difference between
international collaboration and the whole industry being swallowed
up by two giant multinational corporations. I certainly did not
regard such a takeover as the policy of privatization in operation.

The disposal of British Leyland was being treated as a distress sale. My view was that other options should be explored.

On 1 May 1986, Graham Day took over as Chairman of British Leyland and a new chapter in the recovery of the company began. Day, who had impressed Margaret Thatcher in his management of British Shipbuilders, brought both enthusiasm and determination to the new job. About a year after his appointment I went to see him at his headquarters in Coventry. He took me around the design centre and I was able to see the strategy for cars illustrated by the new models being developed. Rather than the plethora of different vehicles which had characterized British Leyland, there was a small 'family' of cars instantly recognizable as Rovers. Rover became the new corporate name and the company looked for *profits* rather than market share.

Part of this strategy was to dispose of subsidiary companies. One of the earliest of these disposals was in 1987 when Leyland Trucks and Freight Rover vans (but not Land Rover) were sold to the Dutch company, DAF. Rover retained a stake in the company and DAF now uses the modern truck assembly lines at Leyland. Production of Freight Rover's vans in Birmingham has increased to 25,000 a year. Exports now make up almost 40 per cent of the total (compared with 5 per cent in 1985) as the company has made use of DAF's European distributors. Jobs in Birmingham have increased to 2,000 and a new partnership with Renault means a £350 million van programme for the mid-1990s.

As for Rover itself, Graham Day concentrated upon developing the core business – the cars and Land Rover. A new model programme was developed from the proceeds of the sales of subsidiaries and a 'total quality' programme introduced to improve reliability. At the same time the link with Honda was strengthened. The discussions with Ford had strained that relationship, for Honda had not been kept in the picture. If British Leyland had been acquired by a competitor then Honda would have been entitled to cancel all arrangements. With the Ford option abandoned, Day was able to sign a joint venture agreement in February 1987 with Honda for a new medium car. This has resulted today in the very successful 200 and 400 series models. Meanwhile within Land Rover a new model, the Discovery, was developed and both production and exports have increased. In

1990 the Land Rover four-wheel-drive vehicle business increased production by 25 per cent to almost 69,000 vehicles. In 1985 production was 30,000.

The goal remained to take the new Rover company into the private sector. Speculation continued that the only way this could be achieved was by selling it to a competitor. The case against that route was put by Day himself: 'We wanted to keep the core business intact in the interests of our various constituencies: the employees, the dealers, the suppliers and those who, in turn, depended upon each.' Instead in 1988 a sale was agreed to British Aerospace. It is not my purpose to analyse the detailed negotiations whereby Rover was bought. I certainly do not defend the withholding of information from the House of Commons. There is, however, a serious danger that in concentrating upon the so-called 'sweeteners' given by the Government to British Aerospace we ignore the undoubted benefits that privatization has brought to Rover.

As with other privatizations, very much the same management team which operated under Government control is now making profits in the private sector. In 1989 profits were £64 million, down to £55 million in 1990 as the recession took hold. Profitability needs to be further improved but the position represents a great advance on the 1970s and 1980s. Total sales have now reached £3.8 billion and Rover directly employs 40,000 people with a further 140,000 jobs estimated to be dependent upon the company. Perhaps most dramatically of all, Leyland's old reputation as an industrial relations disaster has been transformed. Today Rover can claim that over 99 per cent of all available working hours are dispute free.

No one pretends that the recovery is complete. In Graham Day's view that will not be clear until the mid-1990s. No one, however, can deny the progress made in the last five years. My belief is that the recovery of the old British Leyland companies will continue and that what we have today is a great improvement on what was on offer in the early months of 1986. If success comes, then the repercussions of the Westland affair will have proved to have had a decisive effect on the British motor industry.

CHAPTER 13

AIDS – Don't Die of Ignorance

The Posse Sets Off

Guardian

The date was Tuesday 11 November 1986. The place was Downing Street. Television lights pierced the evening gloom. Cameramen and reporters thronged the pavement about fifty yards down from the Prime Minister's office. It was against this backdrop that I conducted one of the most unusual press conferences that even Downing Street has ever seen. Ministers had just ended the first meeting of a special Cabinet committee which had been set up to oversee Britain's response to the threat of AIDS. As Health Secretary I had been deputed to tell the press what we had decided – in itself an unusual step as governments are usually reluctant to concede the very existence of Cabinet committees. I announced that we intended to take the then unprecedented step of sending leaflets to every house in the country explaining the nature of AIDS and that we would be following this up with a major newspaper and television advertising campaign.

'What we wish to achieve,' I said, 'is a campaign that goes directly to the public – not Madison Avenue in style but directed at some of the groups most at risk, young people and those who misuse drugs.' The first message of the campaign was to stick to one partner and the second message was not to inject drugs. But given that there were a whole range of people who would not follow that advice, the government needed to go further. We advised the use of condoms and we warned drug users who were unable to stop injecting never to share needles. The questions went to and fro for the best part of thirty minutes. Just as I was about to leave, a radio reporter took me to one side for a separate interview. 'Mr Fowler,' he asked, 'how would you advise our listeners to conduct their sex lives?'

It was clear that I was embroiled in an issue unlike any that I, or any other health minister since the war, had previously encountered. Advising the public on how to avoid sexually transmitted diseases was not among the things that I expected to be doing as a politician when I first entered the House of Commons in 1970. And yet it was an unquestionably serious challenge which required ministerial action for progress to be made. There were already over 500 AIDS cases and an estimated 25,000 people infected with HIV, the virus that could lead to full-blown AIDS. Although those with the virus were usually healthy in other respects, and without symptoms, they could infect others through sexual intercourse or through sharing needles. We estimated that at that time the numbers infected by the virus might be increasing by as many as twenty to fifty a day. There were also even more tragic signs. Pregnant women could transmit the infection to the foetus and we already had twenty-six babies and small children showing signs that they might have been infected in this way.

The issue was how to respond. One view was that we should not try: homosexuals and drug addicts had brought their sufferings on themselves and they should be left to their fate. Others found the whole subject so distasteful that they did not want to talk about it or discuss it – let alone try to do anything about it. When I went to the United States at the beginning of 1987, I was told that up to that point President Reagan had scarcely mentioned the subject. Yet by then several American cities were in the throes of a crisis far worse than anything we had experienced on our side of the Atlantic. Equally the Governor of California had left AIDS out of his annual address even though San Francisco had one of the worst problems in the whole of the country. But those attitudes were not confined to the United States. There were politicians in Britain who did not like the subject of AIDS one little bit. There were also some journalists who would think nothing of covering a war but who had asked their offices not to send them on stories connected with AIDS.

I found the antipathy towards AIDS sufferers incomprehensible. Disease is disease whether it is sexual or not. Suffering is suffering. You do not have to condone the conduct to want to help the casualties. And some of the casualties were entirely innocent victims of circumstance, like the haemophiliacs who had used infected blood-products imported before the danger was understood. It was clear that our first priority must be to prevent the disease from spreading further. But the problem was that there was no vaccine and no prospect of a cure. We were back to first principles. We had to persuade people to change their habits.

Modern means of communication, particularly television, gave us the opportunity of getting our message across much more widely and much more quickly than ever before. What message should we be setting out? I was not short of advice. I was told that it should be a moral message. That case was best put by Cardinal Basil Hume who argued that promiscuity was the root cause of the epidemic. We were therefore dealing with an intrinsically moral issue, not just a public health issue. He wanted a radical change in popular attitudes so that we could rediscover the joy of faithful love and lasting marriage. As an individual it was an argument that I agreed with but as the minister responsible it left me with a number of difficulties.

Time was short and the problem was urgent. We needed speedy action to prevent the AIDS epidemic from spreading even further. Public education was the only vaccine we had to hand. We had to devise a message which the public would notice and on which they would act. What evidence there was suggested that practical guidance on how the disease could be avoided was more likely to be successful than any other approach.

During the First World War, venereal disease was a scourge of all armies. At one stage, for example, VD accounted for between 40 and 50 per cent of all the sick in Canadian hospitals in England. All countries sought an effective response. The Australians issued so called 'blue light' outfits containing both calomel to prevent syphilis and permanganate to protect against gonorrhoea. In addition their soldiers were advised to use rubber sheaths – although at that stage the sheaths varied in quality and were sometimes very fragile. The Canadians also issued prophylactic tubes and set up early treatment centres where soldiers could be examined confidentially.

The United States Army adopted a different policy. Early in the war they too had issued prophylactic tubes, designed to look like cigars, but had been forced off this policy by public opinion which took the view that it was morally wrong to condone promiscuity. For the rest of the war the Americans placed their faith in a strange form of compulsory treatment. General orders required enlisted men to report for treatment within three hours of intercourse. Nevertheless, whether the soldier reported or not he was court-martialled for neglect of duty if he contracted venereal disease. The only difference was that if he had not reported for treatment then his punishment would be doubled.

As for Britain, one approach was set out by Brigadier-General

A. C. Critchley in his evidence to a government committee in 1919. He relied on the regular lectures he gave to RAF cadets under the headings of discipline, sportsmanship and cheerfulness, loyalty and patriotism, and clean living. His emphasis was on clean living. According to his evidence:

> I talked to them about venereal disease in the most open way possible, not as a parson, nor as a doctor, but as one of themselves. . . . In any talk of this kind there must be no camouflaging or beating about the bush: a spade must be called a spade.

It was an uncertain beginning. Nevertheless, for Britain, the public's concern during the First World War led directly to a Royal Commission on Venereal Disease in 1916 and the setting up of special clinics for sexually transmitted diseases with the assurance of strictly confidential treatment free of charge. By the Second World War there was much greater agreement about the approach. Posters warned against the dangers of VD; condoms were issued to soldiers; and early-treatment centres were established. In the midst of the war the Chief Medical Officer of the Ministry of Health, Sir Wilson Jamieson, warned of the dangers of VD in a special radio broadcast which caused neither surprise nor offence.

AIDS presented a different and far more acute challenge. With AIDS we could not offer a cure. The most we could hope to achieve was to prevent more people contracting the virus. The public, we thought, would accept a hard-hitting campaign provided that it set out the facts objectively. We never argued in favour of a 'condom society', if by that is meant a society in which people simply take the right precautions. We used every opportunity to underline the value of one loving partner. But there is a limit to how effective Government can be in changing the whole moral climate of society. The public will accept the best health advice available to ministers much more readily than they will a campaign that can be labelled a moral crusade. There is no intrinsic reason why Government ministers cannot argue for chastity and sex only inside marriage, but that would not have been remotely enough in 1986. We needed action then and there – and the only way that could be achieved was by a public education campaign.

The logical next step was for the Churches to run a complementary campaign. As a result I arranged private meetings with the Archbishop of Canterbury, Robert Runcie, who had been Dean of my Cambridge college, with Cardinal Hume and with Donald English, the Moderator of the Free Churches. Each one of these Church leaders listened to me with enormous sympathy but somehow the response from the Churches to AIDS has never seemed convincing.

There is no doubt that many Church leaders had serious doubts about the Government's campaign. These were put to me most directly by the Chief Rabbi, Sir Immanuel (now Lord) Jakobovits, at a meeting I had with him in February 1987. He handed me an *aide-mémoire* which complimented me on the 'urgency, boldness and effectiveness' of the campaign which, he said, struck the right balance between hysteria and complacency. He then set out no less than fourteen reasons why he was disturbed by the general thrust of the campaign. These included:

The campaign breeds a false sense of security, not to mention false values. . . .

In effect it encourages promiscuity by advertising it. It introduces to many children and decent young people ideas on sex and marriage entirely unknown to them. . . .

It tells people not what is right, but how to do wrong and get away with it – it is like sending people into a contaminated atmosphere, but providing them with gas masks and protective clothing, or instructing thieves how to escape being caught. . . .

Say plainly: AIDS is the consequence of marital infidelity, premarital adventures, sexual deviation and social irresponsibility – putting pleasure before duty and discipline.

The Chief Rabbi's views no doubt were shared to a greater or lesser extent by all the other denominational leaders. However, it is not unfair to reply: But what did *you* do? If ever there was a time when the public would have listened to the Churches, it was then. But their major campaign never came. Their contribution was to do good quietly, and I do not decry that. The Churches did not publicly challenge the Government's campaign – recognizing, I believe, the damage that such a challenge would have inflicted.

Had we entered into a public dispute, the whole impact of the campaign would have been blunted if not destroyed.

In the early days of the AIDS campaign, the problem was to communicate a sense of urgency to both my colleagues and the public. Initially, policy on AIDS was dealt with by the general Home Affairs, or 'H', Committee of the Cabinet which covered everything from immigration policy to the population census. AIDS was a subject which bristled with difficulties and it was simply impossible to deal with it as one of a number of items on an agenda. AIDS needed an agenda of its own and it needed ministers who could be taken through the background. Unless this was done, we could be sidetracked all too easily. When Barney Hayhoe had been Health Minister, we had been seriously delayed on the wording of a newspaper advertisement we wanted to place. One of the points at issue was whether or not people 'have' sex – a fascinating terminological question but one that is deeply frustrating if you are trying to run a public health campaign. We needed a committee that was prepared to spend time on the subject and was able to authorize action.

Margaret Thatcher has been much criticized for devolving issues to special committees and small groups. It is claimed that this is an autocratic approach. Much of that criticism, however, is based on a misunderstanding of what is now possible in modern government. Devolving issues to Cabinet committees with the time and experience to examine issues properly can provide better government, not worse. Certainly in the case of AIDS, we would not have made half the progress without the creation of a special committee.

If ever there was a contrast between the British and the American governmental response to AIDS, it lay in this. In the United States President Reagan maintained a conspicuous silence; Otis Brown, the US Secretary of Health, insisted that the issue of public education was a local and not a federal matter. Whereas in Britain Margaret Thatcher appointed the Deputy Prime Minister, Willie Whitelaw, to head a special committee and thus unlock the mechanism for quick and effective action. Apart from myself the committee included as regular members Douglas Hurd, the Home Secretary; Kenneth Baker, the Education Secretary; Nick Edwards, the Welsh Secretary; Malcolm Rifkind, the Scottish

Secretary; George Younger, the Defence Secretary; and inevitably the Chief Secretary to the Treasury, John McGregor – inevitably, because the Treasury is represented on every Cabinet committee to ensure that spending decisions are not put through the back door.

The crucial appointment was Willie Whitelaw. He not only had unrivalled experience of government but was essentially a man of action. I had first seen him in operation in the early 1970s when I was a lowly Parliamentary Private Secretary in the Northern Ireland Office. Willie's morning ministerial meetings were dominated by his personality and a joy to attend. He blended together ministers and civil servants as one team rather like the commanding officer of a crack regiment. His attitude to AIDS was entirely straightforward. He did not regard it as his duty to go on television to explain policy – that was my job. His role was to achieve progress as rapidly as possible and this he did. Provided that he and I were agreed, which we usually were, the issue tended to go through. The programme was such that between November and Christmas we had no fewer than seven meetings of the Cabinet committee.

At the Department of Health we had a small team working all hours not only to develop policy and service the committee but also to put that policy into effect. One newspaper said that tackling AIDS had become an obsession with me. I would put it another way. We were all driven by the urgency of the issue. Delay would cost lives. The more people knew, the less the virus was likely to spread. The nightmare was that people could become infected without any real knowledge of the risks they ran.

At one stage Margaret Thatcher said to me that I should remember I was 'more than the minister for AIDS'. Her point was the generous one that my speech at the 1986 Party Conference had gone exceptionally well and there were other political frontiers to consider. Some of my friends believed that I had lost what they regarded as my customary moderation. But it seemed to me that here was a life and death battle in which the Government could do something to determine the outcome. I did not want people in five years' time to turn round and say 'if only they had done more in 1986'. Certainly we still have our critics, but few would dispute the intensity of the effort itself.

There was for me another point. I had been Secretary of State for Social Services for five years. I was now well and truly the longest-serving minister in this post, having passed both Keith Joseph and David Ennals. The social security review was behind me and the Green Paper on family practitioner services had been published. Roy Griffiths had been asked to carry out his review of community care. I had the time to devote to the issue which no new Secretary of State could have managed. A crisis of this kind justifies long-serving ministers.

The Government's first aim was to get the message on AIDS over as directly as possible. We needed to reach the public in general and we needed in particular to reach young people who might be reluctant to accept a message from what they saw as authority. The message had to be hard-hitting but accurate. At one stage our advertising agency – which under Sammy Harari did a magnificent job – came up with the slogan 'Anyone Can Get AIDS'. It was a line which certainly had impact but, as our medical advisers pointed out, it would have added to the belief that AIDS could be transmitted like a cold or from using someone's cup. The truth was that it was really only sexual intercourse or injecting drugs that spread the infection.

We modified the message, but at no stage could we be accused of having clothed our words in generalizations. At a time when the American administration was keeping well clear of the subject, the British Government sent leaflets to 23 million homes which left no one in any doubt about AIDS and how it was transmitted.

The leaflet ran under the banner 'AIDS – DON'T DIE OF IGNORANCE'. Two extracts give the flavour:

Any man or woman can get the AIDS virus depending on their behaviour. It is not just a homosexual disease. There is no cure. And it kills.

We added:

Because the virus can be present in semen and vaginal fluid, this means for most people the only real danger comes through having sexual intercourse with an infected person. This means vaginal or anal sex. (It could also be that oral sex can be risky particularly if semen is taken into the mouth.)

So the virus can be passed from man to man, man to woman and woman to man.

Curiously, it was this last part of the message which proved most controversial. In the main, commentators did not object to the explicit language, but a number did complain that the message was a general one addressed to everybody. We were accused of pandering to the gay community by making the advertisements acceptable to them. But we did not take this step for public relations reasons. We took it because the evidence indicated that the infection's transmission routes were not confined to only one or two groups in society.

Everyone agreed that sharing needles could pass the virus to man or woman and everyone also accepted that babies conceived by infected mothers had a chance of acquiring the virus from them. It was also accepted that in Africa, where there was the greatest AIDS problem of all, the virus was passed from woman to man and man to woman through heterosexual intercourse. The only question was whether the evidence from the United States also pointed the same way. Our medical advice was that there was a risk in heterosexual intercourse. And it was not only British advice. Everett Koop, the Surgeon-General of the United States, who gave sturdily independent advice on AIDS in spite of the personal flak he endured, took the same view. Koop's advice was blunt: 'Heterosexual transmission is expected to account for an increasing proportion of those who become infected with the AIDS virus in the future.' Faced with these warnings, the Government would have been open to very serious criticism if it had simply confined its warnings to homosexuals and drug addicts. Nor has anything happened since to persuade me to change my view.

At the beginning of 1991 the Department of Health published AIDS and HIV figures for the United Kingdom. These figures showed that since the start of the epidemic there had been over 4,000 reported AIDS cases, including 2,000 deaths. The number tested as HIV-positive was over 15,000 – a figure which substantially understates the real problem. Most significant of all, the Government's Chief Medical Officer, Sir Donald Acheson, reported that 'AIDS in heterosexuals was now increasing faster than in any other group'.

When the campaign began, we all had some concern at what the public's reaction might be. Our fears proved groundless, though there were a few rumbles. At one political meeting I addressed in Manchester I was told by a questioner that she would burn any leaflet that came through her letter-box to keep it away from her fifteen-year-old daughter. Another questioner accused me of promoting safe promiscuity. Yet these were only rumbles and overwhelmingly the meeting was on my side. When it came to the delivery of the leaflets at the beginning of 1987, the same was true. There was a handful of complaints but not remotely on the scale of even a routine response to a health service campaign. It spoke volumes for the maturity of the British public. Churchill's advice to trust the people had never been so relevant.

The leaflets were not our only means of persuasion. Before Christmas, we had put up posters all over the country with the slogans:

AIDS – DON'T DIE OF IGNORANCE
AIDS – HOW BIG DOES IT HAVE TO GET BEFORE YOU TAKE NOTICE?
AIDS IS NOT PREJUDICED – IT CAN KILL ANYONE

Under each was the same message:

Gay or straight, male or female, anyone can get AIDS from sexual intercourse. So the more partners, the greater the risk. Protect yourself. Use a condom.

In the New Year we moved on to television advertising with an advertisement using a tombstone theme which became one of the best-known of all public education campaigns. And we followed this up with an advertisement showing the present problem as the tip of the iceberg. At the department we went through the advertising carefully and at one stage we toyed with the idea of a ministerial broadcast. Indeed the Opposition agreed to give up its right to reply. But we had not even had a ministerial broadcast for the Falklands War and the idea was dropped. In any event, there was no evidence that our advertising was going unnoticed.

By the beginning of February 1987 I was able to report to the Cabinet committee that our first follow-up poll showed that 98 per cent of the public were now aware that AIDS could be transmitted by sexual intercourse and drug-taking; that 95 per cent of the public had seen the Government advertisements; and that 95 per cent felt that we were right to run a campaign of this kind. Of course the advertisements were criticized by some, but measured by any sensible objective criterion they had had real impact. From a relatively low level of public awareness a few months before, virtually everyone in the country now knew about the danger.

Not everything could be achieved by advertising, however. We also needed the help of the media – in particular television. Early on in the campaign I went to see both the BBC and the IBA. Television comes in for a lot of stick from politicians of all parties, but in this case the response of both the BBC and the IBA was magnificent. At the IBA I saw George Thomson and at the BBC I met with Marmaduke Hussey and Alasdair Milne, then Director-General. The meetings were short and the only request was 'how can we help?' Later, both television and radio put out extremely helpful programmes, including an unprecedented week of joint programming on AIDS at the end of February. Most of the press – both national and the very important regional press outside London – also helped by repeating the campaign's message in their leader columns and articles.

In making policy on AIDS, public education may have been the most urgent requirement, but it was by no means the only issue we had to settle. There was, for example, a strong view that it was important to identify AIDS sufferers by compulsory testing. It was an issue which came early to the AIDS committee and one which we had little difficulty in rejecting. Compulsory testing is justifiable only if there is a general threat to everyone irrespective of their behaviour, and that is certainly not the case with AIDS. Doctors are very unlikely to agree to compulsory testing in such circumstances, and there is the obvious problem of what to do about those who refuse to be tested. What the advocates of compulsory testing all too often ignore is that the process has to be repeated again and again. There is a period of up to three months after infection when testing for the virus may give a negative result.

There are those who argue that you should simply round up and quarantine all AIDS sufferers – or at the very least issue them with special documents. But unless you are prepared to take such drastic steps, it is difficult to see what compulsory testing would achieve. You can get an accurate picture of the size of the problem in other ways and the Government is now rightly conducting an anonymous testing programme.

Another issue was drugs. Some opposed any special arrangements for addicts unless they were being weaned off drugs. They were not prepared to see addicts helped to maintain their habit. Their argument was that drug taking was illegal and the drug taker was committing a criminal offence. My view was that AIDS presented a new dimension. Dirty needles spread the virus and infected mothers and babies. There was a strong case for launching pilot schemes to see whether needle exchange, together with the offer of treatment, offered a way forward. Again we were in new territory and not surprisingly there was some reluctance to see such schemes proceeding. We did, however, go ahead and today there are some 120 needle-exchange schemes in operation – while the figures for new HIV-infection among drug users in cities like Edinburgh have at last flattened out.

What clinched the gravity of the AIDS threat for me was the experience I was able to bring back from a number of overseas trips. One of my beliefs in making policy is to see how other countries are tackling the same problem. In every department I have ever run I have always made special visits to the United States and to the countries of the European Community. Ironically, it is easier to get information from the USA than from Europe. Indeed it is foolish of the Community not to have sensible arrangements for exchanging information between member states. We are all tackling the same social issues. Yet too often we approach these issues in isolation. AIDS was a prime example of an issue where countries, if not always governments, were putting their mind to a new issue.

My starting-point was the World Health Organization, an agency of the United Nations, overlooking Lake Geneva in Switzerland. Here one of the most distinguished and tireless workers in the field, Dr Jonathan Mann, gave me a sobering account of how he saw the world-wide position. In scale he predicted that by 1992 there would be over half a million deaths from AIDS — and the total could rise to as high as three million. Africa had the most acute problem although accurate figures were impossible to come by. After Africa the United States faced the most serious threat. In Europe the spread of the disease was less developed and therefore the countries of Europe had the greatest opportunity of avoiding the cataclysm.

Dr Mann raised other issues as well. One was sexual tourism, where people from the developed world travel to the under-developed nations of Africa and Asia with the promise of sexual partners, male or female. Nothing better illustrated Cardinal Hume's views on the moral nature of much of the problem. In spite of all that has been said on AIDS over the last five years, such internationally organized prostitution continues today.

My next ports of call were Amsterdam and Berlin. At the time it was being suggested that the Netherlands had the answer to the AIDS problem. It was not remotely the case. Their efforts at public education were, at best, patchy but more interesting were their efforts to reach drug users. Medical staff took the heroin substi-tute, methadone, by bus to drug addicts. In Berlin clean needles were readily available over the counter of pharmacies, and the authorities were making strenuous efforts to reach drug users. The image that remains in my mind is of a visit to a Berlin hospital and of a consultant, gaunt and overwrought, despairing at his impo-tence in the face of a disease he could not cure.

But the most important of my visits was to the United States in January 1987. If the politicians were not doing very much, the same could not be said about the hospitals, the voluntary organiza-tions and at least some of the Churches. I went first to San Francisco which by any standards had a major crisis. San Francisco is the most beautiful of American cities and had become a centre for homosexuals during the 1960s and 1970s. In the words of one of the community workers I spoke to: 'They had become recog-nized and accepted as part of normal society.' They were, of course, never accepted by all, and AIDS confirmed the prejudices of those most hostile to them. Nevertheless, the city had been able to develop a range of community facilities like home-care and special flats. In 1987 there was still a great deal of ignorance about the process of dying for the AIDS sufferer. AIDS patients do not need to be shut away in hospital all the time. They have crises when they must enter hospital but for the most part patients can live at home. As one of the American doctors there said: 'AIDS is essentially an outpatient disease.'

On our second day in the United States we visited the San Francisco General Hospital – an early twentieth-century complex of red-brick buildings on what was once the edge of the city. I talked first to the nurses and again the problems of the staff came through. The longest-serving nurse in the AIDS section had a mere three years' experience. Many others had transferred to other parts of the hospital depressed by the hopelessness of a ward where month after month they had seen patients die without being able to do anything to intervene. We should never forget the effect on medical and nursing staff of caring for predominantly young patients who cannot be cured.

Inside the ward itself one of the patients had agreed to be televised and photographed as we shook hands. I had not imagined for a moment that this picture would go round the world as an example of AIDS not being a contagious disease. I regarded our tour as fact-finding and although reporters had attached themselves to our small Health Department team, we had not sought coverage. Indeed unbeknown to me one of my staff had turned down an interview on *Good Morning America*, which is rather like a footballer passing over the Wembley Cup Final.

Ken Gifford was a young man in his early thirties – the average age in San Francisco for AIDS cases – and his life expectation was only two or three months. He was remarkably cheerful and anxious to talk. He had been a shipping clerk but now there was no prospect of him working, although his employer would have been happy for him to come in even for an hour or so each day. As I left the ward, my way was barred by about twenty or thirty reporters. An American reporter asked: 'Mr Fowler, will you share your emotions with us?' My overriding emotion was that I had just met a man of some courage.

From San Francisco we flew to Washington which was caught in an unexpected snowstorm. If ever you were to attack the United States, you should do it when the snow comes down. Civil servants were sent home and we conducted our meetings in otherwise empty government offices. The best message that came through that day was the vast resources being devoted to research on AIDS. Yet even so, no one was at all optimistic that there would be any vaccine, let alone cure, for at least five or ten years. As we drove back to the Embassy that night, my attention was claimed by an entirely irrelevant picture. It was a scene to gladden the heart of any Land Rover manager. There on a snowy Washington hill was a fur-coated lady pushing a four-wheel-drive Japanese jeep up a slight incline. It was one of the few light moments of our American trip.

The next day we set out to New York by train as all aircraft had been grounded. The problem in New York was drugs. The City Health Department painted a bleak picture of New York, 1987. They estimated that there were about 200,000 intravenous drug users regularly injecting themselves. They were a difficult group to reach. Many of the homosexual community were middle class, well educated and certainly did not want to die. The intravenous drug users were much more apathetic about their future. Yet their conduct affected others. There was the tragedy of babies being born HIV-positive. On my last day in New York I visited the Roman Catholic St Clare's Hospital. There I met two young mothers who were both expected to die in the coming few months. Fortunately their small babies were not infected. They faced a future, however, without parents and would have to be brought up by their grandparents. In a sense they were the lucky ones. As I talked to these two mothers – both in their twenties – the one impression that came through was of appalling human waste.

The American AIDS workers I met made no secret of the fact that they would have preferred their own Government to have run a public education campaign on British lines. They could not understand the official silence given the scale of the American problem. For my part I cast envious eyes at the size of the American research programme which must still be the world's chief hope for a breakthrough in developing a vaccine. Above all, however, I was impressed with the quality of care that I had seen both in San Francisco and in New York. When we got back to London, my department set to work on the financing of community help organizations and the formation of a new voluntary body, the National Aids Trust.

As I look at the AIDS position today, I am struck by how much bleaker the picture has become. The World Health Organization estimate that there have already been 1.2 million cases of AIDS throughout the world and that there are another 10 million people infected with HIV. They believe that by the year 2000 the overall total could have increased to between 25 and 30 million people infected, including 10 million children. Even a public grown sceptical of future projections can hardly challenge the evidence which is now being collected. African nations like Uganda and Zaire face a crisis of catastrophic proportions. The size of the problem in the United States has now been recognized by the formation of a President's Commission on AIDS, with the administration pursuing a much more determined policy of public education. In Latin America, the Caribbean, the Far East and India AIDS is now an urgent public challenge.

In some nations, simple medical steps could save lives. People are still being infected by dirty needles or the transfusion of contaminated blood. In Western Europe the risk of transmission in these ways has been virtually eliminated. The populations of the world's poorer nations are not so fortunate and the innocent suffer and die. If we wish to debate the moral issues presented by AIDS, we could usefully start here.

In Britain the challenge is no different from the one I set out at my Downing Street press conference five years ago. There is still no cure for AIDS and no vaccine. We would be optimistic to believe that the position will change in the next five years and the prospect is that we will have to wait until the next century. Prevention remains the only policy and the need is to persuade people not only to listen but to act. Yet as time goes by the initial message is felt to be less urgent. In spite of the evidence, young people wrongly assume that if they are not homosexual and do not inject drugs, they will come to no harm. Young gay men feel that it is not a problem for them but for an older generation. While, in the words of one medical expert, 'the middle class do not feel threatened'. There is a dangerous complacency about the risks of unprotected sex and drug abuse.

The real question is how to make prevention more effective. We need to inform and we need to persuade people not only to change behaviour but to maintain that change. The challenge of AIDS points to one of the most crucial health issues of the twenty-first century. Our surgeons, physicians and a host of other medical and nursing staff do heroic work in saving life once illness has struck. Yet even today we do all too little in preventing ill health. Health education has no great priority. It is seen as a side-issue – in spite of the illness and death caused by drugs, taking alcohol and smoking. We desperately need not only to increase the effort but to improve the skills at our disposal. We need the same professionalism which is devoted to persuading people to buy goods to be devoted to persuading people to look after their own health.

This is not a plea for a new one-off campaign but for a searching inquiry into the whole area of health education which will examine the effectiveness of our current approaches. As AIDS grimly shows, health education is not some rather cosy, marginal activity but often the only means we have of preventing human disaster. At present we are only in the foothills of development. It might seem curious for a sexually transmitted disease like AIDS to be in the forefront of a much more general policy. We might, however, reflect that the 1916 Royal Commission on Venereal Disease led to a free public medical service a quarter of a century before the inception of the National Health Service. Our methods of preventing AIDS could well find important paths elsewhere.

My hope is that the Government's AIDS campaign saved lives and will continue to do so. The figures show that the incidence of AIDS in Britain is below the European average and well below countries like Switzerland, France and Italy. We may have made mistakes but the nightmare of public ignorance was avoided. For once the health debate was not just about resources but also about judgement and compassion and making policy in a difficult, uncharted area. The challenge now is to persuade the public that AIDS has not gone away and that it still represents a lethal threat. The real test is still to come.

CHAPTER 14

A Third Term

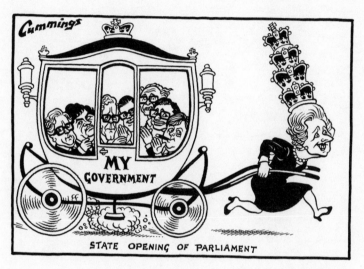

Daily Express

Whenever a new minister joined the team at the Department of Health and Social Security, we organized a 'photocall' at our headquarters in Alexander Fleming House. The photographers were duly invited to attend but the response was usually less than overwhelming. Just occasionally a photographer from a national newspaper with a space to fill made the journey to the Elephant and Castle. More often, our pictures appeared in the ever loyal *Health and Social Services Journal*.

All this changed on the morning of Monday 15 September 1986. At the end of the previous week the Conservative MP for Derbyshire South, Edwina Currie, had been appointed Parliamentary Secretary on the health side of the department. On the Monday morning every press photographer and television crew appeared to be on parade. They crowded into the long, overheated room that had been my office until I moved to smaller but more congenial surroundings. Edwina protested loyally that she was 'just one of the team' but that did not deter the assembled throng. They wanted her picture – and who can blame them? If you were a photographer, would you prefer Norman Fowler, Ken Clarke or Edwina Currie? Of course, it is exactly this drawing power which does not endear her to everyone in the competitive world of politics.

All kinds of theories were advanced in the bars of Westminster as to why Edwina Currie had been promoted. One was that it was all a Machiavellian plot on my part to provide the health service and the press with an alternative political target. Another was that she was forced on me by Margaret Thatcher in spite of my protests that she was too abrasive. The truth is altogether more straightforward. When I knew there was to be a vacancy at the health department, I asked that Edwina should be promoted. She had given us effective support from the back benches in some of the difficult and unpopular debates which are arranged in the House of Commons after 10 p.m. at night. There were not many Conservative backbenchers who wanted to speak on social security at a time when most people enjoying a normal life outside politics are preparing the cocoa and thinking of going to bed. Edwina was always prepared to help and invariably spoke well. I needed a health minister who was ready and able to appear on the media at any time of the day or night and speak intelligently on any one of a hundred health questions. She was an obvious choice.

Edwina Currie earned her promotion and became an effective minister. Things you asked her to do were done. She had a genuine enthusiasm for health and succeeded in bringing preventative health issues dramatically up both the national and health department agendas. Even when the rows came her views could not be dismissed. In my time her most famous row was about diet. At a press conference in Newcastle Edwina dared to venture that not all bad health could be put down to deprivation and unemployment. Diet and personal behaviour were also factors and a nation that spent £900 million a year on potato crisps and hundreds of millions more on cigarettes and drink could hardly complain that bad health was all due to lack of Government resources. This was wrongly interpreted as an attack on the habits of people living in the north, and a few weeks later when I introduced my team to the Conservative Party Conference there was a short spurt of barracking when I mentioned her name. But consider this. Five years later the message that good health is not simply a responsibility of Government and the health service but also of the individual is much better understood.

In the press Edwina Currie's promotion swamped all the other changes in the 1986 reshuffle. Yet politically an even more significant promotion had taken place at the Health and Social Security Department. Barney Hayhoe had retired as Minister of Health and we needed a good replacement as we neared the general election. My choice was Tony Newton who had been in the department for almost as long as I had, albeit up to then always on the social security side. With that move decided, there was a vacancy for Tony's old job as Minister of State for Social Security. I had no doubt who that should be. For the previous twelve months John Major had toiled away as the junior social security minister and had impressed both me and the department with the effective Rolls-Royce way he had dispatched business.

John Major had come to the department highly recommended from the Whips' Office, which has become over the last twenty years the ministerial nursery of Conservative Governments. One of the stories told of him at the time concerned the night he got into a fierce debate with Margaret Thatcher. At issue was whether the Government was persuading the public of the case for tax cuts. John was a supporter of reducing the tax burden but (unlike many of us at the time) doubted whether we were winning the public argument. Margaret disagreed: she believed the case self-evident. Margaret gave not an inch. Much more significantly, John did not give an inch either. He stuck to his guns in the distinctively polite but firm manner that is now publicly much more familiar. Not surprisingly, Margaret Thatcher was impressed with this display of determination.

In 1985 John Major was promoted from the Whips' Office to arguably one of the worst jobs in the entire administration. As Parliamentary Secretary for Social Security he answered letter after letter on everything from pensions to housing benefit. Many of the letters were from MPs and raised very detailed issues from constituents. Standard replies, therefore, did not work. You had to read each letter put before you very carefully. Weekends were dominated by red boxes full of departmental replies. On one weekend, John took home to Huntingdon no less than thirteen red boxes crammed full of letters. He started checking and signing at 9 a.m. on Saturday morning and finally ended on Sunday evening. You now know why politicians in general and ministers in particular do not regard letter-writing as the greatest social pleasure. Indeed it can become a minor nightmare as some recipients of ministerial replies protest at imagined slights. I once had two perfectly good letters returned to me by a Labour Privy Counsellor. He refused to take delivery on the grounds that the letters had been signed by the Parliamentary Secretary and not by me as Secretary of State.

Letter-writing was just one of John Major's trials as junior social security minister. Any change in social security needs the authority of either a full-scale bill or, at least, a Parliamentary order or regulation. Either way, any change requires debate in the House of Commons. Thus John took a leading part in putting the reforming bill that resulted from our social security review on to the statute book. He also had to handle some of the rows that broke over us as a result of the exceptionally cold weather at the beginning of 1987 and the ensuing demands for extra help for

heating. Often the social security debates were angry, but at no
stage can I remember John being flustered or anything other than
calm under pressure. He was not a Tory that Labour MPs loved
to hate. They were disarmed by his style and recognized that he
not only knew the detail of the policies he was defending but
cared about the human effect of the policies. He was one of those
politicians who had few, if any, enemies.

Looking back, I would claim only one contribution to John's
meteoric rise to Prime Minister. When I asked for him to be
promoted to Minister of State there were slightly raised eyebrows.
'Was it not too quick?' 'Did he not need a little more experience?'
My reply was that John had already proved himself an excellent
minister and the promotion went through. The direct result was
that he took part in the 1987 election press conferences at Conservative Central Office. In these he greatly impressed the then
Chancellor of the Exchequer, Nigel Lawson. Once the election
was over, Nigel immediately snaffled him to become his number
two as Chief Secretary to the Treasury and so John entered the
Cabinet.

The promotions of John Major and Edwina Currie and the
transfer of Tony Newton showed part of my own approach to being
a Secretary of State. I am told that there have been Secretaries of
State who have surrounded themselves with junior ministers who,
although worthy, are unlikely to overshadow them. This betrays
an unappealing lack of security and also detracts from the fun of
Government office. You not only want good people to take charge
of policy areas, you also want their ideas. Being a minister is not
just about running the machine; it is above all about developing
new ideas for running it better. My aim at the DHSS was to build
up good teams of ministers and to bring to the Elephant and Castle
some of the future stars of the Government.

In this I was helped by two Chief Whips, Michael Jopling and
John Wakeham, and of course by Margaret Thatcher herself.
Theoretically a Prime Minister has absolute power of appointment.
In practice, a wise Prime Minister seeks to balance the team
between left and right, north and south, young and old – and also
discover the view of the Secretary of State. I never had a minister
forced upon me I did not want and I was usually given the ministers
I asked for. I remember one of my nationalized industry chairmen

telling me that having the right members on his board was crucial to him personally. The same is true of a Secretary of State and his ministers. The chemistry has to be right. To her credit, Margaret Thatcher recognized that if you were in a fight – and at the DHSS you were always in a fight – then you had a right to have a very big say in who was at your side.

During my time at the DHSS, I had the good fortune to be backed by a formidable 'all stars' team. Apart from those now in the Cabinet, there are former social services ministers like John Patten and Nicholas Lyell who are certain to go further in their ministerial careers. Among the excellent Ministers of State who served in the department were Hugh Rossi, Barney Hayhoe and Rhodes Boyson. There were hard-working Parliamentary Secretaries like Geoffrey Finsberg and Ray Whitney and from the House of Lords we had splendid ministers like Jean Trumpington, David Trefgarne and Simon Glenarthur. I never enquired, but I am not sure that every one of the ministerial team had set down the DHSS as their lifetime's ambition. Who can blame them? It was without question one of the most difficult jobs in the Government, as all experience before and since has shown. We had our critics inside Government, too. I remember one of my colleagues opining that the health service had almost lost us the 1987 general election, but his point was rather dented by the size of our majority and when he made clear that he could not possibly take a DHSS job himself. To those who *did* serve, I offer my grateful thanks.

There is one other group whose contribution tends to be overlooked. Every Secretary of State has his own Private Parliamentary Secretary. The PPS is entirely unpaid and carries out his duties in addition to his work as a Member of Parliament. He can sit in on departmental meetings but his major role is as the minister's eyes and ears at Westminster, spotting the issues which can blow up into trouble. Too often the reward of the PPS comes in heaven, but occasionally recognition comes in this life. Two of my PPSs, Sydney Chapman and Peter Bottomley, were promoted. Peter, who did more for road safety than most Secretaries of State, has since left and the Government is the poorer for it. Two others, Charles Wardle and Peter Thurnham (who joined me at Employment), are obvious candidates for promotion. Throughout my time at the DHSS I had an exceptionally able political adviser from outside the civil service in Nicholas True who helped me in both policy-making and speech-writing. Not surprisingly he also impressed John Major and is now in the policy unit at Number 10.

The September 1986 reshuffle was a prelude to the general election expected at some stage in the following twelve months. Although there were no changes in the Cabinet itself, below that about thirty ministerial changes were made to bring a younger face to the Government. All attention then switched to the party political battle. The Government's low point had been the Westland crisis and although we had weathered that storm our recovery was slow and uncertain. The bombing of Libya from British airfields in April 1986 had been fiercely controversial and at home unemployment remained stubbornly above the three million mark. Worst of all, there was a wide perception that the Government itself was still in some disarray and had lost direction. There was one major opportunity to change the mood – the 1986 Conservative Party Conference.

It was an opportunity triumphantly taken and demolished once and for all the claim that party conferences are of no consequence. There was a virtuoso performance by the new party chairman, Norman Tebbit, and strong speeches from Nigel Lawson and Kenneth Baker. But at the heart of the conference was some invaluable preparatory work done by two of the senior figures at Conservative Central Office, Michael Dobbs and Harvey Thomas. The order went out that in their speeches ministers should set out their policy targets in as specific terms as possible. We should look forward to what we intended to achieve rather than backwards at what we had done already.

I found that each year the Party Conference presented a fresh challenge. The next speech is always the worst. If last year's speech has gone badly, you stand up knowing that the conference wants something better. If it has gone well, you must ensure that the standard is at least maintained. I invariably put hours of hard preparation into this annual twenty-minute ordeal (as do most other ministers) and the text went to and fro between Nick True and myself over the space of several weeks. Yet for all my industry, I had not come up with anything particularly striking for 1986. Then, a few days before the conference, we were discussing the new hospital building programme which had steadily expanded during my time as Secretary of State.

We had left far behind the terrible stop-go years of the 1970s when hospital plans were no sooner announced than cancelled. The problem was how to communicate the radical change which was taking place. During a meeting at the department, I came up with the answer when I was shown the computer printout of our current building programme. It was this printout that I held up midway through my speech and the reaction was such that I was unable to continue for a good twenty seconds. As I let the computer printout drop to the conference-hall floor, Anthony Bevins of the *Independent* pounced forward intent on checking it and the *Daily Mirror* put a team of reporters on to investigating the list.

I am glad to say that neither they nor anyone else was ever able seriously to challenge our figures – which is more than can be said for our rivals. When Simon Hughes of the Liberals tried to do the same during the 1987 election campaign, it went disastrously wrong. The printout that he claimed represented the hospital waiting list proved to be a party membership roll.

My speech also provided a fascinating glimpse of the sensitivity of some journalists. No paper has more gleefully reported the problems of the health service than the *Daily Mirror*. Reporters scoured the country for cases which could be used to demonstrate the Conservative Government's hard-heartedness. No paper had attacked health ministers in more personal terms, from Fowler to Clarke and Ray Whitney to Edwina Currie. In my conference speech I dared to reply. I pointed out that the political editor of the *Mirror* was none other than Joe Haines, a valued member of Harold Wilson's kitchen Cabinet with other such luminaries as Gerald Kaufman and Lady Falkender. The audience laughed but the *Mirror* was not amused. 'Why are you conducting this bitter personal attack?' a *Mirror* journalist asked me as I left the platform. The next day my photograph appeared the wrong way up on the *Mirror*'s front page to illustrate my upside-down world, and a very sensitive Joe Haines devoted paragraph after paragraph to reply. Those who dish it out so freely should be a little more sturdy when they themselves become a target.

As we waited for the general election, I settled one issue which had irritated me for a very long time. At the Department of Health and Social Security we had one undoubted and serious disadvantage. We may have been Whitehall warriors, but being South of the River we were a good ten-minute drive or twenty-minute Tube ride from the action at Westminster, the Cabinet meetings at Downing Street and the frequent financial discussions at the Treasury. This had its effect. For civil servants it meant that life was spent in the concrete world of the Elephant and Castle. For us ministers it meant that popping over to the House of Commons for a quick lunch was an impossibility. Our regular Monday alternative was the excellent pizza house where Labour researchers from Walworth Road either strove to hear our conversation or passed us notes warning us of the perils of drinking alcohol. Later on we went over to healthy salad lunches in the department where Jean Trumpington positively refused to follow Edwina Currie's suggestion of low-cholesterol margarine and insisted that butter went back on the menu. From this moment also John Major joined us, having previously found innumerable excuses to avoid the garlic of the pizza house.

Separation from Westminster and Whitehall, however, had more serious consequences. In particular for ministers it meant difficult lines of communication to the House of Commons. No set of departmental ministers were more often on their feet than us, yet no set were further away. I remember one of my ministers having to make a statement on the floor of the House on the basis of an indecipherable hand-written note composed by two civil servants in a taxi. It was a crazy position and after a year or two I began to look for an alternative. Initially I got nowhere, but then in 1986 a note came round saying that it had been decided to move the Overseas Development Agency into the new offices across Whitehall from Downing Street at Richmond Terrace. At this point I blew my top.

I sent off by far the most ill-tempered minute I ever wrote in Government. I pointed out that I had nothing against the Overseas Development Agency but their single minister appeared on the floor of the House of Commons about once every five weeks for fifteen minutes of questions. My team of six ministers were in play constantly with questions, statements, private-notice questions, debates, points of order, ten-minute-rule bills and every other contingency known to political man. My message was that this was the wrong decision and no way to treat an important department. There was a silence – and then one minister came out on my side. Fortunately that minister was Margaret Thatcher. A meeting was arranged at Number 10; the Foreign Office was repulsed; and the decision was rescinded. The Department of Health and Social Security at last came in from the cold.

Since then the department has been split in two on the debatable grounds that the Secretary of State's job was too big for one minister. Whether that is right or wrong, there had always been those who had argued for separation. I did not think it would make much difference one way or the other. Those who supported change were either indulging in the social world's well-known partiality for structural reorganization or in some remarkable way believed that once the health service had a department all to itself then the problems would magically melt away. I have not noticed that health has become politically less difficult as a result of the change. Nevertheless the decision is taken and it is unlikely that the two departments will be put back together again. At least they still have Richmond Terrace.

In March 1987 Nigel Lawson introduced his fourth Budget. The Budget reduced taxes for both individuals and companies, and made a series of beneficial changes affecting the elderly, the disabled and the unemployed. An election fever took grip. By April speculation was so widespread about a June election that Margaret Thatcher warned us in Cabinet not to close her options and to box her into June irrespective of what happened in the local elections. Yet, provided we did reasonably well in the council elections, it was difficult to see how June could be avoided. From inside Government the momentum towards an election felt unstoppable.

A morning's canvassing will usually tell you how opinion is moving. In 1974, for example, it was quite clear on the doorstep that opinion was moving away from us. Just as certainly in 1987 it was clear that opinion was running our way. There was a friendly response which indicated a good support. And so it proved. The result of the May local elections in Birmingham was that we won five seats and from around the country there came the same story of Conservative gains.

On Monday morning, 11 May, at 9.30 I received a call at the

department summoning a Cabinet meeting for 11 a.m. Outside
the Cabinet room on Horse Guards Parade a rehearsal for the
Trooping the Colour was taking place. The meeting was short.
Margaret Thatcher said that she had decided to bring the uncertainty to an end and the election would be on Thursday 11 June.
The reaction of the Cabinet was summed up in the photographs
taken as we left Number 10. There was palpable relief that the
waiting had come to an end.

The next day the manifesto was largely settled, and on Tuesday
19 May it was launched at a good-humoured press conference at
Conservative Central Office. In any election there is a period of
phoney war as the parties make all the last-minute decisions and
arrangements that are necessary. However well-prepared you are
– and in social services we were exceptionally well prepared –
there are always final decisions to be taken. For me the most
important decision taken in those last days running up to the
campaign was the addition of £300 million to the social security
budget to increase the level of the new Income Support. It finally,
and an innumerable number of rows later, established the point I
had always argued – that the social security reforms should be
cost-neutral.

All the predictions before the election were that social security
would be a major issue. We had just completed the most comprehensive review of social security since the war and expected a
major Labour attack. But the attack never came. Labour appeared
reluctant to expose their plans and television and radio producers
feared that audiences would quickly be lost in the complexities of
the social security debate. The issue, as it turned out, was not
social security but health.

Michael Meacher and I toured the television studios of the
country. I counted some ten television debates on health compared with one on social security. The Conservative Party has
never been ahead in the polls on the health issue in any election
since the inception of the National Health Service. That dates
back to our mistaken decision to vote against the introduction of
the new service in 1946. Nevertheless the 1987 election debate on
health did not go too badly for the first two weeks of the campaign.
We were able to point to more spending, more services, more
patient care and more hospital building. We were also able to point

to a better-run health service for, in spite of the early opposition, the management revolution was working. Michael Meacher's attack came down to one point: the Government should spend more money. Yet what was to cause the damage in the 1987 campaign had nothing to do with the issues that Meacher and I had been so regularly debating.

On Thursday morning, 4 June, I went to Conservative Central Office for one of the party's daily press conferences. Social security was on the agenda, but the press was not much interested. With the Prime Minister on the platform a number of other questions were asked, including one about policy in Northern Ireland. But the question that did the damage was floated by Anthony Bevins of the *Independent*. It was to the effect that if the Prime Minister was so concerned about the health service, why did she herself use private health facilities?

The question was, of course, a 'try on'. It had been asked a hundred times before. There was a perfectly good short reply to it. No major party standing at the election wanted to see the private sector in health abolished. Using private facilities did not in any way invalidate support for the National Health Service. This time, however, Margaret Thatcher's patience snapped and obviously quite exasperated she responded with a long, long reply that the press gleefully headlined. In particular they picked on her comment that she was exercising her right as a free citizen to go to hospital 'on the day I want, and the time I want, and with the doctor I want'. There followed an intense and almost entirely bogus row.

The question put to Margaret Thatcher was deliberately personal and concerned her own position. Any Prime Minister is going to be given special treatment in either the health service or the private sector. If Margaret had chosen to be treated in the health service, she would also have been criticized. Some of the public reaction to Prince Charles's treatment in an NHS hospital after his accident in 1990 made that point quite clear and demonstrated how unwinnable the argument is. Security requirements will determine that a private room, and probably much more, is set aside. Treating a serving Prime Minister in a National Health Service hospital is a disruption that most can well do without. It is likely to put back the work of the hospital, not put it forward.

There remains the general argument that no one should have
the right to pay for treatment. Private means undoubtedly confer
a choice of consultant and much more influence over the timing
of an operation. To remove that right means removing the right
of the individual to pay for health treatment out of an income
which has already been reduced by tax to pay for the health service.
Any party that promised the abolition of the private sector in health
would lose the argument with the public. Perhaps that is one of
the reasons why it is not Labour Party policy.

Nevertheless, for all that, Margaret Thatcher's press conference
on what was to become known as 'wobbly Thursday' had one
certain effect. We were back to the old CPRS debate on private
health and the Government's commitment to the health service.
The new position, as seen from an anti-Government standpoint,
was described the next day in a leader in the *Guardian*.

> It is important to realize why health has not previously provided
> Labour with the momentum which it needs in this campaign.
> Most voters approve strongly of the National Health Service.
> Most voters prefer Labour's NHS policies to the Tories'. But
> Mr Norman Fowler has proved a resourceful running repairman
> to the Conservative's image. He has been able to contain the
> Tories' losses by pointing to the Government's record of
> increasing NHS spending over its eight years, by emphasizing
> the new areas of health care and research which the Tories have
> funded and by stressing his record in trying to reform NHS
> management and bureaucracy. Always in his wallet he has had
> the bankability of Mrs Thatcher's 1979 pledge that the NHS
> would be safe in her hands. Mr Fowler hasn't piled up many
> positive points by such tactics. But he has managed to prevent
> Labour's Mr Michael Meacher from landing a real knock-out
> blow. Yesterday's clear endorsement of private health care for
> the few may have destroyed all that crafty work.

There was no question that at this point health came to the centre
of the campaign, but in the event Labour failed to land anything
like a knock-out blow. This was due to two events. The most
important was that we at last succeeded in getting the election
debate on to the running of the economy and the heavy cost of

Labour's alternative plans. This development is usually dated to the press conference at Conservative Central Office on Saturday 6 June taken by the Chancellor, Nigel Lawson. In fact the real initiative was taken on the Friday when by a splendid piece of private enterprise Andrew Tyrie, the Chancellor's special adviser, and Nick True between them took a number of political correspondents through the detailed figures of Labour's plans. 'Labour was forced on to the defensive last night over its plans for a reform of the tax and benefit system,' reported the *Daily Telegraph* in its lead story. 'Exposed: Labour's Tax Fiasco' thundered the *Daily Express*. The pieces appeared on the morning of Nigel's conference.

The second event came when it was revealed that Denis Healey's wife, Edna, had also used private health facilities. You have to feel sorry for Mrs Healey. No one should like politicians' wives being made the target of personal attack. Labour, however, have only themselves to blame. Over the last ten years they have exploited the health issue completely without scruple. They have gloried in the problems that any health service faces and they have raised fears about the future of the service itself which they know are untrue. They have made promises that in their heart of hearts they know they cannot meet. Nothing in Labour's record in Government on health can lead to the conclusion that they have some secret magic remedy.

By most political standards the 1987 election was a famous victory. No Prime Minister had won a third term since Lord Liverpool in the early nineteenth century. It was not a sparkling campaign, but then nor was there much sparkle about the way we won in 1979. It was also true that our campaign got off to a slow start with a bemused press watching a meeting of candidates in Central Hall, Westminster. Equally Labour with their red roses were much better presented than in 1983. That, however, was not saying very much. Labour needed to do more than simply produce a few well-scrubbed faces and soothing but essentially vapid television commercials. They never seemed to have the credibility which was necessary for victory. No election is a certainty but I would have been amazed had we lost in June 1987. In the event Margaret Thatcher romped home with a 102-seat majority over all other parties.

Yet no sooner were the polls closed than an entirely unrecognizable story of the election started to be put around. According to this version, the 1987 general election was an epic battle in which the Conservatives had snatched a last-minute victory from the jaws of defeat. This had been achieved by some inspirational newspaper advertising in the last days of the campaign and some changes behind the scenes at Conservative Central Office. There followed a fierce argument about who had really won the election. Individuals I had scarcely heard of were revealed as the master tacticians behind the victory. Men who had never seen a political shot fired in anger were portrayed as ballot box generals. Advertising copywriters, it was claimed, were the crucial men behind our successful strategy. It needs to be said that all this was the greatest nonsense.

I fear that David Young, who was then Employment Secretary, must take a major responsibility for this misconception. His views are set out in his book, *The Enterprise Years*. According to David Young's diary for Thursday 4 June, nerves had become so frayed that there was a confrontation between him and Norman Tebbit, the Chairman of the Conservative Party. In the most memorable extract from the diary, he wrote:

> I got him by the shoulders and said, 'Norman, listen to me, we're about to lose this f . . . election!'

Like all diaries, David's reveals most about the writer. I do not believe for a moment that we were about to lose the election and nor do I accept that advertising turned the corner for us. Any party prefers to have good advertising rather than weak advertising. It is right that party managers should strive to achieve the best. I entirely doubt, however, whether newspaper advertising in the last few days of the campaign had any serious effect on the outcome. Even less is it credible that any changes in the advertising approach or the script had a serious impact.

Advertising cheers up the party and the candidates but leaves most of the electorate cold. Of course you need advertising, but rarely does it have a crucial impact upon the result. We won the election because our policies had produced low inflation, good economic growth, reduced taxes, more home owners and a range of industries successfully transferred from the public to the private sector. Most people felt better off and they feared that Labour would jeopardize that with ill-thought-out and badly costed economic policies. They distrusted Labour's defence policies and they compared the two leaders. Margaret Thatcher was by now a leading world statesman just back from a historic meeting with Gorbachev. Neil Kinnock was seen as inexperienced and lightweight. Only one thing could have defeated that combination – the impression that at the centre we were disunited and in panic.

Fortunately the divisions that existed were not seen by the public and indeed only rarely glimpsed by ministers like myself who were most often on the road around the constituencies. My own realization that something was wrong came on the Wednesday night before 'wobbly Thursday'. The aim of any election press conference is to produce not just words but pictures which can be used by television. For my first health press conference I had produced a map of flashing lights to illustrate our hospital building programme. This was effective enough to get a round of applause from the assembled journalists, but illustrating social security is not so easy.

We had produced a graph which challenged Labour on the cost of their social security proposals. Arriving in Central Office, I breezed into the room where the graphics were usually checked. I explained what we had in mind. There was a rather shell-shocked atmosphere and quietly I was asked whether I would now explain it all to another group. It became clear that there were now two teams in charge of presentation. Elections are always fraught affairs. There is, however, one rule. There should be one campaign and one team.

Yet what angered me most about the claims for credit which followed the 1987 election was that they pushed to one side the people who really are responsible for election victories. There is the voluntary effort around the country of the party members who keep the associations going in the bad years as well as the good. And there is the work of the party's professional agents – very much including the staff at Conservative Central Office – who provide one of the distinctive strengths of the Conservative Party. This professional organization sets us apart from what Harold Wilson called the penny-farthing machine of Labour. A party is run like any other big organization. You build up the right team

and then you trust in them. You do not change course half
way through an election campaign. History, then, needs to be put
right. But the events of 1987 are more than of just historical
interest. We need to ensure that it never happens again. At the next
election the press will concentrate as never before on detecting
the slightest split in the Conservative campaign. That is the legacy
of all those who sought credit for themselves after our third
victory.

With election night over, I returned to London on the Friday
morning to appear on the host of television and radio programmes
which were keeping going until the last results were through. My
intention was not, however, to bask in the warm afterglow of victory
but to be there in the event of any flak on our handling of the
health service. The opinion polls showed that health was one of
the areas (like education and employment) where Labour had run
ahead of us. It was not a long step from there to the charge that
this was all due to a lack of ministerial presentation.

I went first to Independent Television News who had been
having a good election. Their predictions on the outcome of the
election had proved much more accurate than the BBC's, and
Alistair Burnet put me through my paces in an atmosphere of
well-ordered calm. At the BBC Television Centre at White City
the atmosphere was very different.

The election studio seemed to be divided into warring camps,
with David Dimbleby and Peter Snow on one side and Robin Day
on the other. Dimbleby and Snow reported the results and kept
viewers up with events. Day carried out the political interviews. As
Peter Snow advanced towards his admittedly extraordinary chart
which showed the voting swings, Robin Day let out a very audible
chortle. That over, we got down to a perfectly sensible interview
until our conversation was suddenly, and unexpectedly, interrupted. An outside broadcast was peremptorily inserted into the
programme featuring the familiar health-service cast of a consultant, a nurse, a general manager and a health union representative.
All made their points as if the election was still to be settled. When
the interview ended, an exasperated Robin Day turned to me and
said wearily: 'Well, as far as I can tell they have raised at least a
dozen points there. Choose which ones you would like to answer.'
I made my escape as a film on education was just as suddenly

being inserted into the programme. It was not a good day for the BBC.

From the BBC, I returned to Sutton Coldfield. My own majority had increased to over 21,000 and I went round the streets in my loudspeaker car thanking voters. I then sat back to await developments. After almost six years in charge of the DHSS it was clear that I would be on the move, but the question was where? In politics there is little point in trying to guess your future. Stories were coming through from London that Norman Tebbit was standing down from Government altogether. In Sutton Coldfield the reports seemed scarcely credible. Norman had been Party Chairman in an election when we had won an almost unprecedented third term. He had also fought as hard as anyone for the achievements of the Thatcher Government while, at the same time, being a notably strong performer around the Cabinet table. It seemed inconceivable that he would leave and yet as the hours went by the political correspondents seemed more and more certain.

Norman and I had both come into the House of Commons at the 1970 general election. I saw him most closely after the bomb explosion at the 1984 Conservative Party Conference in Brighton. The explosion had woken me in my third floor room at the Grand Hotel just before 3 a.m. There was what sounded like a fall of masonry and then an uncanny silence. A minute or two later the alarm went but it was only when I went out on to the hotel's central staircase that I began to sense the enormity of what had happened. The scene was like something out of the First World War. There was dust and smoke in the air and down the stairs a long slow-moving crocodile of ministers, MPs and delegates. Keith Joseph was loyally clutching his red box; Patrick Jenkin was wearing only a silk dressing gown; Jock Bruce-Gardyne was fully dressed with the exception of one shoe. I joined up with Nigel Lawson and as we looked back we could see for the first time the damage that had been caused to the Grand Hotel. One section of it seemed to have collapsed like a lift-shaft.

Although we did not know it at the time, underneath the rubble were Margaret and Norman Tebbit, and John Wakeham and his wife Roberta. Tragically, Roberta was among the five killed as too were Anthony Berry, a long-time colleague in the Commons, and Eric Taylor, Chairman of the North-West area Conservatives.

John was seriously injured but made a remarkable recovery and was welcomed back to the Chamber of the House of Commons by members on both sides standing and waving order papers. Margaret and Norman were also badly injured and later I saw them both in hospital in Brighton and then in Stoke Mandeville. Throughout the long months that followed Brighton, they both showed a brand of courage that marks them out as very special people. It was a great blow to the Government when on the Friday after the election it was confirmed that Norman was standing down. The Cabinet lost one of Margaret Thatcher's wisest counsellors and a minister whose political feel was invaluable.

Just before 11 a.m. on Saturday morning, 13 June, I received a telephone call from Nigel Wicks, the Prime Minister's Private Secretary. 'Could you come in to see the Prime Minister at 3.20 p.m.?' he asked. Fiona and I put together our belongings. We packed Kate and Isobel into the car and to the accompaniment of a tape of *Puff the Magic Dragon* drove back to London.

I arrived at 10 Downing Street just before 3.15 p.m. and was directed to the waiting room outside the Cabinet room. There to my surprise I found two ministers already waiting: John Major and John Moore. I say to my surprise because when, in 1981, I coincided in the waiting room with David Howell this was regarded as a mild breach of protocol. Ministers in reshuffles were then kept apart. But even more ministers were to arrive. The next to enter was Ken Clarke and he was followed by John MacGregor. Finally in came Paul Channon. It was beginning to become like a doctor's waiting room.

Fortunately there was little tension about whether we were 'in' or 'out'. The departures had taken place that morning. The official announcements had not been made but we had all heard the lunchtime news. It was clear that John Biffen, who had proved an outstanding Leader of the House of Commons but had seriously fallen out with the Prime Minister, was a prominent casualty. It was also clear that the gathering in the waiting room that afternoon were the changes. Our speculation, then, was reasonably cheerful. Who was going where?

On the basis of my 1981 experience I offered the theory that it all depended on what order we were going in to see the Prime Minister. The person behind the man in front was getting his job.

Thus in 1981 David Howell had taken over from me as Transport Secretary. We compared times and found John Major going in behind John MacGregor. If my theory was right, John Major would be entering the Cabinet for the first time as Chief Secretary to the Treasury. I knew also that Ken Clarke was just behind me and my assumption was that he was to become Social Services Secretary. But then John Moore intervened to say that actually he was between myself and Ken Clarke. That was my first indication – and I suspect John's also – that he was to take over the DHSS.

Personally I believe it would have been better all round had Ken taken over my job at this point. He was one of the very few people in the Government who both wanted the job and had the experience to do it. I suspect that his disadvantage in the immediate post-election period was that he was seen as one of the 'old gang'. He was not likely to produce a radically different approach to the health service but to build on the reforms that had been carried out over the previous six years. John Moore did not have the same social services background but would have made an excellent Trade and Industry Secretary. Or, indeed, he could well have stayed at the Transport Department where he was making an impact and which has suffered from too many changes at the top.

I was still no wiser where I was to go. In order of appearance I was directly behind John Major – but it seemed unlikely that I would take over his job as Minister of State for Social Security. To my total surprise Margaret Thatcher offered me the Department of Employment. I had assumed that Lord Young would be staying in that job but in fact he was going together with Ken Clarke to Trade and Industry. Margaret and I talked for some minutes about the job but the point I remember most clearly was her obvious sadness in losing Norman Tebbit from the Cabinet. In view of everything that has been written about their conflicts in the 1987 campaign, I would only record that she felt that Norman's decision to step down was a real blow to the Government and one that she genuinely regretted.

Downstairs again we compared notes as we waited to go to the Palace to be sworn in either as new Secretaries of State or to the Privy Council. John Major was indeed to become Chief Secretary to the Treasury. John MacGregor was going to Agriculture in place of the unlucky Michael Jopling who did all the right things and paid the price in terms of popularity with the farmers. Paul Channon was moving to Transport and Cecil Parkinson, who was also at Number 10 that afternoon, was returning to the Cabinet as Energy Secretary. John Wakeham was to go from Chief Whip to Leader of the Commons and at Buckingham Palace I met Peter Walker and learned of the strangest appointment of all. Peter was to become Secretary of State for Wales. Before the changes I would have given very high odds on the Welsh job not being offered to him – or for that matter being accepted. Nevertheless, Peter, with all the skill of the old professional he is, proved a resounding success in Wales.

As I left Downing Street *en route* to the Palace there was a sudden thunderstorm. One of the doorkeepers at Number 10 helped me to my car with an umbrella. There then came a picture of absolute journalistic devotion. Standing drenched in the pouring rain was Chris Moncrieff, the long-serving political correspondent of the Press Association. All the appointments would be announced in a couple of hours but Chris Moncrieff wanted, like the excellent reporter he is, to be first with the news. 'What have you got?' he asked hopefully, with water pouring down him. I felt guilty as I avoided the question. 'I am delighted,' I shouted through the downpour.

Indeed I was delighted. I had served longer than any of my predecessors as Social Services Secretary and I wanted to return to an industrial department. Although I had started my political career as a specialist on Home Office affairs, my move to Transport had opened up new horizons. I regarded success in industry as basic to national success. But as I moved I had some rather more personal thoughts. I had been on the Conservative front bench for over a dozen years and for the last six years I had carried out a job which had kept me tied down seven days a week. At times life was fraught; at times it was exciting. One factor, however, remained constant. There was precious little time for anything else. This had not mattered when I had first joined the Shadow Cabinet in the mid-1970s. I was divorced and had no other responsibilities. That had now all changed. I was a member of a family with a wife, two very young daughters and a stepson in his middle teens. It was in this post-election period that I pencilled in May 1989 as the date I would step down. By then I would have served ten years successively in Cabinet and there were not many ministers who had done that this century. Employment, then, was to be my last post. I resolved I would make a success of it and seek to go out with a modest bang not a whimper.

CHAPTER 15

Fully Employed

Independent

M argaret Thatcher had come to power in the wake of the Winter of Discontent and at a time when internationally Britain had become a byword for strikes and industrial unreliability. During the 1970s we lost an average of 13 million working days a year through strikes. The law allowed strikes to be called without a secret ballot of trade union members. Strikers could picket other places of work regardless of whether the workers there had any dispute with their own employer. No limit was set on the number of pickets with the result that factories could be closed by intimidation. It was a dire position and yet there were plenty of people who doubted whether any government could ever correct it. Harold Wilson had given up on his attempt and Ted Heath had been defeated. Why should it be thought that Margaret Thatcher's Government would succeed?

Yet in the years following 1979, slowly and cautiously the law was reformed. In spite of their different political stances the strategy of Norman Tebbit, the hawk, was not that different from the approach of his predecessor Jim Prior, the dove. Both Employment Secretaries eschewed an all-embracing bill like Ted Heath's massive Industrial Relations Act of 1972. Both took the view that any legislation should carry public opinion with it, even if the price was that we were a step behind what was desirable. Each step was consolidated before the next stage was attempted. Industrial relations reform became the art of the politically possible, with separate acts in 1980, 1982 and 1984.

The strategy (far more typical of the Thatcher Government than is generally supposed) was spectacularly successful. Secret ballots were made compulsory; secondary action was curtailed; and the number of pickets was limited. Steadily the position was transformed. There were full-scale battles like the miners' strike but there was no prospect the Government would give way. By 1986 the number of strikes had reached its lowest level for fifty years. In my period as Employment Secretary between 1987 and 1990 the average number of days lost through strikes had come down to just over three million a year. The reform of the labour laws and the improvement in British industrial relations became one of the most important achievements of the Thatcher years.

At the centre of the revolution was the Department of Employment whose role changed almost out of recognition as the 1980s progressed. Traditionally, the job of the Minister of Labour – for that was his title in much of the post-war period – had been to settle strikes. He was there as a last court of appeal. Intervention of this kind was emphatically not the approach of the Thatcher Government. The services of the conciliation service, ACAS, were available but whether they were used or not was entirely up to the parties in dispute. Ministers no longer called in unions and management but concentrated instead on providing the right background of law in which companies could pursue their own policies and negotiations. We had thankfully lost a troubled empire and were now developing a new and more constructive role. Rather than industrial mediation, the new task of ministers and the department was to promote employment, to remove obstacles in the labour market, and most crucially of all to promote training.

On Monday 15 June 1987, I went for the first time to my new department. Our headquarters at Caxton House were almost next door to Central Hall, Westminster. It was everything that the Department of Health and Social Security had not been. It was within walking distance of the House of Commons and the surroundings verged on the luxurious. My office had been designed as a flat and came complete both with bathroom and dressing room. It reminded me of the joke made about a colleague's country garden: on a clear day you could see to the other end. Even so, it was still below the standard that any junior Foreign Office minister might expect to inherit.

In terms of ministers I was lucky to acquire two excellent new signings. John Cope, the former Deputy Chief Whip, came in as Minister of State; and Patrick Nicholls was promoted from the back benches to Parliamentary Secretary. The team was completed by an existing Employment Minister, John Lee, who put his heart and soul into developing the tourist industry with the help of Duncan Bluck who deserved more recognition than he received as Chairman of both the British Tourist Authority and the English Tourist Board. The strong civil-service staff was headed by Michael Quinlan, reputed to be the cleverest man in Whitehall

and certainly one of the nicest. A few months later Michael moved
to Defence, which had always been his first love, and his place
was taken by Geoffrey Holland who had devoted a lifetime to
improving training. For the first time I found myself older than
my Permanent Secretary – albeit only by a few months. I reflected
that serving on Margaret Thatcher's Opposition and Government
front benches was the longest period of continuous employment I
had ever enjoyed.

Other features of my life also remained the same. Not content
with four years of opposing me on health and social security,
Michael Meacher now moved over to Employment. He had
become my eternal Shadow. As Colin Welch asked in the *Daily
Mail*: if Mr Fowler was appointed Governor of New South Wales,
'would Mr Meacher follow on the next convict ship? If he retired,
would Mr Meacher be seconded to the same sunset home?'

I spent the first weeks looking over my new department. While
I was on holiday in August I set out for myself what I saw as my
work schedule for the next couple of years:

My priorities are to reduce unemployment and by the same
measure to improve training – not just for young people but
through life. The days are over when a person left school; took
up a trade; and stayed in the same trade and with the same firm
for the whole of his career without refresher training. Industrial
relations legislation is decided for the first session of Parliament
and industrial relations itself remains important. We must not
be lulled into a false sense of security. We should try to take
the opportunity we now have to develop ways of involving the
workforce. We should give people a sense of ownership – that
it is *their* firm and the success of it is important to them.

Of these aims, there was no doubt which was the most politically
and socially urgent. Unemployment came top of every list of
national concerns. Some say that this did not represent the political
reality and that the public tended to vote on the basis of what
affected them, not someone else. I have never accepted that as a
political theory or as a guide to social policy. There were overwhelming human reasons for wanting to avoid the waste of
unemployment and politically it was an issue which we could not

ignore. On Thursday 18 June, I attended my first Cabinet meeting in my new post and was able to report that unemployment had fallen below three million. In every month I carried out the job I reported further falls. When I started unemployment was over three million and when I left it had almost halved to under 1.6 million. I do not, however, claim that the bulk of the improvement could be put down to us at Employment.

The major reason for the fall was undoubtedly the growth in the economy. As industry and business recovered, job vacancies increased. In the Employment Department we had an important supporting role. We sponsored two of the employment growth areas – tourism and small business – and we ran the Youth Training Scheme to tackle youth unemployment. The major public concern was about youth unemployment, but by 1987 it was clear that the position for young people was changing very much to their advantage. Rather than a surfeit of young people coming onto the labour market, we now faced a shortage. Birth rates in the 1970s meant that there would be a million fewer school-leavers by the early 1990s. Employers were likely to be competing to recruit the young, particularly the young with good qualifications. There were still undoubted problems in inner cities and among ethnic minorities, but the problem that gave me most cause for concern were the long-term unemployed.

Most people who lose their jobs go back into employment fairly quickly. The long-term unemployed have been out of work for more than twelve months. In 1987, they remained without jobs for a whole range of reasons. Many had been caught in the recession of the late 1970s and early 1980s. They lived in areas where traditional industries like ship-building or steel-making had severely contracted or disappeared. New jobs were difficult to come by and what these people most often required were new skills. New skills required new training.

When I took over at Employment, we did not have a programme which provided that training. There was the Community Programme but, although that did valiant local work, it did not provide the people on it with the skills they required. It gave people a taste of work but not a regular path to employment. I remember going to Bolton to see the Community Programme in operation. I met there about a dozen young men in their early twenties. They had cleared and constructed a football pitch on the side of a hill in the bleakest of Lancashire weather. They liked the work and would have liked to have stayed in construction. But their project was coming to an end and they faced going back on the dole. A few miles away I met a number of building employers who were complaining that it was becoming difficult to find labour. It seemed to me that it should not be beyond us to train and to join up those who were looking for jobs with those who had jobs to offer.

The flagship adult training programme I inherited was called the Job Training Scheme. However, although it had been heavily advertised, it had failed to attract the unemployed to it. At no stage did the numbers on it rise above 30,000. This was partly because it was brought on national stream too quickly, but partly for another reason. One of the most perplexing, irritating and intractable issues about unemployment was that substantial numbers of unemployed people refused to be trained.

I had become convinced when I was at the DHSS that there was a substantial 'black economy' in Britain. Everything I now saw at the Employment Department confirmed that picture. Around the country we ran Job Clubs. The idea was simple but effective. Unemployed people were helped and motivated to apply for jobs and everything was provided – telephones, newspapers, writing paper. Yet of those who said that they would go to a Job Club, around seven out of ten failed to show up. It was not that they went to the Job Club and decided it was of no help. They did not go in the first place. Even more dramatically, our fraud drives uncovered abuse with people claiming unemployment benefit and working at the same time. At a major building site in Birmingham, investigators found that 130 of the 450 workers employed there were also drawing benefit. They were in full-time, well-paid work, but they appeared in the total of the unemployed. In any discussion of unemployment we need to recognize that there is a significant minority who for one reason or another do not want to get off the register.

We should recognize one other fact. The conventional theory is that the high level of benefit paid to families with children acts as a disincentive to people coming back to work. In 1988 I commissioned a survey in London of the unemployment position. It showed that, at that time, there were about 250,000 people registered as unemployed and yet there were 140,000 job vacancies. Nearly one in ten of the unemployed had a degree and over half had some kind of qualification. About a third of the vacancies required no previous knowledge or experience. In London over half the unemployed were single and no less than 70 per cent had no dependent children.

Of course, most unemployed people are genuinely unemployed and for them the most likely path back to work is through training. By November 1987 I felt that we were sufficiently advanced to put to Margaret Thatcher proposals for a new unified training programme. This programme was to sweep up all the existing schemes and initially we planned 300,000 places for it. As unemployment dropped dramatically, we reduced that figure to nearer 200,000. The aim was to give about six months' training and to place as many people as possible with employers or in positions where they could go on into full-time employment. Employment Training was by far the most ambitious programme that had ever been introduced in Britain. Contrary to many predictions, we also decided that it should be a voluntary programme. We had a perfectly sensible weapon against abuse and that was the long-standing rule, accepted by Labour and Conservative Governments alike, that benefit could be reduced or withdrawn for those who did absolutely nothing to find work. My instinct to rely on this course was confirmed by a number of visits overseas.

In socialist Sweden training was not compulsory but unemployed people claiming benefit were expected to take the opportunities that were there. If they failed to do so, or simply fell out after a few days, they were brought back in and required to start again. In West Germany similar efforts were made to bring back unemployed people into the workforce. The German view was clear. In Bonn an office block was devoted to both paying out benefit and finding jobs. The benefit part was utilitarian and uninviting; the job-finding part was well carpeted and plush. My approach was confirmed by American experience. In the United States compulsory Workfare, under which benefit claimants are compelled to train, was supposed to flourish. There were, in fact, notably few examples of such programmes in action.

The lesson I brought back from the United States had nothing to do with Workfare and came from Boston. There I saw in operation a 'compact' or agreement between employers and schools for the benefit of children in inner-city areas. Provided the children met certain standards – attendance as well as academic – they were guaranteed a job interview. We adapted that concept to this country and with the imported help of Kay Stratton, an exceptional public servant from Boston, introduced it here. We gave guarantees of jobs and the compacts were welcomed by companies and schools alike. We thought that perhaps we would get five or six compacts established in Britain. At the last count there were no fewer than sixty compacts covering virtually every inner-city area in the country.

If compacts were welcomed, however, that was certainly not the reaction of the Labour Party and many trade unions to Employment Training. Characteristically Michael Meacher came out against ET from the start, but the man in the driving seat was not Meacher but Ron Todd, the General Secretary of the Transport and General Workers' Union. What made his opposition particularly galling was that he was one of the three trade-union representatives on the Manpower Services Commission, the body that had proposed such a training programme in the first place. Consistency, however, had no part in Todd's attitude. It was clear that his union activists were against the programme and as General Secretary he obliged by doing a clumsy somersault. Rather than keeping a discreet silence, he led the opposition.

When it came to the TUC Conference in September 1988, Todd proposed the motion that the TUC should withdraw all support for the training programme and institute a policy of non-cooperation. It was this policy which – in spite of the advice of Neil Kinnock himself – was adopted by the TUC. Kinnock's intervention was an effort to avoid the bad press which inevitably came, but he had only himself to blame for the mess. He had allowed his front-bench team to roam the country campaigning against the programme. The result was that, incredibly, the Labour Party and the TUC proclaimed themselves opposed to Britain's biggest ever programme for retraining the unemployed.

In fact, their attitude had remarkably little effect. There was no evidence that unemployed people were influenced and, indeed, some anecdotal signs that the loud opposition gave the programme a higher profile than it otherwise would have had. Very few training programmes had been launched amidst as many headlines as ET. There was also the clearest evidence that neither employers nor many unions at the local level intended to take the slightest notice of the TUC resolution. The whole episode was far more revealing of the TUC than of the Government's training policies. But it did leave me with one unresolved question.

Employment Training had resulted from proposals from the Manpower Services Commission. This was a tripartite body with representatives from government, employers and unions. The TUC had now voted to withdraw support for the commission's biggest programme. To be blunt, the TUC had demonstrated what the critics already believed, namely that the commission had become a piece of outdated machinery whose only function was to delay action. My predecessor, Lord Young, had sought to abolish it prior to the 1987 election but had lost the argument. Now it was clear that there was no option. The Manpower Services Commission was abolished and, as in the case of the abolition of one or two of the giant metropolitan councils, there was scarcely a murmur of dissent. As for Employment Training itself, we managed to place more than 200,000 people in training within ten months of the programme being introduced. The issue which continued to give concern, however, was the number of unemployed who, having agreed to training, did not show up. The record was better than any other adult programme, but nevertheless something like 40 per cent still failed to make it to the front door.

Over the months one other point had become crystal clear. Training for the unemployed was important, but even more important in achieving better industrial performance was training for the employed. It did not make sense to divide the two areas into watertight compartments. In this I had been much influenced by the German experience. For decades, Germany had been ahead of us in training. There are references to their superiority which go back to the end of the last century. The secret of Germany's success seemed to be that they based their training locally and involved employers closely. Britain had tended to think in terms of bureaucratic national bodies with Whitehall, or at least the Manpower Services Commission at Sheffield, intervening at every level. My view was that the department should certainly monitor standards but we would do much better if the training itself was in the hands of local employers. The Germans based their training on the chambers of commerce and I thought we could largely follow their example.

Here again we had a stroke of luck. Margaret Thatcher had been much impressed by the ideas of the Chairman of the CBI for Scotland, Bill Hughes. As a result we all met together at Chequers on Saturday 3 September 1988, and it soon became clear we were thinking along similar lines. Our plans south of the border were more advanced and in December I published a White Paper which set up the new Training and Enterprise Councils. The idea was that industry would play the major role but that each council would also include members of the local community chosen on merit and not because they represented a particular organization. There might be an educationist or the leader of a voluntary group. I certainly hoped there would be a local trade-union leader on the council, for I had no wish to exclude the unions. Indeed the tragedy of the training debate is that it is polarized, whereas a sensible national aim would be to achieve consensus.

The councils were to take over responsibility for programmes like Youth Training and Employment Training, but their role was also to encourage training by employers. We set up a National Training Task Force to bring the new system into operation, and at once it became clear that we had a great deal of practical support from industry. Normally there is considerable difficulty finding men and women to sit on such a body. For the task force we had few refusals, although it was perfectly clear that the job was anything but a sinecure. The members included Tony Cleaver of IBM, Prudence Leith, Peter Thompson of NFC, Eric Pountain of Tarmac, James Ackers, a former President of the Chambers of Commerce, Allen Sheppard, the Chairman of Grand Metropolitan, and Bill Jordan, the President of the Amalgamated Engineering Union. A real find was Brian Wolfson, the man responsible for transforming the fortunes of Wembley Stadium, to chair the task force. It is thanks to him and his team – ably supported by the staff of the Training Agency – that today we have some eighty councils up and running.

The hope must be that the councils will now be accepted as the way forward. It would be a huge act of folly if we were ever, over the next years, to ditch them and start again with some other form of organization. That does not mean that there cannot be change. The councils, for example, should be given maximum independence. We have recruited some excellent managers up and down the country. They are certainly not going to be content to be quasi-bureaucrats implementing a policy laid down from above. Having embarked on this course, we must have the courage of our convictions and devolve.

In Whitehall the next logical step is for the Departments of Industry and Employment to come together. Both departments have lost much of their traditional role. Employment no longer settles strikes; Industry no longer runs companies. Next to no one wants to go back to the old position. The private sector is the proper place for industries and good industrial relations are best secured by company effort and sensible law. The reduction of the present level of unemployment will depend on the recovery of the economy, but a united department would be in a strong position to advise on the measures which could be taken to soften its impact. Above all, however, their efforts in the post-privatization era should be directed at improving the standards of the workforce. In this agenda better training is of vital importance.

Frustratingly, training is still regarded in Britain as a worthy but rather dull area. Since the war, we have all recognized the importance of education. Great hopes are placed on the Government's present education reforms. I hope, and believe, they will be a success, but we should also remember this. The education reforms will be comparatively slow in their effect. They will not benefit the present workforce. Yet eight out of ten of the workforce in the year 2000 are in the workforce now. The reforms in education must go hand in hand with reforms in training. If they do not, then as a nation we will decline. Training is as important as that.

By the time I became Employment Secretary, many of the long-standing problems affecting the labour market had been tackled. However, there remained one which had been carefully avoided in the ten years since Margaret Thatcher's election. On Thursday 6 April 1989, the Cabinet met at 8.30 a.m. It was the earliest start for a full Cabinet meeting that I could remember since we had come to office. The reason was that President Gorbachev had come to London and was starting talks with Margaret Thatcher at

10 a.m. at Downing Street. It was an important meeting. The Soviet Union was in the first stages of the fundamental reform which was to bring the Iron Curtain crashing down. The Prime Minister's diary had been cleared for the visit. Margaret Thatcher had even dropped out from her regular Thursday afternoon Parliamentary Questions when she faced Neil Kinnock over the dispatch box of the House of Commons. The one part of her diary that remained was Cabinet and that was because we needed to decide on my proposal to abolish the Dock Labour Scheme.

The Dock Labour Scheme dated back to the 1940s. Under the Attlee Government's post-war legislation, over eighty ports (every major port in the country at that time) were brought into the scheme. It even became a criminal offence for an employer to employ anyone other than registered dockworkers on dock work without the approval of the National Dock Labour Board. Registered dockworkers were, in effect, given a statutory monopoly quite unlike anything else in British industry. By the early 1970s, however, cargo handling was undergoing a revolution. Goods were entering ports in pre-packed containers and were being collected and delivered by lorry. Traditional dock work had become outdated. Registered dockworkers then claimed that it was their job to fill and empty the containers. Disputes and strikes inevitably followed.

As the price for ending the 1972 national dock strike, the Heath Government had accepted the proposals of a committee headed by Lord Aldington and Jack Jones, then General Secretary of the Transport and General Workers' Union. These proposals succeeded only in making the position of scheme ports even worse. Port employers were required to retain, on at least basic pay, any registered dockworker regardless of whether they had work for him. In addition, they were required to accept workers allocated to them by local dock boards from employers who had gone out of business. Dockers were given 'a job for life' irrespective of whether there was any work to do. The only comparatively bright spot came in 1978 when, thanks to one or two brave Labour rebels, the Commons threw out an attempt by the Labour Government to extend the scheme even further to half a mile inland.

I had first seen the effects of the Dock Labour Scheme when I had been Minister of Transport in 1979. Serious overmanning was pushing ports like London and Liverpool into heavy loss. In practice, the only way to reduce this surplus labour was by voluntary redundancy. Ports had to buy out the dockers' rights, but even that depended on the offer being accepted. There was nothing to prevent a docker without work simply sitting it out and drawing basic pay which he might, or might not, supplement by other jobs outside the ports. When I left the Transport Department the repeal of the Dock Labour Scheme remained a major piece of unfinished business.

Policy responsibility for the scheme was with the Employment Department and in 1979 Jim Prior had no wish to embroil the new Government in a major dock strike. That remained the position through the first two terms of the Thatcher Government. No one could justify the scheme, but the political risk of abolishing it was regarded as too high – albeit that our action in denationalizing the British Transport Docks Board in the early 1980s had passed off without incident. Wrongly, some felt that the scheme would wither on the vine. The truth, however, was that as long as there were scheme ports there would always be registered dockers. Change could only be brought about by Act of Parliament.

After the general election of 1987, we took a new look at the prospects for repeal. One of the most notable developments over the years had been the growth of the non-scheme ports. An outstanding example was Felixstowe which had been little more than a run-down wharf in 1945 and had thus escaped registration. It was adjudged too small to bother about. Over the years Felixstowe had prospered and so, too, had the dockers working there. There had been no return to casual working, which was the haunting fear of the unions. Earnings were high, but so was productivity. The result had been that Felixstowe had developed into one of the leading ports in the country.

The employers in the scheme ports looked on with envy. For them the scheme meant that the unions had in effect a veto over any employment changes. Management was unable to manage; and only the local dock boards could dismiss, which they very rarely did. Restrictive practices abounded and even had their own special names to describe them. 'Ghosting' was when dockers were paid to stand and watch skilled workers actually doing the job;

'bobbing' was when gang sizes were too large and dockers were simply sent home. But this was not all. As far as investment was concerned, there was a blight on port areas. No one was going to invest in, for example, a new warehouse, when they risked facing a claim that it was covered by the scheme. The ironical result was that the safest investment was highly priced housing or offices. Nor was it possible to claim that the scheme had brought industrial peace. Since 1967 over four million working days had been lost because of disputes in the scheme ports.

It was a lamentable position and the case for abolition was as overwhelming as ever. But would we do it? The Transport Secretary, Paul Channon, was an unqualified supporter of abolition and so too was the Chancellor of the Exchequer, Nigel Lawson. On the back benches I had strong support from Members like David Davis and Nicholas Bennett, who are now both in the Government. Crucial, however, was the view of Margaret Thatcher herself, and her reputation for pugnaciousness overlooked an important part of her character. She also had a natural caution.

Certainly it is true that in crises like the Falklands War, she responded quickly and decisively. The issue was clear; the die had been cast. The Dock Labour Scheme provided a different set of issues. If the Government moved to repeal, we would be initiating the action itself. If the result was a prolonged dock strike, with all the possible economic damage that entailed, there would be many to say that the Government had chosen the wrong target. After all, there were only 9,400 registered dockers. Was it worth the trouble? Margaret Thatcher had been sitting at the Cabinet table at the time of the 1972 dock strike. She did not like the scheme any more than we did but she had to be persuaded that, not only were we right in principle, but that we had a strategy to bring about abolition successfully.

There was one fundamental decision to make. The Transport Department favoured an approach which set the repeal of the scheme in the context of the reform of the ports generally. Under their plan, repeal would be announced in a White Paper and would be followed by comprehensive legislation which would, for example, allow trust ports to go into the private sector. I saw the point of this proposal. It underlined the truth that we were modernizing the whole ports industry. I favoured, however, another approach.

My view was that we should pass a short bill which did nothing else but abolish the scheme. My concern was that with a White Paper we would simply put the unions on notice and give them the time they needed to mobilize their forces. It would provide the long strike we wanted to avoid. My plan contained risks, for its success depended on secrecy being maintained. The strategy would be destroyed if, as so often in the past, we had 'leaks'.

It meant keeping the planning to a small group of ministers and officials in the Employment and Transport Departments. As for timing, I wanted to see a bill introduced early in 1989 and carried through all its stages by July. If there were to be a strike, I wanted to have it over by the August recess. I remembered only too well from the health service in 1982 what happens to an industrial dispute when Parliament is not sitting and the press have nothing else to write about. It gets out of your control.

It was this strategy which was accepted in mid-1988, but only on a contingency basis. No decision had been made to abolish the Dock Labour Scheme. Rather the decision was that *if* we decided to go ahead with the abolition of the scheme, that was how it would be done. In the autumn of 1988 we started to look at the complexities of drafting an abolition bill but it was not until March 1989 that we agreed the compensation terms for dockers made redundant – and even then still on a contingency basis.

The abolition bill and a short White Paper which went with it were agreed by a small group of ministers chaired by the Prime Minister on Monday 3 April. At the Cabinet meeting at 8.30 a.m. on the Thursday, the day Mikhail Gorbachev was in London, the plan was approved. At 1 p.m. on Thursday afternoon, the advance notice went up on the Commons annunciator that I was to make a statement on the 'Dock Labour Scheme' later in the day. Quite exceptionally, that was the first sign the press had had that something was afoot. Even then, however, it was far from clear just what the Government had in mind. A mild reform was one possibility, or even an increase in severance payments.

I arrived at the House in time for what would have been Prime Minister's Questions. When the Prime Minister cannot take them, the Leader of the House of Commons stands in. Thus it was John

Wakeham who rose and in the time-honoured way said he had been asked to reply. 'Why?' asked a number of Labour MPs pretending to be outraged at the Prime Minister choosing to see the President of the Soviet Union rather than themselves. Rather unwisely, John decided to answer. The Prime Minister had decided to 'make herself available to Mr Gorbachev'. There were roars of helpless laughter which went on and on. It is just the kind of *double entendre* that the House of Commons loves. But it had a great advantage for me. It put everyone in a sunny mood and as far as our side was concerned the mood was to last.

According to Simon Heffer of the *Daily Telegraph*, my statement that the scheme would be abolished and a bill introduced the next day resulted in the biggest Conservative cheer in the Commons since the 1979 election. Certainly as I glanced back our side were waving order papers in the air, the traditional sign of a really popular statement. The joy, however, was not shared by the Labour benches. Michael Meacher charged over the top shouting that the announcement was an act of sabotage and would plunge the nation into politically motivated strife in the docks. Eric Heffer, the veteran Liverpool MP, said that the decision would be resisted 'in every possible way' and that Tory MPs who had enthusiastically supported the move were 'lower than vermin'. The scene looked set for industrial war.

On Friday I chaired the first of the daily meetings to oversee progress. The committee was made up of all the Whitehall departments with a direct interest. Employment and Transport clearly had the closest interest. But we also needed the advice of Agriculture on food supplies; Trade and Industry on the effect on the movement of goods; and Scotland, Wales and Northern Ireland to report on the effects around the United Kingdom. My announcement had been met by a walk-out at Liverpool, Tilbury and Southampton, but right from the beginning it was clear that there had not been the spontaneous explosion of anger which some had feared. Most of the scheme ports were working normally as too were the non-scheme ports like Felixstowe. The response of the Transport and General Workers' Union was a remarkable commentary upon how things had changed since 1979. Ten years before, there would have been no question of waiting for meetings, let alone ballots. The strike would have been 'on' from the moment of the announcement. In 1989 wise unions were careful to find out what their members really wanted and to hold a secret ballot.

Our worst scenario was that by the Monday we would be at the centre of a nationwide dock strike. When Monday came, however, virtually all the ports were back at work and the docks committee of the TGWU had still not decided whether to call for a ballot. Apparently they were held up on the question of whether this would be an industrial dispute or a political dispute against the Government. If it was a political strike, it could place them on the wrong side of the law and put their funds at risk of sequestration. The union decided to play safe and called a meeting of their executive for the Friday. Ron Todd's plan was that there should be an attempt to negotiate a new scheme with the employers. He realized that this was doomed to failure but believed the attempt at negotiation would beyond doubt make it an industrial dispute. Inside the union the argument went to and fro but on the Friday Todd's strategy was endorsed.

The result was that, contrary to all our expectations, when the abolition bill received its Second Reading in the Commons on Monday 17 April there was no strike and no obvious signs of conflict. It was not until the following Thursday, after the employers had predictably rejected the union plans for a replacement scheme, that the ground was clear for a ballot. But again there was delay. No one was certain when the ballot would actually take place. From our point of view only one thing had gone wrong. The Department of Trade and Industry had circulated very widely our secret contingency plans – including the likely length of the dispute and critical areas of shortage. This had ended up in the *Socialist Worker* but fortunately no one seemed much interested.

By Tuesday 25 April, the abolition bill was in committee and we were still without any strike or for that matter any ballot. Perhaps the TGWU were trying to avoid the Vale of Glamorgan by-election on 4 May, but it was not until mid-May that the ballot backing industrial action was announced. But then the union became involved in a legal wrangle with the employers. The employers sought an injunction on the grounds that a strike would not be in furtherance of a trade dispute but political action. Slightly to everyone's surprise, the injunction was granted pending a full

Batting for the Employment Department against the press in 1988

Decapitating a wax model of Margaret Thatcher in York in 1989

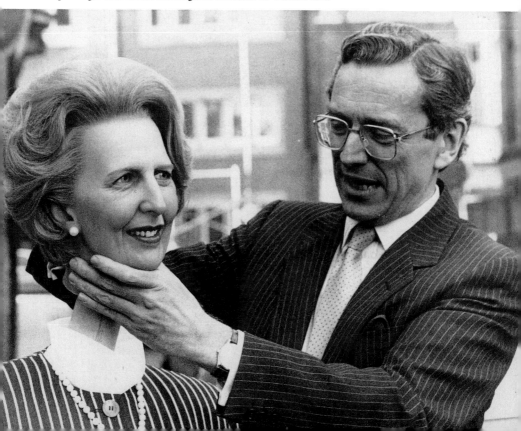

The Cabinet in 1979. *Back row, left to right:* Michael Jopling, Norman Fowler, John Biffen, David Howell, Norman St John-Stevas, Humphrey Atkins, George Younger, Michael Heseltine, Nicholas Edwards, Patrick Jenkin, John Nott, Mark Carlisle, Angus Maude, Sir John Hunt. *Front row, left to right:* Sir Ian Gilmour, Lord Soames, Sir Keith Joseph, Lord Carrington, William Whitelaw, Margaret Thatcher, Lord Hailsham, Sir Geoffrey Howe, Francis Pym, James Prior, Peter Walker. Only Norman Fowler, George Younger, Sir Geoffrey Howe and Peter Walker were still members of the Cabinet in 1989

The Cabinet in 1989. *Back row, left to right*: David Waddington, John Major, Lord Belstead, John Moore, Malcolm Rifkind, Kenneth Clarke, Kenneth Baker, John MacGregor, Paul Channon, John Wakeham, Cecil Parkinson, Antony Newton, Sir Robin Butler. *Front row, left to right*: Nicholas Ridley, Norman Fowler, Peter Walker, Lord Mackay, Sir Geoffrey Howe, Margaret Thatcher, Nigel Lawson, Douglas Hurd, George Younger, Tom King, Lord Young

Fiona on the night of my resignation, January 1990

hearing of the issue. The injunction was finally lifted in June.

Doubtless in union mythology the abolition of the Dock Labour Scheme will go down as an example of a union being entrapped by the tentacles of the law. This is not the right analysis, however. Certainly it is true that the union needed a ballot before industrial action could be taken. Equally it is true that the employers' injunction threw a spoke in the union wheel. But a major part of the delay was the direct responsibility of the union itself. They did not have their heart in a strike.

The TGWU sensed the mood correctly. This was not a dispute that they were ever likely to win. As the weeks went on, it was made clear by local port employers that there was indeed life after the Dock Labour Scheme and that many of their workers could look forward to a well-paid job in a good industry. The dockers themselves knew that there was overmanning and must have been expecting action to correct the position for several years. The £35,000 redundancy payments made to men with over fifteen years of service helped that process. Certainly few other industries have been as generous. The men made redundant in the metal-bashing industries of the West Midlands did not leave with payments of that size. But the real rub for the TGWU was this. Outside the ranks of the registered dockers, there was precious little support for a strike. There was no prospect of a strike going beyond the docks and little evidence of any wider support for a dock strike alone.

On 2 July the bill became law, having passed all its stages through both the Commons and the Lords. A month later, at the beginning of August, Ron Todd called off all industrial action and advised his members to take part in local negotiations. The Dock Labour Scheme was dead. The change was as permanent as any politician can ensure. For although we carried out abolition against fierce opposition, now that it has taken place there is very little prospect that the policy will be reversed. I certainly cannot see the Labour Party pledging themselves to restore the scheme. As for the ports themselves, all reports indicate that there has been a resurgence of activity and new investment. An enormous barrier to the development of British ports had been lifted. And with the Dock Labour Scheme successfully abolished, the way was clear for me to settle my own personal position.

CHAPTER 16

Resignation

Daily Mail

M ay 1989 was the tenth anniversary of the election of the Thatcher Government. Around the Cabinet table there were only five survivors from that team photograph taken in the heady days following our first election success: Geoffrey Howe, Peter Walker, George Younger, myself and, of course, Margaret Thatcher. It was an obvious opportunity (if opportunity were required) for the Prime Minister to have stood down.

Politically the Government was in the doldrums. The local elections in early May had not gone well; we were far behind in the opinion polls; and there were rumours that there might be a challenge to the leadership in the autumn. But Margaret Thatcher was above all a fighter. It would have been entirely out of character for her to have gone when she was personally under challenge and also when there was no certainty as to who would be her successor. The anniversary passed off with a number of low-key celebrations and Margaret made it clear that she wanted to look forward, not back. She recognized that anniversaries can be double-edged affairs. May 1989 certainly marked an exceptionally long period of government but it could also provoke a public response that it was now 'time for a change'.

As these major political considerations were being weighed, I was preoccupied with rather more personal thoughts. It had been many years since ministers had served such long terms in office without any break to recharge the batteries or to reintroduce themselves to their families. Politicians need time away from the demands of running a department if they are going to be able to develop new ideas. I had been sitting round either the Cabinet or Shadow Cabinet table since the age of thirty-seven. I was now fifty-one. Time was not on my side if I was to expand my experience in industry or seriously to put pen to paper again. I wanted also to see for myself some of the developments which were transforming the world, such as the signs of emerging political change in Eastern Europe.

Above all, however, I felt that I had a young family who also had rights at this stage in their lives. My concern was that unless

I did something over the next two or three years my two daughters would be teenagers without my really taking part in their development. Childhood goes so quickly and I had already seen Oliver go from six to his teens in what seemed to be record time. By May 1989 Kate was seven and Isobel almost five. Kate was a great enthusiast prepared to tackle any issue and enter any new activity. Isobel, with her distinctive red hair, gave the impression that butter would not melt in her mouth but was in fact a very determined young lady.

If my daughters had not exactly been born among the red boxes, politics was close to their lives from the beginning. The day Kate was born I was in Sutton Coldfield for the annual Remembrance Day parade. I have always made it a rule to go to the constituency for the ceremony rather than stand in the ranks of Cabinet ministers around the Cenotaph in Whitehall. A telephone call came through that I was required and I hared back to St Thomas's Hospital just in time to be there at the birth. In July 1984 Isobel managed to interrupt a Cabinet meeting. A note was passed in to me which said in capitals: 'YOUR WIFE IS HAVING A BABY. COME AT ONCE.' I passed the note to Margaret Thatcher and sped away over Westminster Bridge. Altogether typically, Isobel kept us waiting and then came into the world feet first.

I am occasionally asked to appear on television programmes as some kind of expert to discuss the family. I am always tempted to reply by saying that I left the Government to learn about the family, not to give advice. My motivation was very simple. I had no desire to reach the age of sixty with my children polite strangers. For one point is crystal clear about a family. However busy you may be, you cannot stop the clock. You cannot put your children on the shelf and say 'Sorry. I will return in a few years' time.' I was a middle-aged father with a divorce behind me. I wanted to take a couple of years out to get to know my own daughters.

Although at Westminster we love to pontificate about family policy, we are peculiarly unqualified to do so. The House of Commons makes no concessions to the family and its absurd working hours keep husbands, wives, and children as far apart as possible. British politics produces more than its fair share of one-parent families with the wife usually bringing up the children by herself. The higher you climb up the slippery pole the more difficult it all becomes. If your children are grown up then perhaps there are no problems, except for the spouse. If your children are young then there are undoubted difficulties and real choices to be made.

Some impression of my feelings over the years comes from an intermittent personal diary I kept. On Monday 2 February 1981, my forty-third birthday, I wrote:

The trouble with politics and particularly ministerial politics is that there is so much to demand your attention that you tend to ignore the basic issues of life itself. When I am doing politics, that takes all my energy and leaves very little for anything else. Clearly you cannot live like that for ever. Now that the early doubts about whether I can do the job at all have to a large extent been dispelled, I really have no excuse. My birthday resolution must be to integrate my life rather more successfully than I have over the previous forty-three years.

On 27 March 1981 I wrote:

For once, a day not dominated by politics. Fiona and I go out to dinner at a little Italian restaurant down by the river in Chelsea. I know that something is up. Even I know that. It is just over three years ago that we first went out to dinner. The restaurant is where I proposed a year later. Fiona breaks the news to me by giving me as a present a small bronze of a young man carrying a baby. We are both excited. Fiona loves children and will be super. What about me? I have been broken into children by Oliver and that has been a tremendous experience. My only fear is that I am rather a distant figure. I bustle off to work in the early morning and crawl back late at night. At weekends I am often away and on Sundays I am normally trying to catch up on the boxes. But of course this life cannot go on for ever. Children have an unqualified right for time to be spent on them and this I must do.

On holiday in France on 31 August 1983, I wrote:

Holidays also give time to catch up on the rest of life – like family life. I rely entirely on Fiona to run the family. I do not say that with any satisfaction. During the year the department and the red boxes take over. I am there for crises but I would be in a pretty mess without Fiona who manages to find time to organize the children, the house and still be my best friend when it comes to advice. Does she know how much I appreciate her?

On 16 February 1986, in the midst of the Leyland row, I wrote:

I am exhausted. I reintroduce myself to Fiona and the girls. They have to put up with a lot. I don't think the girls notice the very many occasions I am not there but I think Fiona feels like a single-parent family.

On Sunday 25 January 1987, after my trip to the United States to look at the AIDS issue, I wrote:

I treat the house as a lodging house. I can make excuses about the unending pressure of the department (which is real enough) but it is not remotely an adequate explanation. It is a matter of priorities. My wife and family should come first – and over the last months they have come last.

While on Friday 27 May 1988, during a Whitsun holiday on the Isle of Wight, I wrote:

Kate is growing up fast now. She can read well and has a remarkably retentive memory. She is a popular and very open girl. Isobel is now almost four – her speaking has come on a great deal, although she still has some difficulty with it. She is small and petite with a mass of red hair. Although there is this difference in age they happily do everything together. Fiona carries a big burden as far as the family is concerned. I am conscious of the fact that I flit in and out. Fiona is the anchor and because she does it so well everyone, of course, relies on her.

Surely, you might say, the pressure of a Cabinet minister's life is no greater than that of any other reasonably busy man? I can think of plenty of jobs where there are immense pressures. From my own experience I have seen the demands that a newspaper puts on editors and writers alike. I have also glimpsed the responsibility that the chairman of a big company and his senior executives face. Nevertheless I doubt whether there are many jobs which more consistently take a man or woman away from their family than being a Government minister. By most measures a minister's job is full time, but as well as running your department you need to remember that you are also a Member of Parliament and a spokesman for both Government and party.

You have been elected to represent your constituents. That does not mean you are a delegate but it does mean that you do your utmost to understand and keep up to date with the issues which are causing concern locally. It also means that you are on hand to help. Advice bureaux on Friday night or Saturday morning have been a regular part of my political life for over twenty years. Problems on housing, social security, tax, immigration, all come over the desk. The advice session is open to anyone irrespective of party allegiance and indeed one of my best-reported victories was for a prominent member of the local CND. What matters is not how they voted but that they live in your constituency. To do the job properly, you also need to have a home in the constituency.

At the weekend, the party will want you to take on speaking engagements in other constituencies. The complaint that Conservative Central Office most fear is the indignant 'We never see a minister here'. The result is that Fridays are booked up for months ahead and quite often Saturdays too. Throughout the week, you will be asked to appear at short notice on one of the ever-increasing gaggle of television and radio programmes. These days not even Sundays are sacred. Sunday programmes operate on the principle that nothing happens on the sabbath and they vie with each other to conduct interviews which will set the political agenda for Monday morning's newspapers. There are not many politicians today who follow the example of one distinguished figure of yesteryear who refused all invitations on the grounds that 'it is against my principles to make political speeches on Sundays'.

Inevitably there are pressures when you try to balance all these factors, as I set out in my diary for the weekend of 14–16 November 1986:

The British system of politics means a division between the ministerial role and the constituency role – although the same person carries out both. At the DHSS, AIDS continues to dominate our thoughts. Following the events of the week it is clearly sensible to have a speech extract from either myself or Tony [Tony Newton, the Minister of Health] for the Sunday papers. We labour over this at the Elephant and finally I manage to get away to Sutton Coldfield at 4 p.m. As soon as I step into my constituency role, the official support ends. I drive my own car away from the House of Commons and spend the next four and a half hours driving myself to Sutton Coldfield. The traffic could not be worse on the M1 – three lanes of traffic on the newly opened M25 join the three lanes of traffic already on the M1. The result is chaos. I finally arrive almost two hours late.

The next morning I have an advice bureau and then drive myself to Bromsgrove for a Conservative Political Centre meeting at an exotic château-style hotel. Back in Sutton Coldfield there is a speech to prepare for the Conservative trade unionist conference at Peterborough. On Sunday I set out driving to Peterborough at 8.30 in the morning; give my speech at 11; and then make my way back to London. The 'weekend' starts at 4 p.m. on Sunday afternoon.

The other serious complication in any politician's life is the eccentric hours of the House of Commons. Business on the floor of the House does not start until 2.30 p.m. in the afternoon and the serious voting at Westminster takes place during the evening. You are lucky to get away before 10 at night and quite often an hour or two later. All-night sessions going through to dawn are happily rare over the last few years. Nevertheless the hours are long and antisocial.

Some ministers add another element to the pressure and start working at an hour when most good citizens are safely and sensibly still asleep. For one period of my life I regularly started work at 5.30 a.m. This was when I had just taken over the Department of Health and Social Security and every issue – big, small and minute – appeared to run through my office. After a few months I came to the conclusion that it was a mug's game. Whitehall would feed you red boxes as long as you wanted to eat. If you were not careful, you simply ended up with the interdepartmental prize for letter signing and a reputation for seeing every piece of paper in circulation at the time. I found it better to devolve and (barring emergencies) to get up an hour later. Hopefully, I also remained reasonably alert for the rest of the day. I had noticed that one or two ministers who made a great deal about how they rose at 5 in the morning looked half dead by 8 in the evening.

It is not easy to choose a typical week in a minister's life to show how all these demands come together. But the following week in June 1989, taken from my official diary, gives some idea of what has to be packed in:

Sunday, 18 June
15.00 Settle down to the red boxes from the department which contain papers to be cleared, letters and Government correspondence.
22.00 To Broadcasting House for the BBC Radio 4 European Election results programme with Brian Redhead.
Midnight Depart Broadcasting House.

Monday, 19 June
09.30 Chair daily meeting at the Employment Department on the progress of the dispute about the abolition of the Dock Labour Scheme.
10.00 Meeting with my constituency secretary, Caroline Bell.
11.00 Meeting with ministers and Department of Employment officials.
12.00 Meeting with ministers and political advisers.
13.30 Lunch in the House of Commons tea room. Return to my department.
14.30 Briefing for an International Labour Organization meeting in Geneva on Wednesday.
16.00 Weekly meeting to review progress on the Training and Enterprise Councils.
17.00 Weekly meeting to review progress on the Employment Training programme.

18.00   Meeting on public spending.
19.45   Diplomatic Banquet at the British Museum. With Fiona. Black tie.
23.30   Arrive home. Work on red boxes.

Tuesday, 20 June
08.45   Arrive at my department.
09.30   Daily meeting on the dock dispute.
10.30   Internal meetings at department.
11.30   Briefing for Employment Questions in which ministers are questioned on the floor of the House of Commons.
13.30   Lunch in the House of Commons tea room.
14.30   Employment Questions in the Chamber.
15.15   Sit in for Prime Minister's Questions.
15.30   Return to department.
17.00   Leave for Heathrow Airport.
18.45   Depart from Heathrow for Geneva. Flight BA 732.
21.15   Arrive in Geneva.
22.00   Briefing for tomorrow's meeting.

Wednesday, 21 June
09.30   Arrive at the headquarters of the International Labour Organization in Geneva.
11.00   Make speech at the conference. Meetings with other national ministers.
12.30   Official lunch followed by meetings with other ministers. Depart Geneva for London.
16.55   Arrive at Heathrow Airport.
18.00   Return to my department.
18.30   Political meeting in the House of Commons.
19.00   Vote in the House of Commons on Opposition motion on food safety.
20.00   Dinner in the House of Commons.
23.00   Arrive home. Work on red boxes.

Thursday, 22 June
09.00   Daily meeting on the dock dispute.
09.30   Meeting of Home Affairs Committee in the Cabinet Office.

10.30 Cabinet. Downing Street.
11.30 Meeting of the Cabinet committee on the community charge.
13.00 Lunch with political correspondents.
15.15 Prime Minister's Questions. Return to my department.
16.00 Meetings in my department.
19.00 Anniversary dinner with my first private office from the Department of Transport.
23.00 Arrive home. Red boxes.

Friday, 23 June
08.45 Daily meeting on the dock dispute.
09.45 Depart Euston.
13.15 Arrive Oxenholme in the Lake District.
13.45 Arrive Brathay Hall Trust, Ambleside. Buffet lunch followed by tour.
18.30 Speech to Westmorland and Lonsdale Conservative Association, Windermere.
Night as the guest of Michael and Gail Jopling.

Saturday, 24 June
09.00 Train to Shipley, Yorkshire.
12.00 Lunch meeting of Shipley Conservative Association.
15.00 Train to Birmingham.
17.30 Arrive Sutton Coldfield. Red boxes.

Lest it should be thought otherwise, let me make one point quite clear about this life. I enjoyed it immensely. I enjoyed the challenges and the ability to be able to decide policies and institute change. I enjoyed working with a whole range of able colleagues and excellent civil servants. Obviously I did not enjoy every moment of it. I did not enjoy being stranded on Rugby railway station at 1 a.m. on a Sunday morning in a snow storm. I did not enjoy staying up to the early hours in the morning to vote through some piece of legislation against the votes of the Opposition – or, even worse, of our own side – particularly when you knew that the next day began with a breakfast meeting. I did not enjoy the mountain of red boxes which dominated Sunday afternoons and evenings. But for all that, the adrenalin flowed. I woke up enthusi-

astic for the next day – always a sure test of whether you are doing
a job you want to do. My complaint is not that I did not enjoy
being a minister. Far from it. Rather it was a feeling that the
process had become dangerously all-devouring. It pushed out
everything else.

That superb Conservative politician Iain Macleod once told a
doubting Richard Crossman that 'being a minister is the only thing
worth doing in the whole world'. Like Crossman I would not go
as far as that, but there is no doubting the fascination of a life
where you are at the very heart of political events, sometimes at
crucial times. You become immersed (sometimes totally immersed) in policy-making and the affairs of the Government.
Everything outside the ministerial world seems tame in compari-
son. And there is the problem.

The other side of the coin is that your life lacks balance. Your
family can become a poor second or third. It is not a story of total
neglect. You transfer the habits of political life to domestic life.
You put in an appearance and trust that is enough. You dash into
the school sports day and just as speedily dash away. Your general
life outside politics also suffers. You never know when you can get
away from the House of Commons, so you dare not organize a
supper for friends in mid-week in case you have to cancel. You
cannot even plan your summer holiday with any certainty. Each
July there is the rumour that 'we will have to sit into August'. We
rarely do, but even so Scottish MPs regularly return home to find
their children preparing to start school.

Obviously there is an inevitable pressure about ministerial and
Parliamentary life. If you do not like pressure then you are in the
wrong profession. That said, it should not be the end of all discussion. Politicians hesitate to complain about this life. They can
always be told that if they do not like it then there are many who
would give their eye-teeth to change places. But even politicians
have a right to a more sensible life than is offered at the moment.
In particular the ways of Parliament need to be urgently reformed.
It is basically absurd that Parliamentary life should be as haphazard
as it is. It is difficult to regard it as one of our great democratic
traditions that four days a week the House of Commons should
start at 2.30 p.m. in the afternoon and finish, at the earliest, at
10.30 at night.

These hours – which have been largely unaltered this century*
– belong to an age when the House was dominated by practising
lawyers. The theory was that with hours like this the lawyer could
get back to the House in time for any votes and be back in uninterrupted action in the courts next morning. The hours presuppose
that his wife is back at home looking after the children and the
Member of Parliament has no family role or no wish to have any
role. The general position is archaic enough – but what happens
when the Member of Parliament is a woman?

Periodically the press and public deplore the fact that there are
so few women in the House of Commons. Currently, out of 650
MPs, there are 42 women. Given the hours of Parliament it is
something of a marvel that there are so many. It is certainly difficult
to imagine a more trying system for a woman with young children.
Imagine the indignant accusations there would be if it was revealed
in some other walk of life that mothers left the house early in the
morning and abandoned their children until late at night. The
press would thunder back about 'Midnight Mums – Your Breakfast, Lunch, Tea and Dinner Are in the Oven'. Members of
Parliament would demand urgent inquiries.

We are running Parliament in a silly and outdated way. The
hours take no account of the fact that many MPs and ministers
are parents with young children who want to take some part in
their family's life. Even worse is the total uncertainty about the
arrangements at Westminster. I imagine that many MPs would
settle for a weekly routine where the House sat for two days up to
midnight if the *quid pro quo* were two other days when the House
finished at 6 or 7 p.m. If the price of that arrangement was one or
two days of morning sittings, so be it. Doubtless there are other
variations, but the point is that an attempt should be made *now* to
modernize our procedures. Of course there are those who say that
nothing can be done. It is pointed out that Richard Crossman's
brave attempt to reform the position twenty-five years ago ended
in tears. But it would be a sad commentary indeed upon political
parties with pretensions to radical reform if they were unable to

* In 1902 the House of Commons met from 2.00 p.m. until 11.30 p.m.
This was altered in 1906 to 2.45 p.m. until 11.30 p.m. Since 1945 the
normal hours for sitting have been 2.30 p.m. until 10.30 p.m. – but the
closing hour can be and frequently is extended to around midnight.

decide on changes of procedure in the House of Commons itself.

After the 1987 general election, I had pencilled in May 1989 as the date I would stand down from the Government. When May came, however, we were in the midst of abolishing the Dock Labour Scheme and a strike threatened. I could not conceivably leave at that stage and the same reasons still applied in July when Margaret Thatcher carried out a further substantial reshuffle of the Cabinet. Two Cabinet members, George Younger and David Young, decided to leave at this point; and two others, Paul Channon and John Moore, were unlucky casualties. Paul had helped me very substantially on the abolition of the dock scheme and was an exceptional ministerial colleague; while John paid the price for being put in the wrong department. The DHSS had now been divided into two and I was amused to see two old Elephant and Castle hands presiding over the separate pieces: Ken Clarke at Health and now Tony Newton at Social Security. The dock dispute lumbered on for a few more weeks and then at the beginning of August all industrial action ceased. The way was now open for me to leave.

I spent August on the beach in the Isle of Wight setting out in notebooks my first thoughts on what has become this book. I decided that my timetable would be to see Margaret Thatcher after the Party Conference and after my other bill, the 1989 Employment Bill, had completed all its stages through Parliament. The obvious time to go seemed to be between the end of one Parliamentary session and the start of the new session in late November. In the meantime there were one or two pieces of unfinished business.

In Europe we faced a battle on the European Community's proposed Social Charter. A number of other European governments could not understand our opposition to this blanket regulation of the labour market, given that this was what they already had in their own countries. For us, however, there were important issues of principle and practice. We had one of the best records in Europe on employment growth, but this had not been brought about by regulation of the labour market. Equally we strongly supported better employee involvement, but again we did not equate better employee involvement just with stronger trade union representation and more regulation, which was what the Social Charter envisaged. It remains the greatest pity that the European Commission should spend so much energy on harmonizing regulations throughout the Community when all common sense suggests that they should recognize different national arrangements and customs in pursuit of the same goal.

A more hopeful development concerned the further reform of the labour laws. I spent my last months at the department preparing the legislation which became the 1990 Employment Act. If ever there was a sign of how times had changed on the reform of industrial relations, this was it. One of my chief proposals was the total abolition of the trade union closed shop. This would mean that no one could be barred from employment because he refused to join a union. At the beginning of the 1980s that was seen as a step too far by many Conservatives and no action was taken. In 1990 the proposal was accepted by the Labour front bench.

On Thursday 26 October we had a brisk Cabinet. Margaret Thatcher had just returned from the Commonwealth Heads of Government meeting in Kuala Lumpur and there was nothing much on the agenda to delay us. It was very much end of session. A number of Labour backbenchers were seeking to delay the progress of bills in the Commons which might in turn hold up the Queen's Speech and the opening of the new Parliament. In the Lords there were difficulties in seeing the Housing and Local Government Bill through its last stages. Cabinet over, I returned to the Employment Department and at 1 p.m. my former special adviser, Nick True, came in to join me for a salad lunch. We settled down to drafting my resignation letter.

It needed no great powers of prophecy to realize that my resignation would be carefully scrutinized. The press could easily jump to the conclusion that I had had a serious row with Margaret Thatcher or disagreed on some aspect of policy. I was also exceptionally pessimistic that hard-bitten political correspondents would accept that a politician wished to spend more time with his family.

Nick and I worked on the letter for about an hour and, following lunch, I went over to the House of Commons for Prime Minister's Questions. Over the past week while Margaret had been away a fierce argument had developed between Nigel Lawson and Sir

Alan Walters who, in Nigel's increasingly angry words, was 'a part-time adviser' on economic affairs to the Prime Minister. At issue was the Government's attitude to the European Monetary System, a system which Walters had described as 'half baked'. Given that this comment was entirely contrary to the Government's declared policy, it was not surprising that he and Nigel were at serious odds. For months Government ministers led by the Prime Minister and the Chancellor had repeated the formula that Britain would join the European Monetary System 'when the time is right'. It was a pound to a penny that this would be the issue that Neil Kinnock would raise at 3.15 p.m.

And so it proved. What was the Government's position? asked Kinnock. Who ruled: the minister or the adviser? Margaret Thatcher replied: 'Advisers advise; ministers decide.'

It was a noisy question time but no worse than many others. To most of us it seemed that would be the end of the row. Back at the department I settled down to a long meeting with my own advisers on the Social Charter. There was to be a meeting of European Employment Ministers on Monday in Brussels which promised to be difficult. We had one or two allies, but in seeking any form of compromise we faced the unnecessarily inflexible opposition of the EC Commissioner responsible. Just before 6 p.m. we broke to allow my opening statement to be typed up but almost immediately the door opened again and one of my Deputy Secretaries, Graham Reid, returned with the news, 'the Chancellor has resigned'.

Nigel Lawson's resignation was a great blow to the Government. It has become fashionable to say that he took the wrong path in the aftermath of the 'Black Monday' stock-market crash of 1987. If he did so, he was not alone. The Labour Party urged more demand in the economy and distinguished commentators like William Rees-Mogg predicted that we were on the verge of a great slump like that of 1929. What the critics forget is that Nigel Lawson was the major architect of the Government's 1987 election victory and had proved one of the great tax-reforming Chancellors. I had had more than my fair share of policy differences with Nigel when I was at the DHSS but I never felt that they were anything more than that. He certainly pulled no punches in his arguments but there was no personal side to our disputes. I do not think he cared very much for lobbying behind closed doors. All of which, I suspect, made his dispute with Sir Alan Walters hard to bear.

I also had the greatest sympathy with Nigel's position. I certainly supported his views on the European Monetary System rather than the Walters version. More than that, I felt he was Chancellor of the Exchequer and Chancellors should not and cannot be double-guessed by advisers. It was clear that Nigel felt his position was being undermined. As he said in his resignation speech, the Walters article on the EMS 'represented the tip of a singularly ill-concealed iceberg, with all the destructive potential that icebergs possess'. No self-respecting minister could conceivably put up with a situation like that.

Much of this book describes how it was ministers who made decisions in spite of the advice of often distinguished advisers. Ministers rejected the advice of the Central Policy Review Staff and maintained a free, tax-financed National Health Service. Ministers rejected the advice of Sir Alan Walters himself to abandon plans to electrify the railway system and to cut down the rail network. If ministers had left the pace of policy to civil-service advisers, we would not have made the rapid progress we did on privatization or deregulation or the reform of industrial relations law. This is not intended to devalue the role of the adviser, whether civil service or drawn from outside Whitehall. But it is important to be clear that there are different roles. Advisers put their experience and judgement at the service of ministers. In the final analysis, however, it is ministers who decide because it is ministers who are accountable for the decision. They are accountable to Parliament and they are accountable to the public. If they get it wrong, it is their heads that roll and not the heads of their advisers. Advisers can influence policy but they cannot determine it. Even less can an adviser be allowed to undermine it.

Over the weekend I rang up Nick True to say, with some understatement, that I thought the timing of my resignation had become a little tricky. Morale in the party was not good and it looked as though Margaret Thatcher was going to face a symbolic challenge to her leadership from the Conservative backbencher, Sir Anthony Meyer. There was a great deal of sympathy for the former Chancellor and a sense of loss. There were quite enough problems for the Government without the Employment Secretary strolling in to offer his resignation. We now had a new Chancellor – my old friend and colleague, John Major, who I knew had always had this ambition – and we badly needed to get back on course. I needed to wait a few more weeks.

In coming up to resignation I would have liked to have explained the position to more of my friends than I did. Clearly the wider the circle who knew, the more the chance the news would leak out. It was not that, however, which was my concern. The views of the few political friends I did speak to were unanimously and solidly against resignation. 'Don't you think you will regret it?' 'Why not take a week or so off and see how things seem then?' 'Your friends will miss you.' It was all extremely kind but not at all helpful to someone who had already decided to go.

On Monday 20 November I went over to Number 10 just before 11.45 a.m. Margaret Thatcher was finishing a meeting in the Cabinet room. That completed, we went up to her study on the first floor. I explained the position. By January, I said, I would have served with her for fifteen years, including over ten years in her Cabinet. I had enjoyed it and I hoped I had made a contribution. But I felt that the time had now come for a change. I wanted to stay in the House of Commons, but over the next few years I would like to see more of my family and my constituency, do some writing and also take part in industry. I had now seen the two bills for which I was responsible on to the statute book and I would like to go before becoming entangled with the next Employment Bill. I would obviously time my resignation for her convenience but I thought the best moment to leave would be just after the Christmas break.

Clearly there had been some speculation at Number 10 on why I wanted a private one-to-one meeting with the Prime Minister. After Nigel's resignation she must have been just a little wary about private meetings with Cabinet ministers. I do not think then that she was altogether surprised. Her first reaction was: 'It's a blow, Norman. I had hoped to go on with the same team until the election.'

She then asked: 'You're not ill?'

'No,' I replied, 'I have never felt fitter.'

'Well, that's a relief.'

We talked for, I suppose, twenty minutes. Margaret was very generous about what I had done in Government and the discussion went far and wide. At the end we agreed to keep the decision strictly between ourselves. We were both due in the reception rooms of Downing Street for a party for all ministers to hear the contents of the following day's Queen's Speech. As we left Margaret repeated: 'It's a blow – a great blow.'

At lunch at L'Amico, nearby in Westminster, Fiona and I reviewed the position in hushed terms. Hushed because the restaurant seemed to be more than usually full of politicians and political correspondents. I suspect with a resignation that you only know for certain whether you have done the right thing after you have tendered it. My immediate reaction was relief that in spite of all the delays the decision had now been taken. Although I had one or two twinges before resignation day itself, I have never had any doubt that I took the right course. In the weeks following my meeting with Margaret Thatcher, there were suggestions that the resignation should be postponed. My strong feeling was, however, that once the decision had been made and communicated it should go ahead as quickly as possible. In retrospect that view was confirmed by the case of Peter Walker. Unknown to me, Peter had also said that he would be leaving the Government but delayed his departure. The result was that he had the decision announced for him in the weekend press. There is something to be said for seeking to control events.

There was one last event I did have to await, however, and that was the leadership election, now set for Tuesday 5 December. Sir Anthony Meyer was described by his friends as a stalking horse and by his enemies as a stalking donkey. The possibility was not that he would win but that there would be sufficient votes for him and abstentions to amount to a vote of no confidence in Margaret Thatcher.

A small group of MPs had never been reconciled to her leadership. The most prominent was Ted Heath. In May I had been on the receiving end of his continuing hostility. We had been flown over to Paris by the BBC to contribute to a programme on Europe in the luxurious setting of the Hotel Crillon. Ted had been interviewed first and within seconds was on the attack. Margaret Thatcher, he said, was deliberately 'misleading' the nation on

Europe. Her policy would leave Britain as a 'second-rate power in a second-tier community'. I was left as best I could to defend the position – although it is never easy to do that effectively when the attack comes from your own side and from a former party leader to boot.

In 1975 I voted for Ted Heath. It is the greatest tragedy that Ted should have chosen to spend the next fifteen years sniping from the wings. At Chequers, each Prime Minister is allowed a glass window and coat of arms to commemorate their period in office. Ted has never put one up. Perhaps he harboured the ambition that one day he would return to Number 10 and therefore his period as leader was interrupted, not ended. Whatever the reason, he would have done much better to have sought a role where his formidable talents could have been used. History will probably deal generously with his achievement in bringing Britain into the European Community during the three and a half years of his premiership. I cannot believe, however, that it will take the same view of the years since defeat.

But Ted Heath was, of course, not the only malcontent. There were some who had never supported Margaret Thatcher's policies and others who simply wanted a change of leadership. Added to these were a few former ministers who had been sacked by her and a few more who could not forgive her for her inexplicable failure to promote them. As party leader since 1975, Margaret had inevitably made enemies.

When it came to Tuesday 5 December I went up the stairs to Committee Room 12 of the House of Commons. I had just answered my last set of questions as Secretary of State for Employment. Outside the committee room were the cream of the political correspondents of what used to be Fleet Street – Robin Oakley of *The Times*, George Jones of the *Daily Telegraph*, Anthony Bevins of the *Independent*, Gordon Greig of the *Daily Mail*. Simon Heffer had even transferred his *Telegraph* sketch to the scene outside the polling station. Inside the committee room the only other voter was Norman Tebbit. We left together muttering about the need for new laws to restrain journalistic picketing. A few hours later the result was announced that Margaret Thatcher had secured a comfortable victory with 314 Conservative MPs voting for her. Anthony Meyer had secured only 33 votes with a further 27 abstentions. For me it was the first time I had voted for Margaret Thatcher in a leadership election. I did what with the benefit of hindsight I should have done in 1975. Margaret now looked set for the next election and I agreed with Kenneth Baker, the Chairman of the Conservative Party, who after the poll said that 'the leadership question is now settled'.

I resigned from the Government on the afternoon of Wednesday 3 January 1990. The Christmas celebrations had come and gone. I had attended my final Employment Department carol service in St Margaret's Church at Westminster and gone out to a Soho restaurant with my private office for our Christmas lunch without being able to tell them that in a few days I would be leaving. With one possible exception no one really guessed the position – even given what I at any rate had thought to be a host of mysterious calls and visits to Downing Street. At home I was just a little preoccupied as the children opened their presents and relations and friends called in for meals and drinks. On a number of days I woke up feeling 'What on earth are you doing?' I had even (irony of ironies) begun to wonder why I was leaving this safe, secure ministerial life.

On New Year's Day itself Margaret and Denis Thatcher had invited Fiona and me to join them for lunch at Chequers. A few colleagues were there, among them Douglas and Judy Hurd and Ian and Jane Gow. Ian was in irrepressible high spirits and showed the obvious and natural affection he had for the Prime Minister he had served as an outstanding Parliamentary Private Secretary. The atmosphere was very much that of a family lunch. Margaret and Denis were relaxed hosts; Mark snapped away with his camera. Even at this point very few people knew about my impending resignation. But one man who did was Denis Thatcher. As we left the lunch table, he took me to one side. 'I am horrified to hear you are going,' he said. 'You are the linchpin of the Government.' It was a wonderful exaggeration but altogether typical of a kind and generous man.

Before I left Chequers I had a few minutes alone with Margaret Thatcher. There was only one thing wrong with my resignation letter, now I came to read it yet again. At one point I had written with an oratorical flourish: 'The time has come to leave the Government.' As Margaret observed wryly, 'that sounds as though everyone should leave the Government'. I conceded that perhaps the words did seem a little close to Nelson's exhortation at Trafalgar. As I left, the one thing that surprised me was Margaret saying 'See you on Wednesday'. I had somehow doubted whether a formal meeting to bid farewells would be necessary – given that I had just enjoyed a generous informal one.

I faced the Wednesday with some foreboding. I remained pessimistic that the press or the public would accept my family reasons as sufficient explanation for resigning from one of the top jobs in the country. However, I need not have worried. On Wednesday I explained the position to a number of political friends I had not been able to telephone the previous night. The reaction of one senior minister gave the flavour of the response. 'I am surprised, Norman, but I fully understand the position,' he said. 'I have missed out a great deal on my children growing up and I resent it.'

To my slight astonishment I received just the same reaction when I explained the position to the political correspondents in the afternoon. They were surprised, but when I explained the pressures on my family there was almost immediate understanding. We politicians forget that the journalists who cover Westminster live as strange a life as we do. I had also failed to appreciate that around the country there were men and women who in their different spheres faced the same dilemma. I received some flak on leaving, but overwhelmingly the public reaction seemed to be that this was a healthy issue on which to resign.

At Westminster some politicians felt quite clearly that it was altogether good that ministers should decide when they wanted to resign. It was good for the Cabinet trade union that members should leave with the public asking 'why?' rather than shrugging 'at last'. Indeed, one former Cabinet colleague in the House of Commons came up to say: 'You know, that was the best ministerial resignation since the war.' Another kind exaggeration – and it did not remotely feel that way at the time. My main reaction was relief that the resignation process was over.

For days afterwards the feature writers, television interviewers and photographers poured in to see us both in London and in Sutton Coldfield. Fiona and the children withstood the assault magnificently. For a while Kate and Isobel were the two most

photographed girls in Britain – and on one or two occasions even
Oliver consented to smile at the cameras. Then about a week later
mercifully the phone stopped ringing and we could get back to
planning our new life.

I was inundated with letters. Predominantly they were generous
but there were one or two which did not quite fall into that category. A doctor in Westminster took the trouble to write: 'Good
riddance, but why didn't you take Kenneth Clarke with you?' A
gentleman in Wales observed: 'Dictators go in the Philippines,
Panama, Eastern Europe – so at last they've caught up with you.
Let me know when you come up for trial. I would like tickets.'
The Fees Office in the House of Commons were also in touch
about my new financial position. My salary would go down from
£55,000 to a Member of Parliament's salary of £26,700. Nevertheless, I had my pension to look forward to. My service of eleven
years around the Cabinet table would entitle me to a ministerial
pension of £6,800 to be paid when I reached the age of sixty-five.

Two weeks after my resignation I had breakfast with Jeffrey
Archer at the Savoy. A few months before, he had told me that if
ever I intended to write a book not to do a thing before contacting
him. He would put his ten years' experience of writing at my disposal
and guide me through the publishing jungle. When we met, Jeffrey
said that he had noticed my ears pricking up when we had talked of
writing. He had been puzzled, knowing that ministers hardly had
the time to write a cheque let alone a book. But in the midst of working hard (and he does work very hard) on his latest bestseller he had
put the conversation out of his mind. Now all was revealed. Over the
next hour Jeffrey did what he promised and gave me the invaluable
advice of a successful professional writer.

Jeffrey Archer was not the only old friend from the past I saw
in the aftermath of leaving the Government. The day my resignation was announced I received a telegram from Jorgen Philip-
Sorensen, the Chairman of Europe's biggest security company,
Group 4. A man of infectious enthusiasm with whom I had worked
back in the 1970s, Jorgen now wanted me to join his board. A
week later Peter Parker was in touch. Would I like to come on to
the board of Evered, the building materials company, based near
my constituency in the West Midlands? While Peter Thompson,
the Chairman of NFC, wrote to me and after intensive interviews

with the executive board members and the non-executives (which made political selection seem like a piece of cake) I joined. It was almost ten years since I had privatized the company and that length of time met any stipulation about former ministers joining privat-ized companies. In the voluntary sector I accepted an invitation to become a trustee of the National Aids Trust.

Some say that MPs should not have outside interests in industry. I entirely dispute that. Indeed, an MP, particularly in the West Midlands, *should* have industrial links. It is ludicrous to accept that politicians can be paid for appearing on television and for writing articles and books but not for working in industry itself. Of course, there have to be rules about what involvement is proper and about disclosure. But the net result of no involvement is that the House of Commons would become a place where members talk and talk – with less and less to say.

My position was, and remains, that I am staying in politics and, the electors willing, in the House of Commons. When I left the Government I was resigning, not retiring; it was stepping down but not stepping out. There are many issues on which I would like to campaign and, hopefully, with my years of Cabinet experience I may be more effective than otherwise. But politics remains my life. My belief is that the role of a backbench MP is an honourable one and that you can successfully practise the essential art of changing things for the better.

But wait a minute. Were you not going to spend more time with your family? The answer is that I do. There is a little more time to do those things – going to the theatre, going to the park – which could not be fitted in before. The big change, however, is that I am around. It helps having your office at home and it helps not being pursued by the red boxes. I am still wearing L-plates but I am enjoying life in a way I have not done before. I have even struck a glancing blow for a more sensible Westminster life. The Government whips now talk about 'a Fowler day'. That is code for 'There is no vote tonight. You can all spend the evening with your wives and children.' There are worse epitaphs than that.

So what do I miss? At times of crisis, like the Gulf War, I would like to be around the Cabinet table once more. But any time I feel nostalgic I remind myself of the baleful visits to the Treasury to talk about public spending. Unlike some former ministers, I do

not miss the chauffeur-driven car. There is a limit to what a
politician based at Westminster can do with a chauffeur-driven
car. One of the experiences I will always remember is travelling
by Underground just after my resignation. Total strangers came
up to wish me luck.

My one area of undoubted loss is the private office. In my last
job at the Employment Department I was cared for by an office of
four graduates who divided the policy responsibilities between
them. In addition I had a personal secretary and one unfortunate
who had no other role but to juggle my diary. That last job was
reckoned the worst in the department. I doubt if ever again I will
have such a large and skilled staff directly organizing my life. Over
the years the private office threw up some undoubted stars. At
Transport there was Genie Flanagan and the marvellous Tony
Meyer who was both bright and sharp. He now prospers in the
private sector. At the DHSS there were Private Secretaries like
Don Brereton who was an outstanding part of my inheritance from
Patrick Jenkin; and Steve Godber who was as good as anyone I
ever worked with in Whitehall. He too has gone to the private
sector. Perhaps we should be taking note. At Employment I started
with a quite exceptional Private Secretary in John Turner, who
had worked his way up from the bottom and I hope will not stop
until he has got to the top, and ended with Clive Norris and a really
capable all-woman trio. My wonderful, but overworked, House of
Commons secretary Caroline Bell has now to combine all these
functions.

The contrast with Whitehall is most marked in the working
surroundings of Westminster. In Whitehall it is not only ministers
who live reasonably comfortably. Senior civil servants rightly have
decent rooms with sensible accommodation for their secretaries. In
contrast much of Westminster is a slum. The room I was eventually
allocated as an ordinary MP once more took me back to Abbey
Gardens whence I had come a decade before. What intrigued me
was that, previous to my arrival, no fewer than three MPs had
occupied the space. They probably set some world record on a
par with the number that can be stuffed into a Mini or a telephone
box. The cream of Whitehall would not remotely contemplate
working in the kind of conditions that are the lot of many MPs.
Even less would they put up with pathetically inadequate office

accommodation for secretaries. It is a good thing that the Palace of Westminster is not covered by the Offices and Shops Act for otherwise it would be closed down.

In over twenty years in politics, however, I have neither regrets nor complaints. My feeling immediately after stepping down from Cabinet was that it had all been an enormous privilege. That remains my feeling today. Few people have had the opportunity of serving for almost eleven years in succession in the Cabinet. Few people have had the opportunity of serving with the same leader for fifteen years. I count myself fortunate in having been part of a team of ministers who secured some fundamental improvements in the Britain of the 1980s.

CHAPTER 17

Full Circle

"I'M JUST GOING OUTSIDE, I MAY BE SOMETIME."

Independent

M any former ministers complain that the change to a political life outside government office is difficult, if not impossible. I did not find that. I had not been on the back benches since 1974 but I had always liked the House of Commons in spite of some of its antiquated ways. I liked the easy conversation of the tea room (although I am not a great one for the smoking room) and the working atmosphere of the library. I found that after resignation old political opponents came up to talk. Above all my new position gave me a political freedom I had not enjoyed for many a long year. If I disagreed with the Government's policy I could say so; if I had proposals to make there was no Cabinet committee I need convince. Yet even amidst the personal euphoria of a new life, I could see as clearly as everyone else that 1990 was not going at all well for the Government.

In March we lost the Mid-Staffordshire by-election with a swing to Labour of over 21 per cent. In May we lost seats in the local council elections and in July the Trade and Industry Secretary, Nicholas Ridley, was forced to resign for some unguarded and mistaken remarks about Germany's position in Europe. As we came up to the summer recess the Government was under siege. We were way behind in the opinion polls and many Tory MPs felt that action was urgently called for if we were to avoid losing the general election which had to be called by June 1992 at the very latest.

Within the party there was wide agreement that 'something had to be done' about the community charge or poll tax as it was generally called. The reform of the domestic rates system had produced a storm of opposition. Back in 1974 I remember being told on doorstep after doorstep in Sutton Coldfield about the iniquities of the rating system. The example always given was of the widow living next door to three wage-earners but paying the same bill. The idea of reform had many supporters but in practice the actual charge had come out way above what was predicted. In Birmingham, for example, we were forecast to be one of the so-called 'gaining' areas with at one stage a charge below £200

per person. In the event the charge had worked out at £406. The
local council itself was responsible for some of the increase but so
too was the safety-net arrangement whereby gaining areas made
contributions to losing areas. Thus Birmingham made a contribution of some £70 a head to the Exchequer for general
distribution to other areas. Complaints came from all over the
country. The public seethed and the party grumbled.

Inevitably this led to another suggested course of action: the
time had come to change the leader. Margaret Thatcher, not
unfairly, was identified as the author of the poll tax and responsibility was put at her door. It was the latest in a long list of
complaints made by her critics. They did not like her position on
Europe. They complained that she 'didn't listen' to public concern
on health, education and the public services. Above all, they did
not like her style of leadership. They saw her as too strident, too
autocratic and too insensitive. So, fifteen years on, how did I feel
about Margaret Thatcher as a leader and as a person?

When I had first entered the Shadow Cabinet I had not been
at all sure that I would like working with her. I ended up both
liking her and enjoying working with her. Like many other Cabinet
ministers who served with her for any length of time, I had my
battles. I had a major dispute over Leyland and others on health
and social security. I doubt whether I ever succeeded in converting
her to my point of view, but she had a certain regard for obstinacy.
There were ministers who were intimidated by her directness of
style. They would have preferred to set out their proposals to a
traditional committee chairman. She was never going to be that
kind of leader and we would not have made the progress we
did if Margaret Thatcher had simply taken the temperature and
summed up at the end. She was not someone who found solutions
to problems by dividing in two. She led from the front and if you
did not like that style of leader you were unlikely to like her.

Had the style been less direct then ministerial life would have
been quieter. But would it have been half as much fun? It is true
that at times you lived dangerously but at other times you had the
inestimable pleasure of seeing your colleagues do the same. The
way in which a minister withstood a Thatcher barrage sorted out
the men from the boys. Among the men, Kenneth Baker stands out
for negotiating his education reforms past his most distinguished

predecessor as Education Secretary. He has a resilience which always ensures that he comes up smiling.

In 1975 I was also not at all sure whether Margaret Thatcher was electable. That was not because she was a woman. I had never regarded that as making any difference one way or the other in electoral terms. It was because in the mid-1970s she appeared to the public as aloof and most certainly not one of them. Although she had come up the hard way, she gave the impression that she was to the manor born. This was not an accurate picture of the woman but that was how she was seen. In the years after her election she was given media advice which she was wise enough to take, but above all she began to project her real self. A much grittier Margaret Thatcher emerged.

So what was the secret of a leader who had won three elections and survived crises that would have toppled a lesser person? Stamina obviously; courage certainly; but if I were to choose one factor, it would be professionalism. Her attitude to the televising of Parliament is a case in point. She was a strong opponent of televising the House. She thought it would change the character of Westminster and, I suspect, put more power in the hands of the media, including her *bête noire* the BBC. At times I felt that she regarded me – a supporter of television and a former journalist – as personally responsible for this invasion. Yet when the decision was made and a majority, including half the Cabinet, voted for television she settled down to work. Most of the rest of us took the view that there was not much you could do. You would either come over well or not. Margaret Thatcher studied the angles of the cameras, considered how the pictures would be appearing in sitting rooms all over the country, and emerged as the undoubted star of Westminster. Whatever may have been Neil Kinnock's hopes of this new opportunity – and remember that Kinnock made his first national reputation on television – he lost.

It was the same professionalism which took Margaret Thatcher from an Opposition leader without experience of foreign affairs to one of the world's best-known and most respected statesmen. It was the same professionalism which drove her into the early hours of the morning working on the multitude of red boxes produced by the departments of Whitehall. The same quality took her into the tea room and the dining room of the House of Commons rather than taking the night off; and at party conferences she was entirely tireless as she went from one function to another. She did not much like the annual trial of her speech at the Conservative Party Conference. She would sit there all week listening to her best lines being used by other speakers but knowing that the delegates would expect a sparkling performance at the end. With her speech writers she would be up half the night preparing her text. It was the price that the Leader of the Party had to pay and she paid it willingly. It was this complete professionalism which set her apart.

Margaret's family provided the indispensable background rock of support, and a clear and uncomplicated instinct about what was right and wrong provided the certainty of direction. She had a strong feeling of what was honourable and what was not. She was intensely loyal to the officials who most closely worked with her. If she ever lost her temper it was because of attacks on advisers like Bernard Ingham or Charles Powell. She regarded an attack on officials who could not answer back as basically cowardly. Critics were trying to get at her through her advisers. To her this was a particularly despicable example of dishonourable conduct.

Her view of ministers was more complex. She was loyal to them in the midst of a dispute and under attack but she also felt that they should be capable of looking after themselves. However close she might be to a minister (for example, Nicholas Ridley), if the minister insisted on digging himself into a hole then ultimately he had to live with the consequences. The interests of the Government took precedence over the interests of an individual minister. The same is true in a rather less stark way of the frequent reshuffles. Ministers were moved out of jobs in the interests of keeping the Government's face fresh. In the process quite a number were roughly treated. Leon Brittan should not have been moved from the Home Office; Patrick Jenkin should have been moved from the Environment Department, not sacked; Peter Rees should not have had to suffer the entirely avoidable fate of reading about his demise in the papers for week upon week before it happened. All the Thatcher Governments would have benefited had ministers stayed both longer in jobs and longer as ministers.

Ultimately, however, success as a political leader is not measured by skill in the television studio or how you appear to your colleagues. It is about what you achieve. Political leaders have to win elections, but it is much more important that they win respect for doing the right things rather than an easy reputation for geniality. Margaret Thatcher's achievement was to take over a country which gave every appearance of being down and very nearly out and turn it round. The change was slow and at times painful but the chances are that much of the change is permanent. She took over a country which had been brought to its knees by uncontrolled trade union power and presided over a decade of reform. Any party which seriously tampers with that record does so at its electoral peril. She took over a country where too much industry and too much activity was controlled, not very successfully, by the state. Virtually no one today believes in widespread renationalization and a reintroduction of controls. She took over a country where millions of people were excluded from ownership. With the sale of council houses and wider share ownership important steps were taken to extend the traditional Conservative aims of one nation and a property-owning democracy. And she also took over a country where for decades tax rates had been too high but where it had become accepted that that was the inevitable way of things. Tax rates came down and my estimate is that most people in Britain would now like to keep them that way. These were real and substantial reforms which singled Margaret Thatcher out as one of the most successful political leaders this century.

When it came to the summer of 1990 I believed that she should remain as leader of the Conservative Party. We still had the best part of two years to go before there needed to be an election. In that time the Government could recover. It was true that a snapshot taken then revealed Margaret Thatcher as an unpopular leader. But that picture could, and in my view would, change. The row about the poll tax was subsiding and in August Iraq's invasion of Kuwait promised a very different political agenda over the next months. If there were war, Margaret Thatcher had all the qualities that the public would rate highly. I put this view in a television discussion and was immediately attacked by Roy Hattersley for warmongering. It was certainly not that. It was a recognition that if, as seemed likely, a war were to take place then Margaret Thatcher would be rated by the public as the person best qualified to lead the country.

In October at the Party Conference in Bournemouth I spoke at the dinner of the Conservative constituency agents. My own excellent agent, Michael Parr, had become the national chairman. There was no doubt that the support and affection for Margaret was still very strong among these hard-headed and skilled professionals. As the conference progressed the old magic seemed to be working and I felt that we were through the worst. There was the prospect that not even a stalking horse would struggle to its feet to contest the leadership when the House of Commons resumed. There then came a development which changed the whole course of recent political history.

On the evening of Thursday 1 November, Geoffrey Howe resigned. The resignation came without warning and left the party in a state of shock. Geoffrey had been regarded as a rock. He had been there since the beginning. It was the Thatcher revolution but it could not have taken place without Howe. Everyone knew that his relations with Margaret Thatcher were not good but they did not appear any worse than they had been for years past. In the summer of 1989 he had been moved from the Foreign Office which he loved to become Leader of the House of Commons. After negotiation he had also acquired the title of Deputy Prime Minister but no one pretended that Geoffrey occupied the same position as the last holder of this title, Willie Whitelaw. Had he wanted to resign from the Government, 1989 would have been the time to have done it and he would have gone with the understanding of the whole party. There is no doubt that Geoffrey carefully considered that course but in the end decided to stay on the grounds that he wanted to see the changes started in 1979 through to success. He did not intend just to slip away leaving the process incomplete. So why was he resigning now, fourteen months later?

Ostensibly, Europe was the issue. In his resignation letter, Geoffrey said that he found himself unable to share the Prime Minister's views:

I am deeply anxious that the mood you have struck – most notably in Rome last weekend and in the House of Commons this Tuesday – will make it more difficult for Britain to hold and retain a position of influence in this vital debate.

The difficulty with this explanation was that we had all heard Margaret Thatcher defend herself in the House of Commons on Tuesday 30 October. She was under attack for not preserving British interests in the European Council meeting at Rome the previous weekend. It was certainly true that Margaret had gone beyond her rather anodyne statement. It was also true that the House glimpsed some of the fire and spirit that sometimes came into our discussions around the Cabinet table. In particular this was evident when the Prime Minister dealt with the views of Jacques Delors:

> The President of the Commission, Mr Delors, said at a press conference the other day that he wanted the European Parliament to be the democratic body of the Community. He wanted the Commission to be the Executive and he wanted the Council of Ministers to be the Senate. No. No. No.

It was a spirited defence and the bulk of the party (irrespective of their views on Europe) counted it a significant Parliamentary triumph. To find that this had been Geoffrey's breaking-point only added to our puzzlement.

The truth, I suspect, is that the events of that week brought to a head a range of issues which had been troubling Geoffrey over a long period. There was no question that the two were far apart in their basic attitude to Europe and always had been. Margaret Thatcher distrusted Geoffrey's enthusiasm for the European ideal and European institutions. Geoffrey Howe was irritated by Margaret's clear scepticism of most things European and the direct way she expressed these views. There had been disputes in the past, notably on the European Monetary System before the Madrid summit in 1988 when Geoffrey had threatened to resign. Yet difficult as the division on Europe was, it was not the whole story. By the autumn of 1989 Geoffrey appeared marginalized in the Government, unjustly sidelined. Geoffrey's formidable contribution to Britain's recovery had gone largely unremarked and apparently unrecognized by the Prime Minister. Man management at this level was never Margaret's strong suit. The result was that the personal rift between the two leading figures in the Government grew wider and wider. Disaster beckoned.

By itself, Geoffrey Howe's resignation was not fatal. The Government had weathered the resignation of Nigel Lawson as Chancellor of the Exchequer and with a little luck and a little help could do the same again. The death blow to Margaret Thatcher's leadership came not from Geoffrey's resignation but from his resignation speech. When Nigel had left twelve months earlier, he had ended his resignation speech by looking forward to a fourth election victory under Margaret Thatcher. To the dismay of at least one of his friends, Geoffrey Howe offered no such comfort. His speech seemed deliberately moulded on Leo Amery's famous call to Neville Chamberlain in 1940 in a debate on the conduct of the war. Quoting Cromwell, Amery had said:

You have sat too long here for any good you have been doing. Depart, I say, and let us have done with you. In the name of God, go.

Geoffrey Howe was not as direct as that, but few who were there that day could mistake the message. Geoffrey had resigned in the period between the old Parliamentary session ending and the new one beginning. The result was that his personal statement had to wait until the House of Commons was sitting again and it was not until Tuesday 13 November that he rose in his new place, three rows back below the gangway on the back benches. The official line on the resignation had been that there was no fundamental division between Sir Geoffrey Howe and the Prime Minister. It was all a question of style. Geoffrey's joke that he must be the first minister in history who had resigned because he was in full agreement with Government policy was an elegant reply appreciated by both sides of the House.

It is, however, not the beginning of a resignation speech which matters; it is the end. Geoffrey's case was that Margaret Thatcher's attitude towards Europe was running risks with the future of Britain. Her casual comments and impulsive answers risked minimizing our influence in the Community. The gap between them could not be bridged. Geoffrey concluded:

The conflict of loyalty – of loyalty to the Prime Minister (and after all in two decades together that instinct of loyalty is still very real) and of loyalty to what I perceive to be the true interests of the nation – has become all too great. I no longer believe it possible to resolve that conflict from within this Government. That is why I have resigned. In doing so, I have done what I believe to be right for my party and my country. The time has come for others to consider their own response to the tragic conflict of loyalties with which I have myself wrestled for perhaps too long.

The impact of that speech cannot be overstated. In twenty-one years in the House of Commons, I cannot remember a speech like it. I do not speak with admiration. It was an attempt at assassination, and that is perhaps the greatest tragedy of all. Few politicians can have worked together as closely as Margaret Thatcher and Geoffrey Howe and it was a total negation of their fifteen-year partnership. Politics is a hard business, and there were issues of principle and belief at stake. Nevertheless, I prefer to remember Geoffrey as the young politician brimful of ideas whom I had supported for the leadership in 1975; or the dogged Chancellor sticking to his economic policies when under colossal political attack in 1981. Doubtless his speech will go down in the history books but Geoffrey Howe deserves to be remembered for much more than that.

I had spent the week preceding Geoffrey's speech arguing publicly and privately against a leadership contest. The Conservative Party outside Westminster did not want an election and the most likely beneficiary appeared to be Neil Kinnock. On the very morning of Geoffrey's speech I had published an article in the *Birmingham Post* saying there was a time for leadership elections: 'Such a time was January 1975. I do not believe that the same claim can be made for November 1990.' Geoffrey Howe's resignation speech altered all that. It became practically certain that Michael Heseltine would now challenge the Prime Minister.

Michael Heseltine had been waiting in the wings for almost five years since Westland. On the back benches he had played a difficult hand with great skill. He had supported the Government and was one of the party's most sought-after speakers. He was my favourite candidate to succeed Margaret. But I did mean succeed.

I was wholly opposed to a contest between the two and I made this clear.

A leadership election at this point was not in the interests of the Government, the party or for that matter Michael Heseltine. It was entirely legitimate for Michael to want to lead the Conservative Party. He had the qualities required of a leader and a wide public following. Ironic as it might seem, Michael was well placed to carry forward the changes of the Thatcher years. He had set out his views in a book, *Where There's a Will*, published a year after his resignation. I was attracted by his emphasis on Europe, the importance of industry and new policy for the inner cities. Michael could give the party a sense of direction which might be badly needed when Margaret stood down.

None of this argued for an election in 1990, however, which would be bitterly divisive. Although Margaret Thatcher had defeated an incumbent leader in 1975, Ted Heath had not been notably popular with the party or conspicuously successful in winning elections. Margaret Thatcher, on the other hand, was idolized by much of the party and had won three elections in a row. The Conservative Party was going to be deeply unhappy with both a challenge and the challenger.

Some of Michael's supporters argued that a challenge in 1990 would be just like the challenge to Ted Heath fifteen years before. As was predictable, however, an election in 1990 was likely to be very different. Victory was not going to go automatically to the first serious candidate to put up against Margaret Thatcher. It was by no means certain that a candidate who entered on the second round would meet the same fate as Willie Whitelaw in 1975. The party would not forget and forgive the defeat of Margaret Thatcher in the same quick way that they accepted the removal of Ted Heath.

Nevertheless, Michael had hastened into what proved to be a decisive step towards a contest in the immediate aftermath of Geoffrey Howe's resignation. On 2 November he was about to leave on a trip to the Middle East. Before he went, he drafted a letter to his constituents in Henley. The letter amounted to a slashing attack on Margaret Thatcher's stance on Europe. The resignation of Geoffrey Howe had caused a 'crisis of confidence'. The Cabinet should now exert its collective authority on Europe.

He went on: 'If decisions continue to be taken or imposed that do not carry this collective endorsement, the stresses will continue to show and could be our undoing.'

The die was cast. Rather than awaiting developments, Michael had in effect thrown down the gauntlet. For the next few days all the guidance coming from Margaret's camp was that the sniping had continued for too long: 'Heseltine should either put up or shut up.' You did not need to know much about Michael to realize that if his courage were impugned he would stand. No attempt was made to reduce the temperature and on 12 November he was confronted head-on by Margaret Thatcher in her speech to the Lord Mayor's Banquet at the Guildhall in London. Using a series of cricketing metaphors, she set out her position in a totally uncompromising way:

> I am still at the crease, although the bowling has been pretty hostile of late. And in case anyone doubted it, can I assure you there will be no ducking the bouncers, no stonewalling, no playing for time. The bowling's going to get hit all round the ground. That's my style.

No one who watched Margaret's speech on television could doubt that she would set about the task with rather more determination than the unhappy English cricketers in Australia.

Margaret Thatcher's Guildhall speech marked the start of her re-election campaign. The decision had already been taken to go for an early election. Nominations would open on Thursday 15 November and any election would take place on Tuesday 20 November. If a second round were necessary, that would take place on the following Tuesday, 27 November, with nominations closing on the preceding Thursday. No one could accuse Margaret of 'playing for time' but, as yet, there was no rival candidate.

From the moment the House resumed, events moved at breakneck speed. On Monday 12 November Margaret Thatcher made her Guildhall speech; on Tuesday Geoffrey Howe made his devastating resignation speech; and on Wednesday Michael Heseltine announced that he would stand for the leadership. I heard the news in Birmingham. In normal times I would have supported Michael as a successor but not in the way now proposed. I thought

Margaret could win a fourth term and like many Conservative MPs and party members, I did not want Margaret to be ejected in this way or the Thatcher years to be ended by such a contest. I wrote to both candidates telling them what I intended to do. Elections are pretty miserable affairs but at least you can be honest. I have no time for those who give assurances all round and not much for those who combine a sphinx-like public silence with passionate private campaigning. Over the next days I appeared for Margaret Thatcher on more television and radio programmes than ever before in my political life.

At just before 6.30 p.m. on Tuesday 20 November I heard the result of the election on air in ITN's Westminster television studio. My prediction had been that Margaret Thatcher would gain the 56-vote majority which was necessary to win on the first ballot. Under the party's election rules, a candidate needed a majority plus a 15 per cent margin. In the event the result was:

Margaret Thatcher   204
Michael Heseltine   152

That gave Margaret a majority of 52: four frustrating votes short of the total necessary for an outright win. 'What now?' asked Alistair Burnet. I replied without hesitation that Margaret would stand again. It would have been out of character for her to do anything else. Minutes later, she announced in Paris that she would contest the second-round ballot the following Tuesday. Margaret was much criticized for this decision on the grounds that it was too quick and she should have consulted other ministers. I do not agree. Just imagine the speculation that there would have been had she sounded an uncertain note at that moment. If she were to win on the second ballot, she needed to show absolute confidence.

The much more important point was that Margaret was in Paris. It was the decisive mistake of the whole election. Had only two people changed their vote in the first-round ballot, she would have won outright. Had she been at Westminster, she would certainly have achieved that and probably much more. Margaret's whole strength was her personality. But she left for Paris on Sunday 18 November for a two-day meeting of the Conference on Security and Co-operation in Europe. By her choice it was a whirlwind campaign, but for the last forty-eight hours Margaret was absent from the main action.

By deciding not to campaign personally, she discarded the most potent weapon at her disposal. Face to face Margaret could have won over some of the doubters. It was a commentary upon her strength of personality that she had always been at her most vulnerable to criticism when out of the country. In the immediate aftermath of the vote it was the campaign team at Westminster, headed by George Younger, which took the blame. In truth, it is difficult to run a campaign without the presence of the candidate.

So why did Margaret decide to go to Paris? Certainly it was an important conference. It was the symbolic end of the Cold War in Europe. Her presence there showed that it was business as usual and demonstrated her position as a world statesman. But Tory Members of Parliament did not need convincing of her role as a statesman. What was needed was some good old-fashioned pressing of the flesh. A few drinks with backbenchers could have achieved a great deal. The others at the conference – men like George Bush and Helmut Kohl – were politicians as well. They knew the score. They knew that the first rule of political leadership is to remain the political leader. Margaret Thatcher was needed back home and had she stayed she would have won.

Right from the start of Wednesday morning, 21 November, it was clear that the Thatcher campaign was in serious trouble. In the tea room of the House of Commons the mood had changed. It was now possible to find ministers who openly declared that if she continued she would lose. Backbenchers who had the day before voted for Thatcher were now talking of switching to Heseltine. A curious theory put forward was that some in the party felt they were obliged to vote for Margaret on the first ballot but not on the second. There was no doubt that the party was all over the place as rumours circulated freely that former Thatcher supporters were changing their position. The switches were, however, difficult to quantify and even more difficult to explain. If you had voted for Margaret on the first ballot, I could not see why you would not vote for her on the second. That was certainly how I intended to proceed.

As the day went on, backbench nerves seemed to steady.

Margaret made a strong Commons statement on the Paris meeting and at tea the Thatcher campaign was still proceeding. Nominations were to close at midday on Thursday and the assumption remained that it would be a straight fight between Thatcher and Heseltine. It was at this point that the ministers took over. To my astonishment, just before 6 p.m. I learned that Margaret had asked the Cabinet to come to see her one by one to tell her their views on whether she should continue. It was at that moment I realized her leadership was at an end.

It was clear there were some Cabinet ministers who were opposed to her continuing as a candidate. In the main this was not because they had lost confidence in her but because they thought she would lose. Their fear was that Michael Heseltine would become leader of the party and other possible candidates like Douglas Hurd and John Major would have been prevented from standing. The vast majority of the Cabinet, however, would have supported her had she continued without consultation. But ministers were now being asked their views and they had a duty to give them honestly. The trouble for Margaret was that it was a no-win position. If the majority said she should stand down then she had little option; and even if only a minority took this view then the news of the poll would be all over the weekend press. Resignations could not be ruled out. The Thatcher campaign would have been left in ruins.

Fiona and I had been at the opera on the Wednesday night. I made my excuses and returned to Westminster early, arriving there just before 10 p.m. to find the Cabinet floor in turmoil. The overwhelming advice from ministers had been that Margaret should stand down. The most common view was that if she went on she would lose. Everyone was now awaiting her decision. Nothing had been announced, but it was impossible to see how she could continue. She had asked for advice and ministers had decided her fate. Her position was now untenable. She would have been utterly destroyed had the events of Wednesday evening become public while she was still a candidate.

Were there any circumstances in which Margaret Thatcher could have won a second-round victory? Had she simply persevered and not asked for ministers' views, she could just have won. It would have been a close-run thing. It would have left her

weak and probably contemplating resignation early in 1991 after
the Gulf War. That was the most optimistic outcome. I remember
once in a Cabinet committee just having the edge on a proposal I
had made for new legislation. Margaret's response was that such
a narrow majority was not the best foundation on which to proceed.
If that was true of an issue of policy, it was even more true of the
leadership of the party.

Margaret's crucial mistake had been during the first round of
the election when greater involvement would have won the day.
The mistake was compounded by her uncharacteristic action in
inviting the Cabinet to give their views. The idea was to ensure
that ministers were united behind her in what was going to be a
difficult few days. They were not. In this they were not being
disloyal to her. The majority of the Cabinet took the view that the
likeliest result would be ignominious defeat for Margaret Thatcher
and the election of Michael Heseltine without any other contender
inside the Cabinet having the chance to stand.

Margaret Thatcher announced her resignation to the Cabinet
at just after 9 a.m. on Thursday morning, 22 November. In the
afternoon she came to the House of Commons to reply to a motion
of 'No Confidence' which had been put down by the Labour
Opposition. Neil Kinnock's plan had been to exploit the difficulties
inside the Government. Instead he provided Margaret with an
unforgettable final curtain. As she entered the chamber Conservative MPs stood and cheered. Of course there was guilt that she
had been forced so unceremoniously from office but there was
also undoubted affection and admiration for a woman who had
achieved so much. For her part Margaret Thatcher spoke with a
freedom, eloquence and humour that in the past had not always
come easily to her. At the very end she turned to the position in
the Gulf and set out her essential faith:

Twice in my time as Prime Minister, we have had to send our
forces across the world to defend a small country against ruth-
less aggression: first to our own people in the Falklands and
now to the borders of Kuwait. To those who have never had to
take such decisions, I say that they are taken with a heavy heart
and in the knowledge of the manifold dangers, but with

tremendous pride in the professionalism and courage of our armed forces.

There is something else which one feels. That is a sense of this country's destiny: the centuries of history and experience which ensure that, when principles have to be defended, when good has to be upheld and when evil has to be overcome, Britain will take up arms. It is because we on this side have never flinched from difficult decisions that this House and this country can have confidence in this Government today.

On Friday 23 November a new campaign began. Michael Heseltine remained in the lists and he was now joined by the Foreign Secretary, Douglas Hurd, and the Chancellor of the Exchequer, John Major. I now faced a very difficult personal choice. I had opposed Michael's decision to stand against Margaret and I had not voted for him on the first round. But, like it or not, Margaret Thatcher was no longer Prime Minister. We now needed a leader to win the next election and in all likelihood steer the country through a Middle East war.

For me there was an additional complication. John Major was a candidate who in most circumstances I would have supported. He had started his ministerial career with me at the DHSS and we had kept in touch ever since. He was one of the few politicians I had warned of my own resignation at the beginning of the year. I liked him as a person and admired him as a politician. He was much aided by his attractive wife, Norma, who in a busy life had somehow found time to write a biography of Joan Sutherland. I had not expected John to be a candidate for the leadership so early, but at the age of forty-seven there he was as a front-runner. I reflected that I only needed Ken Clarke to enter the fray and I would have three friends battling it out. Over the weekend I considered the position. I was meeting with my executive in Sutton Coldfield on Monday night and I intended to tell them first of my decision.

It is now suggested that John Major's campaign was on the ground days before Margaret Thatcher had made a decision to stand down. As it happens, I am in a strong position to rebut those claims. In his book, *The Quiet Rise of John Major*, Edward Pearce reports that 'originally it had been intended that Norman Fowler should run the campaign but he withdrew'. In fact there was no question of me withdrawing for the good reason that I never accepted the offer. I was complimented by the approach and there are few politicians I would rather have helped. But running a campaign for John would inevitably have involved campaigning *against* his chief rival, Michael Heseltine. I was not prepared to do that. I should record, however, that at no stage in the days leading up to the first round election did John himself make any attempt to enlist my support in case Margaret was defeated. It was only when Margaret's resignation was a certainty that I talked with Norman Lamont. This was shortly before midnight on the Wednesday night – a mere ten hours before the announcement became public. Thus even at that stage there was no campaign manager in waiting. Ultimately it was Norman Lamont himself who took on the job but in no sense did he press himself forward.

After reflecting on the position over the weekend, I decided to vote for Michael Heseltine. Having talked with my executive on the Monday evening, I announced my decision very early on the Tuesday morning of the second-round election. Following my announcement, an anonymous lady from Fulham took the trouble to ring my London office to suggest that this was a piece of political opportunism. I can only say that anyone who declared for Michael Heseltine on Tuesday morning thinking he was jumping onto a winning bandwagon lacked all political judgement.

John Major was walking away with the election. On Tuesday morning I met Norman Lamont in the tea room and predicted that his candidate would win on the first ballot. Norman was doubtful but the fact was that party opinion had turned against Michael. As I had predicted three weeks earlier, he was being blamed for Margaret Thatcher's fall. John had a natural support and Margaret's vote moved over to him almost *in toto*. He was also the surprise beneficiary of the votes of those who were sceptical on Europe. They were unlikely to vote for Michael or Douglas, although I doubt if John's position on Europe is much different from either. Very early on in the new contest, John Major took a decisive lead.

I was one of a handful of former Thatcher supporters who moved to Michael on the second round. Others included David

Hunt, the Welsh Secretary, and the junior Industry minister, Edward Leigh. I did not feel like simply turning away to back the winning horse. Nor had I changed my view that Michael would make a good leader and I certainly hoped that he would be brought back into the Cabinet now that Margaret had gone. It would have been foolish of the Government to have ignored his talents. I hoped also that I could demonstrate one other point. It was perfectly possible for loyal Conservatives to back Michael Heseltine. It was clear that some of Michael's supporters would be brought to account by their local associations and conceivably my action could be of some help.

On Tuesday 27 November, John Major was elected Leader of the Conservative Party. The voting was:

John Major	185
Michael Heseltine	131
Douglas Hurd	56

It was not quite the overall majority required in the second round but it was as near as made no difference. I heard the news in yet another television studio and saw for myself Michael Heseltine's brave speech conceding defeat. John Major had become the youngest Prime Minister this century and virtually overnight the party came together.

For an earlier draft of this book I had written at the end of the chapter on the Falklands about the acid test for a leader:

When the issue arises of Margaret Thatcher's successor, a good criterion for judging rival claims would be which of the candidates would have the determination and ability successfully to fight a Falklands campaign.

With the succession settled, there seemed no reason to keep the passage in the book. As it happens it has proved to be a remarkably accurate commentary upon John Major. Few Prime Ministers have been tested so completely as early on in their period of office. He has emerged a successful and respected national leader – as every opinion poll showed.

When John Major took over, there was much comment that he

would not be his own man. That was always a misconceived criticism. He had certainly been Margaret Thatcher's protégé but he
had never lost his independence. He had shown what he was made
of early on in his career in his Whips' Office debate with her. He
established then that he was never likely to accept an argument
simply because it was the view of the Prime Minister. His real
achievement, however, was that he was able to persuade her when
others had failed.

Two examples, big and small, make the point. In October 1990
John had been the Chancellor who had taken Britain into the
exchange rate mechanism of the European Monetary System – the
very issue that had provoked the resignation of his predecessor,
Nigel Lawson. In his first Budget six months earlier, he had
announced tax relief for workplace nurseries which Margaret
Thatcher was solidly against, fearing the creation of a generation
of crèche children. Those who feared that the new Prime Minister
would live in the shadow of his predecessor did not know their
man.

What John Major brought to Number 10 was a different style
and a different approach. In Cabinet he sought the views of his
colleagues; on television he spoke with that quiet fluency which is
now so familiar; at the dispatch box in the House of Commons
he disarmed his questioners with his politeness. Where Margaret
challenged her questioners and took them head on, John tried to
bring them with him and persuade. Margaret Thatcher had the
obvious authority of a leader who had been in power for over
eleven years. To begin with, in the House of Commons, John
Major seemed nervous. There is an innate modesty about John
which makes him question whether he can handle a new job, be
it Chief Secretary to the Treasury or Foreign Secretary. But he
soon relaxed. What then became clear was that on some issues he
spoke with more natural authority than his predecessor.

If the questions to the Prime Minister in the House of Commons
were on the economy or foreign affairs, Margaret Thatcher was
quite plainly in a different class from Neil Kinnock. Where she
was less at home was on the issues of social policy like health and
social security. It soon became clear that John Major could deal
with those questions more effectively and was also prepared to
follow up his words with action. Soon after his election, he

defused the gathering row on haemophiliacs and AIDS where the Government policy of refusing compensation was becoming increasingly difficult to defend. In February 1991, the spell of snow and blizzards brought back the question of cold-weather payments to old people. John had been the Social Security Minister in charge of the policy in the winter of 1987. He knew not only the impossible politics of the subject but also the genuine suffering that can take place. He simply cut through the regulations which surrounded the area and ordered immediate payment.

The first months of John Major's premiership were dominated by war. There is no doubt that the public have responded to his new appeal and also no doubt of the way he has acquitted himself. Before his election he was that rare political figure: a man without enemies. Today he is much more than that. He has emerged as a substantial and determined political personality but still with few enemies. In his first months he was also given one other advantage. To her great credit, Margaret Thatcher remained determinedly in the background. Whatever her views on policy, or for that matter on her defeat, she did not parade them.

John Major now has the opportunity to set out his own agenda. Ultimately it is that which will determine the Government's fortunes. So what should it contain? In this book I have already argued for a greater emphasis on industry. The past decade saw a small revolution as industrial relations law was reformed and industries went from the public to the private sector. That change has substantially been achieved and the next challenge are the policies to be pursued in the post-privatization world. Government can only do so much, but it can certainly encourage employee participation and shareholding. The 1990s will also see a growing population of older people which in turn will place great demands on our health and social services. The challenge will be to achieve partnership rather than conflict between the statutory services and the private and voluntary sectors. In our cities the environmental challenge will be to maintain and improve what we have, and that may well require radical policy-making. While underlying everything is the need for a strong, low-inflation economy.

There are three more priorities for the 1990s. *First*, and fundamental, is Europe. We are a European power and yet we behave at times as if the decision is still to be taken. Both politicians and businessmen often find it easier to deal with Washington and New York than Brussels, Bonn and Paris. We understand American customs more easily than European ones; we understand their language while we struggle with French and German. And yet so much of our tradition and culture is European. There are crucial business and industrial opportunities in the market of the European Community.

In spite of the disappointing response of some European nations to the Gulf War, there are also political opportunities. Made up of nations with immense political experience and history, Europe has the potential to be a power for stability in the world. That is why some of us supported entry in the first place. Certainly we must fight our corner in the endless negotiations at Brussels, but that should not obscure the potential that Europe offers. John Major is probably better placed than any other politician today to find a sensible, middle course on Europe which avoids either federalism or isolationism.

Second, there is education and training. It was Jean Monnet, the founding father of the European Community, who commented shortly before his death: 'If I could do it all again, I would start with education.' Instinctively we all recognize his meaning. If young people can be given the right foundation and the right approach to acquiring knowledge then that will last them a lifetime. During the twentieth century, Britain has not kept pace with countries like Germany. Our grammar schools and our apprentice schemes provided some excellent standards but only for the few. We are now embarked on the task of raising standards generally. What is needed is consistency. The education reforms are taking place; the new basis for training has been established with national standards and local delivery through the Training and Enterprise Councils. The main requirement is that we should develop what we have rather than seek out yet further new directions. Politicians are always happiest announcing radical new plans, but sometimes a period of calm development is a much more important priority.

Third, there is equal rights. That will become one of the crucial issues of the 1990s and rightly so. A central aim must be to give new opportunities to ethnic minorities. Inner-city policies will need not only to continue but to develop. I suspect that we are just scratching the surface of the needs of many of the young people

living on the estates, in the tower blocks and in the run-down areas
of our cities. Just as crucial will be the need to provide the same
opportunities for women as well as men. We sometimes agonize
about the role of the woman and the mother in society. The solution in principle is reasonably straightforward. We need to
provide a position where women themselves can make a choice
about what they want to do and how they want to arrange their
lives. It is about the ability of my daughters Kate and Isobel to
have the same choices as my stepson Oliver. But it is also about
the ability of Kates and Isobels who do not have the backing of
graduate middle-class parents to be able to develop to their full
potential. Equal rights is no longer about the statutory woman: it
is about realizing the potential of all women.

All these issues represent formidable challenges for the new
Prime Minister. John Major will be a very different leader from
Margaret Thatcher but, just as she was in 1975, he is a figure of
his time. He represents many of the public's aspirations for the
1990s. When Margaret Thatcher came to office, whether Britain
had a future or not had to be tackled head on. Had another leader
been destroyed by a national strike or been exhausted by what was
becoming perceived as the impossibility of governing the country,
then the outlook would have been bleak. The test for the 1990s is
different. It is to make progress without the set-piece trials of
strength like the coal strike which sapped our energy even in the
1980s. It is not a soft option. Having escaped disaster, Britain
must establish itself in the first division of industrial and economic
nations.

For me, the great disappointment was that Margaret Thatcher's
extraordinary career ended in the brutal way that it did. It was also
a personal tragedy that her Government ended with the alienation
of so many of the people like Geoffrey Howe, Nigel Lawson and
for that matter Michael Heseltine who had contributed so much
to her success. All kinds of empty explanations were advanced in
the aftermath of her fall: 'All political careers end in tears.' 'No
leader ever knows when to step down.' Now the dust has settled,
it is perhaps easier to see a more complete picture. In John Major,
Margaret Thatcher had the successor she wanted. What he
achieves will be different, but it will be built on the foundation of
the Thatcher years.

Index